The Myth of New Orleans in Literature

The Myth of New Orleans in Literature
Dialogues of Race and Gender

Violet Harrington Bryan

The University of Tennessee Press / Knoxville

Frontispiece: The Tremé cultural district of New Orleans. Drawing by
Amy Elizabeth Bryan.

Library of Congress Cataloging in Publication Data

Bryan, Violet Harrington, 1948-
    The myth of New Orleans in literature : dialogues of race
and gender / Violet Harrington Bryan. — 1st ed.
            p.   cm.
    Includes bibliographical references and index.
    ISBN 0-87049-789-8 (cloth: alk. paper)
    1. American literature—Louisiana—New Orleans—History and criticism.
2. Literature and society—Louisiana—New Orleans—History. 3. New
Orleans (La.)—Intellectual Life. 4. City and town life in literature. 5. New
Orleans (La.) in literature. 6. Race relations in literature. 7. Sex role in
literature. 8. Myth in literature.   I. Title.
PS 267.N49B78   1993
810.9'3276335—dc20   92-42846
                                                            CIP

Ⱳ

To my parents, Miriam Hart Harrington and the late
James W. Harrington, Sr., and to my husband, Trevor George Bryan,
and children, Amy Elizabeth, Alma-Catherine, and Courtney Lara,
for your inspiration and support

Contents

ய

Illustrations

Ⴏ

Preface

Why write a book about so many writers, some major, others not, who have written about New Orleans, particularly in a one-volume study? Can justice be done to Kate Chopin, William Faulkner, Tennessee Williams, and Walker Percy? The selection of texts and authors, and their interrelation, have been major obstacles in this study of the development of the myths of New Orleans. I have been tempted to avoid writers generally considered "major," but some readers have counseled me to omit such "minor" texts by white writers as Robert Tallant's *Mrs. Candy and Saturday Night,* Edward Larocque Tinker's *Toucoutou,* and John Kennedy Toole's *A Confederacy of Dunces.* Some have said that a discussion of their works could be a part of my analysis of the other writers. The most interesting part of the book to many is my treatment of little-known African-American writers, including Marcus Christian, director of the Black Louisiana Federal Writers' Project of the Works Progress Administration; Alice Dunbar-Nelson, who has been added to the canon mainly through the diligent research of Gloria T. Hull; and contemporary writers Brenda Marie Osbey, Sybil Kein, and Tom Dent. But the dialogue among these writers has been my subject from the beginning; my contribution will be to discover the dialogic connection between these writers and to demonstrate the dominance of culture across lines of gender, class, and race.

The texts are related by their various appropriations of the *culture* of New Orleans—a particularly complex aggregate of beliefs, customs, attitudes, art forms, morals, and laws. The city's unique history and population link it intimately with Caribbean, African, and European cultures as well as other North American countries. While I attempt to discuss the city's culture, the intersection of culture and literature, not either separately, is the focus of my inquiry. Therefore, the analyses of the literature and the culture are not exhaustive except as these interact. The perspectives of the writers toward the culture reflect the influences that they have had on each other as contemporaries and across generations. George Washington Cable, Charles Chesnutt, Grace King, Kate Chopin, and Alice Dunbar-Nelson are linked not only by their treatments of "the color line" at the turn of the century but also by the prevailing discourse of Social Darwinism and "the woman question." Across race and gender, the images and themes of their literary works reflect the historical moment of which they were all a part and the influence that each had on the other. Thus Ishmael Reed and Walker Percy may be seen as sharing cultural themes as well as comparable literary responses to a period of impending political and racial dilemmas. The similarity of their literary techniques for capturing the period of racial anxiety is remarkable.

Every book is the product of numerous contributors. I acknowledge with gratitude the many who have helped me in this project. I am indebted to the Southern Education Foundation for a year's fellowship in 1986–87, when I developed the book proposal and first contacted the University of Tennessee Press. I am grateful to Carol Orr, former director of the University of Tennessee Press, for her encouragement through the hectic intervening years of research, writing, and teaching. Mrs. Florence Borders, former head archivist of the Amistad Research Center, New Orleans, has been a treasure trove of ideas and resources. I owe thanks to Beth Howze and the Special Collections Department of Fisk University Library for assistance with my research in the Charles Chesnutt Collection, and the South Central Modern Language Association for its Travel and Research Grant of 1988, which covered the expenses of the trip there. I am most grateful to Quo Vadis Gex-Breaux, poet and colleague, for lending me all of her original copies of publications of the BLKARTSOUTH group. I am indebted also to the Dillard University Library, the Archives and Manuscripts and the Special Collections departments of the University of New Orleans, and the Tulane University Library's Special Collections.

I owe special thanks to Dr. Samuel Dubois Cook, president of Dillard University, for his continuing encouragement. For reading the whole manuscript through various stages, for suggestions and support, I am especially indebted to Barbara Ewell, professor of English, Loyola University of New Orleans. For reading and commenting on various drafts, my appreciation goes to Professors Alma Young, Marguerite Bryan, the late Clifford Bryan, Helen Malin, Brenda Marie Osbey, and Paulene Washington.

I am most indebted to my husband, Trevor Bryan, who from the conception of this project to its completion has contributed major ideas and raised the critical questions that have helped to define the book and its contribution. His support and that of our children—Amy, Alma-Catherine, and Courtney—whose sacrifices have been numerous, have made this book possible.

ONE

Ш

Literary Dialogues
and the Development
of an Urban Myth

L and of Dreams," "City of Sin,"
"The City That Care Forgot,"
"The Big Easy"—New Orleans
is an American southern city that
holds a unique place in our culture; it has always been a center of myth and
legend and a popular setting for literature, film, art, and song.[1] Founded in 1718
by the French as a strategic site at the mouth of the Mississippi River, and later
ceded to the Spanish, New Orleans was nearly a hundred years old before it
became a part of the United States in 1803. As an international port city, it has
from its earliest days attracted settlers of diverse nationalities and social and
political traditions—Native American, French, African, Spanish—and the city
has had waves of immigration from Canada (Quebec and Nova Scotia), Germany, Ireland, the Canary Islands, Italy, and Greece, as well as from Santo
Domingo/Haiti, Cuba, and other Caribbean countries. The extent of
"Creolization," or synthesis of various cultures and intermarriage of ethnic
groups, that has taken place in New Orleans is unique in American history.[2]

Myth, according to Roland Barthes, is a "second-order semiological system," which can be interpreted not only by recognizing the sign (word, speech)
but by understanding the concept, the myth-maker's purpose.[3] In the novels,
poems, and plays studied here, I argue that writers have appropriated the culture of New Orleans—as defined by Clifford Geertz, its "religious, philosophical, aesthetic, scientific, and ideological 'programs'"—in order to develop es-
sential themes of their works.[4] For example, in reading Cable's *The*

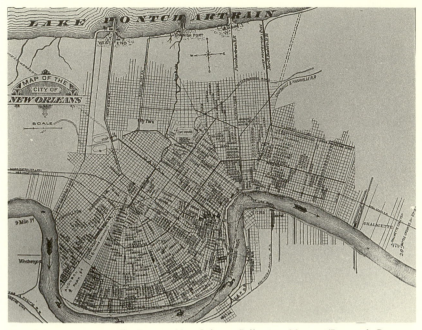

New Orleans. Courtesy The Historic New Orleans Collection, Museum/Research Center, Acc. No. 1990.51.2.1.

Grandissimes, the reader must interpret the legend of the African slave-hero Bras-Coupé in light of Cable's ideological and poetic purposes. Ishmael Reed's rendering of hoodoo, Doctor John, and Marie Laveau may not be historically accurate, but Reed's re-creation of the legends serves the purpose of his fiction. The writers have "appropriated" the rituals, language, and artifacts of the culture to represent their poetic "truths." As Barthes observes, "Myth is speech stolen and restored. Only, speech which is restored is no longer quite that which was stolen: when it was brought back, it was not put exactly in its place. It is this brief act of larceny, this moment taken for a surreptitious faking, which gives mythical speech its benumbed look."[5]

My project is to study the evolving myth of New Orleans as it has been created and re-created by writers from 1880 to the present, to show how the writers' creation and use of the city's myth is related to "the historical moment" during which each of the authors wrote, and to trace the important roles that gender and race have played in determining what voices would be heard and which *silenced* in the creation of the city's myth.[6] Such connections of myth and language are highly significant because, as M. M. Bakhtin explains,

> the living utterance, having taken meaning and shape at a particular
> historical moment in a socially specific environment, cannot fail to

> brush up against thousands of living dialogic threads, woven by
> socio-ideological consciousness around the given object of an utter-
> ance; it cannot fail to become an active participant in social dialogue.
> After all, the utterance arises out of this dialogue as a continuation of
> it and as a rejoinder to it—it does not approach the object from the
> sidelines.[7]

Applying Bakhtin's conception of the dialogic nature of language to the development of myth, I have linked the dialogue of New Orleans literary myth-
makers with many of the voices of the community heretofore silenced. Similarly, Cheryl A. Wall, editor of *Changing Our Own Words: Essays on
Criticism, Theory, and Writing by Black Women* (1989), speaking primarily of
the writings of African-American women, suggests that "after or concurrent
with . . . first readings should come more relational readings that put individual
texts in dialogue." Her interest is in reading black women's texts in relation to
their "multiple contexts," popular and literary.[8]

I view the works of literature studied here as rejoinders in a continuing dialogue that work together to develop myths of New Orleans culture. Sometimes
it is an explicit dialogue, as that which took place between Charles Chesnutt
and George Washington Cable at the end of the nineteenth century. They
worked together in the Open Letter Club to give voice to the Silent South on
matters of race. They also corresponded frequently about their writing projects
and the dominant national discourse about "the Negro question." Sometimes
the dialogue is implicit, and sometimes it is silenced by prejudice, censorship,
or fear. Prevailing ideologies have played a major role in determining what
voices are heard through published texts. The dialogue that we can imagine
between Lyle Saxon and Robert Tallant of the white Louisiana Federal Writers' Project and Marcus Christian of the Negro Writers' Project of the WPA
has to be reconstructed, using the voluminous letters and unpublished manuscripts of Christian.

African, Afro-Caribbean, and African-American traditions and folklore
have played a vital role in designing the New Orleans cultural landscape. In
the 1840s Alexis de Tocqueville commented on the interesting situation of the
races in Louisiana. He observed that Louisiana was one section of the United
States where there was "a third race," and he predicted that racial mixture was
the only solution to the problem of race relations after the abolition of slavery
in America: "There are but two chances for the future: the Negroes and the
whites must either wholly part or wholly mingle. . . . In some parts of America
the European and the Negro races are so crossed with one another that it is
rare to meet with a man who is entirely black or entirely white."[9] Rodolphe
Desdunes, Alice Dunbar-Nelson, Charles B. Roussève, John W. Blassingame,
and many other scholars have studied the situation of New Orleans's *gens de*

THE OPERA HOUSE.

The Old French Opera House. Built in 1859 in the Vieux Carré on the corner of Bourbon and Toulouse streets, the building was destroyed by fire in 1919. The Santo-Domingan refugees of the late eighteenth century were instrumental in making New Orleans the first American city to have a French opera and to maintain a continuing opera company. Courtesy The Historic New Orleans Collection, Museum/Research Center, Acc. No. 1974.25.36.24.

The Lyric Theater. Opening on February 24, 1919, the theater was exclusively for the African-American New Orleans population. At the corner of Iberville and Burgundy streets, it featured such performers as Josephine Baker and Florence Mills before being demolished in 1928. Courtesy The Historic New Orleans Collection, Museum/Research Center, Acc. No. 1974.25.36.70.

couleur libres, men and women joined by their culture and separated by a social and political hierarchy based on class and caste distinctions.[10] As early as 1724 their legal status as *quasi-citizens* had been defined by the French *Code Noir* (Black Code). They could have slaves and own real estate and be recognized in the courts, but they were restricted from voting, from marrying white persons, and from contact with slaves "because of deep-seated suspicions that they were liable at any time to encourage rebellion."[11] They were required to include the letters *h.c.l.* or *f.c.l.* or the English equivalents, *f.m.c.* or *f.w.c.* for *free man* or *free woman of color* after their names on all public and legal documents. Further distinctions were made between free blacks, with degrees of color classifying them in both public and private documents as *griffe,* the offspring of a mulatto and a Negro; *mulatto,* of a white and a Negro; *quadroon,* of a white and a mulatto; and *octoroon,* of a white and a quadroon. "For convenience's sake, the word Mulatto was commonly used to refer to all of these people of mixed blood, regardless of the amount."[12] Based on mistrust engendered by the April 1795 slave conspiracy at Pointe Coupée, Louisiana, and exacerbated by the Santo Domingan Revolution of the 1790s, whites increasingly watched the free persons of color for fear they would incite slave revolts. By 1830, there were almost twelve thousand *gens de couleur libres* in the city, and according to Blassingame, they owned $2,214,020 in real property, much of it in the center of the city.[13] The identity of this group of the population, the attitudes of whites toward them as the Others, and their own response to whites, are central themes in the literature of New Orleans and contribute significantly to the city's myth.[14] The relationship of New Orleans Creoles and the Santo Domingans who immigrated to New Orleans during the Santo Domingan Revolution is also a major theme in the literature, as can be seen, for example, in George Washington Cable's *The Grandissimes,* Charles Chesnutt's "Paul Marchand, F.M.C.," and Edward Larocque Tinker's *Toucoutou.*

The liaisons between white men and Creole women of color form what Sister Audrey Marie Detiege has called "a spicy chapter in the history of old New Orleans."[15] Such liaisons led to so-called *plaçage* arrangements, whereby the white men maintained their quadroon "mistresses" financially, sometimes even having their arrangements blessed by the church; they cared for the children of these unions, often baptizing them in their name and educating them in France. Such arrangements were historically widely accepted. Armand Lanusse describes the perplexing situation of a Creole mother facing the imminent *plaçage* of her daughter in his poem "Epigramme," published in *Les Cenelles* (1845):

> "You really do not want to renounce Satan,"
> A good preacher was saying to a certain zealot
> Who, every year, came to present him
> Her interminable list of rather mortal sins.
> "I do want to renounce him," says she, "for ever,
> But before grace sparkles in my soul,
> To remove henceforth all incentive to sin,
> Why can't I, father—what?—*establish* my daughter?"[16]

Unfortunately, the white men would often marry a white woman and support a family with her as well. The tradition of *plaçage* arrangements and the "quadroon balls," where the white man and the quadroon woman met, has also been a major theme in the literature about, and histories of, New Orleans.

African folklore has contributed significantly to New Orleans culture and its myth. Jazz, the creation of "downtown" Creoles of color and "uptown" blacks; the *bamboula* and *calinda*—songs and dances that George Washington Cable, Lafcadio Hearn, and Louis Gottschalk recreated in their histories, fiction, and music; the folktales of slaves, ghosts, and plantation life made popular in the local color stories and later histories of New Orleans; voodoo, or *hoodoo,* as it is popularly known in the African-American community; the whole mystique of the peculiar color problem of the city with its quadroons, octoroons, griffes, blacks, and whites: all of these aspects of black history and culture are strongly reflected in the literature of New Orleans. The mulatto theme, black Louisiana folklore, and the influence of jazz are apparent in works as diverse as George Washington Cable's *The Grandissimes* (1880), Alice Dunbar-Nelson's *Violets and Other Tales,* (1892), William Faulkner's *Absalom, Absalom!* (1936), Ishmael Reed's *The Last Days of Louisiana Red* (1972), and Brenda Marie Osbey's *Ceremony for Minneconjoux* (1983).

New Orleans has variably been called "la grande dame in grand tenue," "courtesan," "Queen City by the River," and "mon amour."[17] Thus the city's image is intimately tied to the myths of the southern belle, the beautiful quadroon women of the quadroon balls, the madames of Storyville, and the voodoo queens, especially the most well-known—Marie Laveau. Myths of the city as woman are based on the literary productions of authors both male and female, black and white. For example, the white writer Robert Tallant creates "a flamboyant portrait" of Marie Laveau in his books *Voodoo in New Orleans* and *The Voodoo Queen,* which remains the best-known characterization of voodoo and its "queen."[18] Marcus Christian, black scholar and writer, researches the historical bases for many of the stories of Laveau and emphasizes the spiritual side of the woman as healer. Zora Neale Hurston's image of Laveau was published but remained largely unread because she was an outsider looking in, a black woman writing about another black woman and unknown traditions. Her work *Mules and Men* is just beginning to be valued, not because of its accuracy but because of the portrait the author draws of herself and her position vis-à-vis the African-American folklore she studied.[19] Ishmael Reed, Brenda Marie Osbey, and other contemporary writers have continued to explore the traditions of voodoo as folklore, way of seeing, and spiritualist healing.[20]

In post-Reconstruction New Orleans, while George Washington Cable, Charles Chesnutt, Grace King, Kate Chopin, and Alice Dunbar-Nelson were creating literary texts set in New Orleans that contributed to, and commented on, myths of the city, one of the major elements of the prominent discourse was the redrawing of lines between black, white, and Creole and the developing of racial stereotypes in conjunction with, or counter to, the southern plantation myths being created by Thomas Nelson Page and Joel Chandler Harris. The discourse was also dominated by the woman suffrage movement and the building up of women's networks through the women's club movement, as well as by new questions about marriage and divorce, the role of motherhood, and women's careers. Women at the turn of the century were leaders in the anti-lynching campaigns, the establishment of juvenile courts and orphanages, the development of schools for blacks, and the temperance movement. The prevailing ideology—social and scientific—was Social Darwinism. All of the writers studied here were at least conscious of Spencerian thought toward sex, race, and class. George Washington Cable based many of his ideas about culture and class on the new sociology. Chopin and King both read the works of Huxley, Darwin, and Spencer and commented on their readings in their journals.[21]

Although color distinctions were important all over the nation, only in New Orleans were color and cultural distinctions so intimately connected with social and political hierarchy. American writers were fascinated with the phenomena of Creole versus American and white Creoles versus Creoles of color. In the post-Reconstruction period, Cable, Chesnutt, King, Dunbar-Nelson, and Chopin were contributors to images that would yet be hardened into stereotypes regarding blacks. Given the city's unique cultural mix, especially the influence of the Caribbean and its racial classifications, New Orleans was also the site at the turn of the century of several court cases based on racial issues, the most famous being the *Plessy v. Ferguson* decision of the Supreme Court in 1896. Edward Larocque Tinker wrote *Toucoutou* (1928) about an actual court case that dealt with the matter of racial identity and passing. Charles Chesnutt wrote about a hypothetical case, dealing with the ironic story of a young man who discovers that he is white, although he has been raised as a free man of color.[22]

In the New Orleans of the 1880s and 1890s women played an important role in determining matters of race relations, women's rights, and social reform.[23] Their dominance in determining literary tastes is evident in the achievements and friendships of such female writers as Eliza Jane Poitevent (pseudonym Pearl Rivers), the publisher of the *Daily Picayune* (1876-96), Elizabeth Gilmer (Dorothy Dix), a newspaper associate, and Grace King and her neighbors, Mollie Moore Davis and Ruth McEnery Stuart.[24] Though Grace King, Alice Dunbar-Nelson, and Kate Chopin were, like Cable, interested in portraying the life of Creoles and Creoles of color in New Orleans and environs, they were also engaged in a dialogue with each other not only about the role of blacks in the life of the South, but also about marriage and women's roles in the home and the workplace. In Chopin's *The Awakening* and in many of her stories, New Orleans is both the site of male-identified culture—the business world and its clubs, the horse races, the mansions and other architectural expressions of material achievement—and a place where women like Edna Pontellier can remove themselves from familial connections and come to some recognition or understanding of their separate identity. The women writers of the late nineteenth century tended to represent the city in their fiction differently from their male counterparts. Susan Squier alludes to this divergence, noting: "Whether they praise the city or blame it, women writers respond to the urban environment in a significantly different way from men. . . . Considering not only *what* women writers have written about the city, but also *how* they have used the city to express both personal concerns and cultural critiques, the essays in this volume suggest the rich array of symbolic structures and narrative techniques with which women writers have addressed these issues."[25]

The 1920s was a well-known period of literary activity in New Orleans, as it was in Greenwich Village, Harlem, and the culture capitals of Europe. The post-World War I group of writers who met in the French Quarter and started *The Double-Dealer* literary magazine in 1921 often used New Orleans as a setting in their novels. William Faulkner, who began his career as a writer of fiction in New Orleans during those years, developed the idea of the city as courtesan in his sketches written for *The Double-Dealer,* and in material that would later appear in his novels *Mosquitoes, Absalom, Absalom!* and *The Wild Palms.* In these representations of New Orleans as courtesan, he showed the influence of Modernist writers and artists and emphasized the conflict between agrarian Old South values and the cosmopolitan, though often decadent, values of the modern metropolis. He also entered the prominent dialogue about the role of "the new woman."[26] In *Absalom, Absalom!* Bakhtinian *dialogization,* or the diversity of individual voices and social speech types— especially the various voices of characters regarding race and gender—becomes central to the novel's style and theme.[27]

Lyle Saxon, who played a major role in the renovation of the Vieux Carré (French Quarter) during the 1920s, became director of the Louisiana Federal Writers' Project of the 1930s and 1940s. During the days of *The Double-Dealer* he was a leader of the intelligentsia and a host for writers and artists. In the 1930s and 1940s he continued in that capacity, and in time many knew him as "Mr. New Orleans."[28] In this book I explore the dialogue between Saxon and Robert Tallant, a member of his Writers' Project who published prolifically during the period, and Marcus Bruce Christian, African-American writer, newspaper reporter, researcher, and director of the Negro Division of the New Orleans Writers' Project.[29] Their dialogue took place in the context of an African-American literary movement led by writers such as Langston Hughes, Sterling Brown, Arna Bontemps, and Zora Neale Hurston that emphasized the rich folklore, language, and music of the Negro folk.[30] The new movement in African-American literature was paralleled by a renewed interest of white writers in black folklore and the publishing of such books as Roark Bradford's *John Henry* (1931) and Tallant's *Voodoo in New Orleans* (1938). Christian's voluminous research on voodoo, Marie Laveau, John Henry, Melrose Plantation and the Metoyers, and the historical, social, and intellectual life of Afro-Louisianians remains largely unpublished, while the writings of the white WPA and of Tallant, Saxon, and Roark Bradford forge the established written image of New Orleans and of African-American folklore.

Since World War II, authors have created increasingly satirical or parodic portraits of the city, or they have freely used an older folklore to create new myths.[31] The emphasis on satire and the creation of myth has led to new visions of the city. Tennessee Williams envisions New Orleans in *A Streetcar Named Desire* as a part of the New South, where the "Snopeses" are taking over; the city can no longer be home for the Old South pretensions of a Blanche DuBois. Blanche, broken though she is by circumstances, belongs on the Belle Reve (Beautiful Dream) Plantation. Like Faulkner, Williams continues to fabricate the courtesan image, and Blanche, who seeks desire rather than death, eros over thanatos, becomes a part of the evolving myth of New Orleans. In Williams's fiction and drama, New Orleans becomes "the city of night," "the exotic unreality"; in *Suddenly Last Summer* the city's Garden District becomes a metaphor for "rapacious nature" or deep-set psychic horror.[32]

Walker Percy's Binx Bolling of *The Moviegoer,* wounded in World War II, returns to New Orleans as a man alienated from its culture, particularly from its code of southern stoicism. Binx conducts a search for meaning, or knowledge, that will enable him to connect with the world and with God. He avoids the traditional upper-class New Orleans culture by moving to Gentilly, a rather undistinguished suburb of the city, virtually unknown to outsiders, and by evading all "intersubjective" communication with others until he marries his cousin Kate Cutrer and decides to make her his responsibility.[33] Binx Bolling's detachment from his environment makes him more of an observer than a participant in New Orleans culture. In Percy's third novel, *Love in the Ruins,* the protagonist, Dr. Thomas More, is literally separated from the city in a fictional Feliciana Parish outside of New Orleans. A more concrete, referential city setting would have restricted Percy from developing the kind of satiric, diagnostic fiction he had already begun to explore in *The Moviegoer;* the city of *Love in the Ruins* has "not yet articulated itself, does not even have a name."[34] An analysis of setting and theme in *Love in the Ruins* makes clear that in *The Moviegoer* the New Orleans culture was used primarily as a metaphor for a temporary connection with the mundane before the city and its culture could be transcended; the latter novel is also one of Percy's most elaborate attempts to explain the racial issue in America and to show how it is connected to the nation's spiritual dilemma.[35]

In the period following the civil rights movement of the 1960s, African-American writing about New Orleans has taken on revisionist strategies in reclaiming and redefining the traditional folklore. Tom Dent, Kalamu ya Salaam, and other members of the *BLKARTSOUTH* Workshop, which followed the Free Southern Theatre in New Orleans, connected themselves with the national Black Aesthetic Movement of the 1960s and used poetry to refer to actual black experiences, to create new images that would counter prevailing stereotypes of blacks, and to open up the lines of communication between the races.[36] For Dent and Ishmael Reed, a member of the *Umbra* Workshop of poets in New York during the early 1960s, the old myths are dead; Reed re-creates them and gives them a new name, and uses voodoo (hoodoo) and jazz as technique in and subject of his fiction. Past, present, myth, history have no necessary divisions in the hoodoo aesthetic he adopts. Reed, like Walker Percy, portrays New Orleans satirically; while Percy's characters search for a way by which they can accept Christian grace and live instead of die, Reed's characters refute Christian doctrine altogether and accept hoodoo.

Brenda Marie Osbey and Sybil Kein, two New Orleans African-American women poets, add new voices to the dialogue; in their poetry they are retrieving the often "appropriated" images of black women, particularly Creole women, adding a more personal perspective to the myth of New Orleans.

Writers and texts have been selected in this study to demonstrate the growth and development of an urban myth and the dialogue between various literary voices of the culture—the published and the unpublished. I have selected texts from the various genres—fiction, poetry, drama, nonfiction—because all the literary genres are involved in the development of an urban myth, as are such other creative expressions as film, music, visual art, and oral and written histories.

ɰ

Cable, Chesnutt, and the Dialectic of Race

George Washington Cable

The early works of George Washington Cable—*Old Creole Days, The Grandissimes,* and *Doctor Sevier*—are all a form of dialectic, in which clashes between Creole and American cultures, the African and European races, rational thought and the irrational, civilization and the wild, poor and rich, are dramatized. Donald Ringe labels this dialectic "the double center," using Cable's own term in "Café des Exilés." Just as the short story turns around two characters, Galahad Shaughnessy and Manuel Mazaro, "as on a double center," Ringe argues that in *The Grandissimes* there is an "important dialectic embodied in their [Honoré's and Frowenfeld's] relationship, a dialectic that provides the book with its basic meaning.[1] Indeed, Cable uses dialectic in all of his best fiction and essays in order to demonstrate that the opposites he observes, often between his moral ideas and the prevailing ideology of postbellum America, can always be resolved through reason.

"Cable had no natural bent for the conventional kind of romance," Edmund Wilson noted in *Patriotic Gore*; "his interests and his capabilities all lay in the direction of imaginative history and realistic social observation."[2] From Cable's earliest days as a writer for the *Picayune* and as a writer of fiction, he argued for reform. During the time that Cable wrote the stories of *Old Creole Days* and the novels *The Grandissimes* and *Doctor Sevier* (1873-84), New Orleans, the South's largest city and the fourth largest in the nation, was faced with a waning Reconstruction, accelerating racial hostilities, and a growing northern interest in "The Great South."[3] In a column headed "Drop Shot" featured in the New Orleans *Picayune,* Cable attacked the Louisiana Lottery Com-

George Washington Cable at his desk. Courtesy of the George Washington Cable Collection, Manuscripts Department, Howard-Tilton Memorial Library, Tulane University, New Orleans.

pany, which, since its chartering by the state legislature in 1868, had involved ex-Confederate generals, legislators, banks, and businesses in associated corruption. Cable worked energetically for prison, asylum, and public health reform. When the Cotton Centennial Exposition was held in New Orleans in 1884, the city's cotton industry received an economic boost, but visitors to the Exposition viewed a city that had as yet no sewerage system and no adequate garbage collection, open drainage canals causing dangerous, unsanitary living conditions, and drinking water collected in cisterns. Samuel Clemens wrote in *Life on the Mississippi* (1883), "The city had not changed—to the eye. It had greatly increased in spread and population. . . . The dust, waste-paper-littered, was still deep in the streets; the deep, troughlike gutters alongside the curbstones were still half full of reposeful water with a dusty surface. . . . The people cannot have wells, and so they take rain water. Neither can they conveniently have cellars, or graves, the town being build upon 'made' ground; so they do without both, and few of the living complain, and none of the others."[4]

As Cable noted in "My Politics" (written in 1889), it was impossible for him to write novels without being conscious of the social problems of his time.[5] In his dialectic Cable incorporates major ideas of the popular discourse on Darwinism, particularly as translated by T. H. Huxley and by Herbert Spencer, whose book *The Study of Sociology* had a major influence on the founding of American sociology.[6] But Cable also knew the liabilities of such an all-encompassing worldview. In *Old Creole Days* and *The Grandissimes* he demonstrated the importance of accepting the diversity of peoples and the undercurrent of folk cultures, which refuse to be limited by narrow conceptions of caste stratifications. In *Doctor Sevier* Cable faced the issue of Social Darwinism directly. Through the method of dialectic he attempted to answer several questions: What does America owe to its poor? Can the wealthy separate themselves from the poor? Will the Anglo-Americans still be the survivors as the cities become more diversified with immigrants from Europe, Africa, and the Caribbean?

As both a horticulturist and a social reformer, Cable believed in careful empirical research, not large theories. He was not a determinist, and, like T. H. Huxley, thought that environmental conditions sometimes had to be adjusted to the plant, and not just the plant to life conditions. He would have readily assented to T. H. Huxley's comparison of the ethical process to the work of the gardener: "Like horticulture, human ethics defies the cosmic process; for both horticulture and ethical behavior circumvent the raw struggle for existence in the interest of some ideal imposed from without upon the processes of nature."[7] Cable refused to accept the theory of life processes as determining human destiny, as the Social Darwinists seemed to argue, but believed with the later Progressivists in the psychological and moral relatedness of all people and the necessity for collective social action rather than reliance solely upon individuals.[8]

His early works, even when they created seductive pictures of the Creole past, were also social arguments, employing dialectic to persuade his readers to use reason to ameliorate conditions of the present. As Edward Larocque Tinker commented in his "Cable and the Creoles," the reformer finally won out over the creative writer ("His pedagogic excesses murdered his creative ability"), but in the early stories Cable was seduced by the Creoles, and that seduction gives his early writings their passionate appeal: "Perhaps the describing of their [the Creoles'] volatile emotions may have assuaged his own inhibitions, and writing of their warm, exotic, impetuous love affairs, and of the quadroon balls, may have given him a certain psychological release."[9]

Old Creole Days

According to Cable's comments in "My Politics," the stories collected as *Old Creole Days* were not political. Even "'Tite Poulette," a story about the tragic situation of quadroons in Louisiana, which might be interpreted as political, "was chosen for its romantic value," Cable asserted.[10] It is difficult to believe, however, that he had no political intentions in writing the stories, since while still writing them, he had already become involved in the area of Negro rights with his 1875 letter to the editor of the New Orleans *Bulletin,* in which he argued the case for integrated schools following the ignominious forcible expulsion of all the Negro pupils from the Girls' High School.[11] He had signed the editorial "A Southern White Man" to emphasize that he spoke as a native, not as an outsider. Moreover, his first story, "Bibi," was rejected by *Scribner's, Appleton's,* and the *Atlantic* because of the "unmitigatedly distressful effect of the story"; his emphasis in that story, which became the central episode of *The Grandissimes,* was overtly political, as it emphasized the colonial Black Code (*Code Noir*) and its most inhumane applications during the period of slavery in Louisiana.[12]

Written in the 1870s, "'Tite Poulette" is an early development of the story of the tragic quadroon and octoroon, those women of color whom Cable described as "a survival of the fairest through seventy-five years devoted to the elimination of the black pigment and the cultivation of hyperion excellence and nymphean grace and beauty."[13] Cable's romantic rendering of the Creole women of color, whom he unfailingly labels as *quadroons* or *quadroones,* never as Creoles, is echoed in the later descriptions of the women by Lafcadio Hearn as "uncommonly tall . . . citrine-hued, elegant of stature as palmettos, lithe as serpents . . . daughters of luxury. . . . Art has lost something by their extinction." [14] Cable's and Hearn's descriptions of these women and the traditional *plaçage* arrangements, whereby well-to-do young white men of New Orleans often arranged common-law marriages with them in spite of a formal marriage with a white woman of their own social position, reflected a rather decadent *fin-de-siècle* fascination with beauty and exoticism. The shock of a Puritan sensibility and an apparently worldly, but irrational, system of race and caste colors the narration and characterization of "'Tite Poulette," *The Grandissimes,* and *Madame Delphine.*" Cable's image of New Orleans and the Creole women of color had a major influence on later writers who used the New Orleans setting in their fiction and treated the themes of unclear racial identities, "miscegenation," and women's sexuality, such as Charles Chesnutt's "Paul Marchand F.M.C.," Grace King's "The Little Convent Girl," Kate Chopin's "La Belle Zoraïde" and "Desirée's Baby," Alice Dunbar-Nelson's "Sister Josepha," and William Faulkner's *Absalom, Absalom!*

The melodrama of "'Tite Poulette" revolves around the contrast between the innocent daughter of Madame John and the sensual New Orleans atmosphere, "the wicked city," as Kristian Koppig, the newly arrived Dutch accountant, calls it. He rather voyeuristically watches the activities of the quadroon Madame John and her daughter from his dormer window across the street. The narrator describes 'Tite Poulette as "one of those whom the taint of caste has cursed. She lives a lonely, innocent life in the midst of corruption, like the lilies. . .in the marshes."[15] The fight within the young Dutchman's mind over his apparent "horror of mixed blood" (87) and his evident attraction to the young woman was a dilemma that Cable and his northern reading audience could easily identify with. The story, noted Edward Larocque Tinker, "was as warmly received as Boucicault's *Octoroon*."[16] In spite of the portrayal of Koppig and 'Tite Poulette as extreme innocents, the reader cannot help but feel that Cable attempts to tantalize by rendering his "world of sin." The quadroon balls—both in the old days when Madame John had been a young woman who "had danced, and laughed, and coquetted under her satin mask, even to the baffling of that prince of gentlemen, dear Monsieur John himself" (83), and at the time of the narration, when, now widowed, she dances the paid "dance of the shawl"—serve as a metaphor in this story for the beautiful exterior and the decadent, morally corrupt interior of New Orleans.

Cable writes of a "large hall, a blaze of lamps, a bewildering flutter of fans and floating robes, strains of music, columns of gay promenaders, a long row of turbaned mothers lining either wall, gentlemen of the portlier sort filling the recesses of the windows, whirling waltzers gliding here and there—smiles and grace, smiles and grace; all fair, orderly, elegant, bewitching" (95). His vision of the quadroon balls is not nearly so condemnatory as Faulkner's later portrait, when Mr. Compson in *Absalom! Absalom!* describes the quadroon women presenting themselves as "a corridor of doomed and tragic flower faces walled between the grim duenna row of old women and the elegant shapes of young men trim predatory and (at the moment) goatlike.[17] Cable, in effect, tantalizes the reader but, as Alice Petry has noted, "appears unsure about how much to explore the sensitive issues of religion, money, and sexuality—all of which are vitally concerned with the story's key issue, racial discrimination."[18] At the end of the story Kristian Koppig proposes marriage to 'Tite Poulette in spite of his reluctance to go against the law and his moral principles. Luckily, he and 'Tite Poulette are saved at the last moment by Madame John's production of sworn papers that 'Tite Poulette is not her daughter, but the daughter of Spanish parents who died of yellow fever in her boardinghouse. It was an ending acceptable to many northern readers, but it was rightly seen as a *deus ex machina* by the quadroon woman who wrote Cable a letter asking him to write a story that portrayed the real situation of Louisiana's Creoles of color.[19] Everything from the description of 'Tite Poulette's "black eyes" to the conversation between mother and daughter about the plight of quadroon women, who have "no place in this world," prepares the reader for the financial and social dilemma of the free woman of color, who was expected to depend on a white man for her sustenance, but could not legally marry him. Referring to, but finally evading the issues of Catholic religious practice in a city where religious ethics were only a sham in view of the race and caste stratification, women's dependence on men for making a living, and the sexual attractiveness and allure of the women-of-color, Cable ended his story neatly with what must have seemed to many of his readers as simply a lie.

The result of his frustration with "'Tite Poulette" was his novelette, *Madame Delphine,* which he published one year after *The Grandissimes.*[20] Madame Delphine, like Madame John, is a quadroon, but her daughter Olive *is* in fact an octoroon. Madame Delphine denies her motherhood in order to enable her daughter to marry the white Ursin Lemaitre, "a pure-blooded French Creole who would trace his pedigree back to the god Mars" (195). Cable, in an effort to protect his moral stance, portrays Olive as a virtual saint, who is "as white as Cynthia" (219). Ursin Lemaitre is portrayed as one of the Baratarians, the group of Louisiana privateers led by the notorious Jean and Pierre Lafitte in the early 1880s.[21] Lemaitre is converted to Christianity when, during an act of piracy, Olive handed him a Bible to read. Madame Delphine, on the other hand, is not as bright as Madame John and is described as "a small, rather tired-looking, dark quadroone" (194). Even though the French Quarter is often as seductive as in the earlier story, Cable also depicts the area as "a region of architectural decrepitude, where. . .upon everything has settled down a long sabbath of decay" (190). While he sets the time period of the story in 1821–22, as in "'Tite Poulette," in *Madame Delphine* Cable emphasizes more dramatically the changes that have occurred in the twenty years since the golden period of Creole life; he paints boldly the atmosphere of decay in the Quarter and suggests that the newly Americanized Esplanade area on the outskirts of the Quarter would also suffer as a result of its complicity in the racial sins of the area.

The moral consciousness of *Madame Delphine* is voiced by Père Jerome, a Creole Roman Catholic priest who is "remarkable among Cable's characters as being one of the very few Catholics who are sympathetically portrayed as Catholics."[22] Instead of blaming Madame Delphine or Ursin Lemaitre for their wrongdoing, he blames the society: "We all have a share in one another's sins" (203), he preaches in the pulpit of St. Louis Cathedral. "To you, Mme. Delphine, as you are placed," continues Père Jerome, "every white man in this country, on land or on water, is a pirate" (210). The whole society, Père Jerome preaches, is guilty of both the actions of the Baratarians and the actions of the quadroons. Nevertheless, in the tradition of sentimental fiction, Cable has Madame Delphine die in the confessional on the Sunday following her lie to the friends of Ursin Lemaitre, when she swore that she was not the mother of Olive and produced pictures of her white lover (the natural father) and his sister (dead before Olive was born), whom she professed to be the natural mother. While *Madame Delphine* was much more insistently moralistic in teaching that the racial problem was the sin of all Americans, not just southerners, or Louisianians, than the earlier "'Tite Poulette," Cable still felt it necessary to voice his respect for religious and societal order. It was necessary that Madame

Delphine be punished, though Olive *would* become a member of an aristocratic New Orleans "white" family. Racial stratifications could never be rationally contained.

The Grandissimes

If Cable disavowed the evident political intent of his early stories, he was less disingenuous about the novel that brought him infamy in his native city and region. In "My Politics" he wrote, "It was impossible that a novel written by me then should escape being a study of the fierce struggle going on around me, regarded in the light of that past history—those beginnings—which had so differentiated the Louisiana civilization from the American scheme of public society."[23]

The "fierce struggle" going on around him as he wrote *The Grandissimes* was what he would later designate "The Negro Question," the inextricable key to the "Southern riddle." In 1877 Reconstruction had ended in the South, and immediately Democrats, White Leaguers, and other conservative forces began to rescind the rights just granted the slaves freed by the Fourteenth and Fifteenth Amendments. Poll taxes and examinations curtailed or prevented execution of the franchise by blacks. The "strange career of Jim Crow" began its conquest of the South, and the lines of hatred and hostility between the races hardened; enlightened, rational thought was increasingly silenced.[24] But when *The Grandissimes* was published in 1880, Cable was certain that the racial question could still be viewed from the perspective of its causes, and an ethical and moral solution could be found.

In *The Grandissimes* Cable planned to influence the rational thinkers of post-Civil War America by pointing out the antecedents for the racist behavior of white southerners after Reconstruction in the intolerant and irrational actions of the Creoles at the time of Louisiana's cession to the United States. The study would demonstrate the truth of the Spencerian idea that history was a continuum and could be examined scientifically to discover antecedents to the present actions of a nation or people. Herbert Spencer had shown Americans the importance of studying every aspect of life scientifically, including history. The editor of the *Century Magazine* summed up Spencer's theory:

> What the citizen needs to know is the natural history of society,— every fact which can help us to an understanding of the way in which nations grow, and the conditions under which they prosper or languish. Not only do we need to know in minute detail the structure and methods of governments, political and ecclesiastical, but we should study the history of industry, the economic circumstances of every community, the state of commerce and of the arts, the prevailing habits of thought, down even to the commonest superstitions, the

habits of life, the homes, the aesthetic culture, the literature,—
everything, in short, that goes to make up the life of a people.[25]

Cable, a true Spencerian and Darwinian spirit, had amassed numerous details
on subjects of Louisiana life. Two years after *The Grandissimes* he prepared a
history of New Orleans that was published by the Census Office in connection
with the social statistics of the city.[26] His information on so many aspects of
Louisiana (and southern) life led many to view Cable as "the first authority on
all matters dealing with the people and history of Louisiana."[27]

Influenced by the Social Darwinists in his approach toward history, Cable
was also affected by the current evolutionary ideas of culture, a topic under
much discussion by Darwin, Spencer, and William Graham Sumner, as well
as contemporary writers, particularly Turgenev. Hjalmar Boyesen had written
to Cable in 1877 after reading his outline for *The Grandissimes,* "Yours is going to be the kind of novel which the Germans call a 'Kulturroman,' a novel in
which the struggling forces of two opposing civilizations crystalize and in
which they find their enduring monument."[28] By the "crystallization" of two
opposing cultures into their "enduring" monument, Boyesen suggests that the
opposing cultures would eventually merge, each keeping the strongest, most
durable, aspects of its identity. Definitions of culture and theories of how cultures change and are transmitted were just being formulated in Cable's day.[29]
While many believed that cultures were biologically determined and that
"primitive" cultures were by nature inferior to more "civilized" ones, which
would eventually lead to the termination of the "inferior" group, Cable's beliefs were not so clear-cut. He appreciated the relative strengths of the various
cultures he observed in cosmopolitan, yet provincial, New Orleans and recognized the need to understand them.

Through careful observation and documentation Cable portrayed the city
of New Orleans in *The Grandissimes* as the scene of cultural conflict—Creole
and American, on the one hand, black and white, on the other. Just as the Creoles and Americans learned from each other in their interaction, so did the two
races learn the inextricable connections between them. As Joseph Frowenfeld
confirms the white Honoré Grandissime's internal sense of justice, Frowenfeld
also learns from Honoré to be sympathetic toward differences and relents in
his feelings of northern superiority to the inhabitants of Louisiana. Therefore,
the white Honoré returns the land, which his uncle, Agricola Fusilier, had won
in a card fight with the young DeGrapion, to DeGrapion's widow, Aurora, and
her daughter, Clotilde. Because of the increased financial liabilities that this
transfer of land entails, especially in light of the new conditions for land titles
that the French transfer of Louisiana to America entailed, the white Honoré is
propelled to propose a merging of finances with his well-to-do brother, Honoré,
f.m.c., or free man of color. While the Creole patriarch, Agricola Fusilier, is

too stubborn and proud of his race—white (even though he is also proud of his Native American ancestry)—and of his ethnicity, Louisiana Creole, to make the kind of overtures that the white Honoré makes, Cable encourages the reader to see parallels between Agricola and the African Bras-Coupé, the rebellious slave who violates the *Code Noir* and runs away, is caught and hamstrung, but who dies uttering the words, "To Africa."

The violent deaths of Agricola, Bras-Coupé, and Clemence, the voodoo worshipper and cake merchant, reverberate in the description of the New Orleans setting, which Cable paints as a place where beauty and death/violence coexist. Cable thought that by drawing the oppositions of his dialectic clearly as they pertained to the American purchase of Louisiana and the turmoil that it caused, southerners would draw the inference that the cultural conflicts brought out by the Civil War and the Reconstruction must be handled logically and forthrightly, as experience taught the white Honoré Grandissime. The carefully drawn political history, which forms a large part of the novel's background and is based largely on fact, would, Cable thought, lead the reader to accept the novel's deeper meaning—his comment on the cultural history and moral values of the South.

The central historical and political episode in the novel is the transfer of Louisiana to the United States, a cession that occurred during a time of significant social change in New Orleans. Trade on the Mississippi had increased; boatmen and traders from the West as well as merchants from the North and Midwest flowed into the city hoping to make their fortunes. The Frowenfeld family had come to the city for just that reason. Frowenfeld describes New Orleans to Aurora and Clotilde as "a little city where wealth was daily pouring in, and a man had only to keep step, so to say, to march into possessions."[30] Unfortunately, the Creoles, in his view, did not take advantage of all that potential because they despised the humbler sorts of labor and handed "industry . . . over to slaves" (200). War with France had forced Spain's decision to cede the Louisiana Territory, which the Treaty of Paris had secretly transferred to the Spanish throne in 1764, back to the French. France, for its own political reasons, decided to sell Louisiana to the United States in 1803. On December 20, 1803 the French Prefect Laussat delivered the keys of the city to the new American Governor Claiborne, in a ceremony at the Place d'Armes.[31]

In the historical romance *The Grandissimes,* Cable writes that the Cession called for an American reconstruction in the city, which often led to acts of violence; for instance, the mob ransacks Frowenfeld's shop and threatens to assault him when he enters the Creole coffee-house in his search for Sylvestre to stop the approaching duel between the young man and Agricola. "The American reconstruction went harder with the Creoles than the Spanish," wrote Grace King, Creole apologist, in her history, *New Orleans: The Place and the People.* "A thousand common traits congenialized the French and Spanish

Bayou Teche. The Frowenfeld's introduction to the city was to "a land hung in mourning, darkened by gigantic cypresses, submerged; a land of reptiles, silence, shadow, decay." Courtesy The Historic New Orleans Collection, Museum/Research Center, Acc. No. 1974.25.31.23.

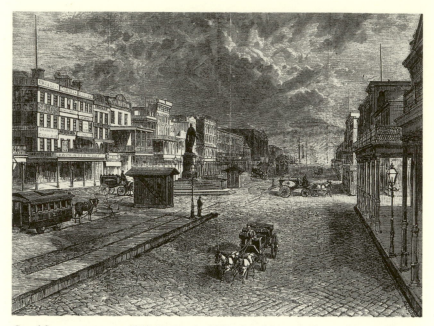

Canal Street gutters, ca. 1880. During the 1880s Canal Street had open drainage canals along the sidewalks. Courtesy The Historic New Orleans Collection, Museum/Research Center, Acc. No. 1981.216i (page 22) and Acc. No. 1980.137.23 (page 23).

character. Intercourse with the Americans, barbarians they were called, re-vealed only antagonisms."[32] Cable implicitly parallels the American Louisiana transfer of 1803 and the Southern Reconstruction of 1865–77. In both events the violence resulted largely from culture-based confrontations and new power relationships that the political events determined.

The culture of New Orleans that Frowenfeld studies has despite its apparent gaiety and festivity the element of violence and death, which is reflected in the natural and urban landscape. The Frowenfelds' introduction to the culture of New Orleans was immediate on their approach to the city. On board ship, they are disappointed by the darkness and wildness of the land, "a land hung in mourning, darkened by gigantic cypresses, submerged; a land of reptiles, silence, shadow, decay" (9). Similarly, Lafcadio Hearn wrote that in his first impressions of the city, there was "one idea running through them all—Love and Death. . . . There are tropical lilies which are venomous, but they are more beautiful than the frail and icy-white lilies of the North."[33] From Cable and Hearn to William Faulkner and Tennessee Williams, writers have used the seductive lushness of the beauti-ful tropical landscape and the eminence of death through natural or human-caused violence to epitomize the romantic myth of New Orleans.

Recurrently, the narrator of *The Grandissimes* emphasizes that the city is just a spot of civilization, virtually an island, surrounded by deadly swamps and the Mississippi River, lakes and bayous, some of them unnavigable. It is very nearly a part of the wild swamp itself. John Cleman notes that Cable depicts New Orleans as a community in its early stages of formation, when the conflict between man and environment was still vital, as in an earlier romance,

Hawthorne's *The Scarlet Letter*.[34] Cable describes the urban landscape in *The Grandissimes* much as Mark Twain described New Orleans in *Life on the Mississippi*; there are open drainage canals along the sidewalks outside the heart of town, and the sidewalks themselves are "only a rough, rank turf, lined on the side next the ditch with the gun-wales of broken-up flat-boats—ugly, narrow, slippery objects" (70). The upper boundary of the city is Canal Street, which will become the main thoroughfare of the commercial district, but is then an open canal with "foul crawling waters" emptying into the swamp on the other side of it (384). The other boundary of the city is not far from Esplanade Street, where the Grandissime mansion, a house held up by white-plastered brick pillars "fifteen feet up from the reeking ground," is located (222). The forest and swamp where Clemence is killed by the Grandissime men is contiguous with the plantation. The infecting climate of the swamp has an impact on the city, being largely responsible for tuberculin conditions like that from which Dr. Keene suffers and certainly for the yellow fever epidemics with which the city was constantly threatened historically.

As Cable illustrates repeatedly in the novel, the cultural landscape of New Orleans can be rife with the same contrasts as the physical setting. When the young American innocent Frowenfeld, proud of his capacity for reason and straightforward behavior, takes on the study of the Creole community he had recently joined, he becomes "involved among shadows. . .in an atmosphere of hints, allusions, faint unspoken admissions, ill-concealed antipathies. . .whisperings of hidden strife" (133). He learns that the culture he confronts is vastly different from his. Like the landscape, it is seductive, but also wild, violent, and often irrational, qualities that are personified in the patriarch of the Creole community, Agricola Fusilier; as the name implies, he is tied to the land (Agricola) and at the same time is a "tinderbox."[35] Lover of Louisiana, he is also an example of the typical chauvinistic white southerner, intolerant, proud, irrational in his adherence to established mores, particularly the established hierarchical social order which regulated race, caste, and gender.

Agricola's "antithetical double"[36] is Bras-Coupé, the runaway slave and former Jaloff chieftain. The irony of their parallel descriptions and destinies is the essence of Cable's dialectic in *The Grandissimes* specifically and his overall myth of New Orleans and the South generally. Honoré, f.m.c., stabs Agricola to death when the latter, seeing the Creole of color wearing his hat in Frowenfeld's pharmacy, orders him to take it off. Honoré, f.m.c., answers in French, "I wear my hat on my head" (463). When Agricola, in turn, strikes him on the head with his staff, Honoré, f.m.c., stabs him three times in the back. Ironically, Agricola dies at the same time that the Grandissime men shoot Clemence in the back, laughing as she limps forward from the trap in which they caught her, and shouting, "Run, Clemence . . . Courri! courri, Clemence!

The Place d'Armes of the 1880s, later Jackson Square. Courtesy The Historic New Orleans Collection, Museum/Research Center, Acc. No. 1981.247.12.92.

C'est pou to' vie! ha, ha, ha—" (470). Clemence is killed as a punishment for laying the voodoo gris-gris (curse) under Agricola's pillow. Agricola, fearing Clemence, has misread the coolness of the other person of color (Honoré), thereby living through what Cable thought was one of the South's greatest fears: "It was not when Clemence lay in irons, it is barely now, that our South is casting off a certain apprehensive tremor, generally latent, but at the slightest provocation active, and now and then violent, concerning her 'blacks'" (457).

The Bras-Coupé story is the center of the cultural history that Cable recreates, as the cession is the center of the political history. It also gives focus to the novel's symbolism and brings all the characters into a definite relation to each other. Since in his depiction of Bras-Coupé, Cable makes use of an old story of Louisiana folklore and history, most New Orleanians would have recognized the story and its several versions while reading *The Grandissimes*. Certainly Cable felt that some of them probably criticized his liberal adaptation of the story to fit his moral purposes. R. O. Stephens has traced various developments of the story.[37] In most of the accounts Bras-Coupé had actually lost one of his arms; some accounts attribute the loss to self-mutilation. Cable chose to use the name as a symbolic one that the African adopted for himself: in losing him, his tribe would feel that their right arm had been cut off. The larger significance of the name was, however, that he became the "type of all slavery, turning into flesh and blood the truth that all slavery is maiming"

(243). In many of the accounts Bras-Coupé committed a number of violent acts; his death, usually by hanging, was to be expected. Cable, however, intended to reveal the harsh applications of the Louisiana Black Code in his story, even though the code was no longer followed at the end of the eighteenth century when Cable's Bras-Coupé carried out his exploits.

In the novel, Bras-Coupé runs away only after assaulting his master. As the Black Code exacted death of a slave for such an act, Bras-Coupé has no choice but to escape to the swamps, but before leaving he lays a voodoo curse on the plantation. He is eventually captured and punished according to the Black Code; hamstrung and ears shorn off, he becomes the mutilated form suggested by his name. In the eyes of the reader and the Grandissime family, as they remember and retell the story in the eight years following Bras-Coupé's death, he has died a martyr. On his deathbed he had heroically assured all that he was going to Africa and to freedom. Cable makes the African chieftain/ slave a more honorable character than he appears to be in many accounts. He also places the episode at the same time historically as the St. Malo conspiracy, a part of the slave insurrection at Pointe Coupée, Louisiana, and Toussaint L'Ouverture's insurrection in Haiti (1794-95).[38] Palmyre has hoped to train Bras-Coupé in the methods of revolution; to her he is "the gigantic embodiment of her own dark, fierce will, the expanded realization of her life-time longing for terrible strength" (175). Similarly, Honoré, f.m.c., feels that he is incapable of becoming another Toussaint l'Ouverture, even though he recognizes the need for such a leader. He fears that he will become a Bras-Coupé instead.

The story of Bras-Coupé is told by three different persons in the center of the novel, following the fête de grandpère in the Grandissime family mansion. Throughout the novel, from the time that Frowenfeld's family approaches Louisiana on board ship until Agricola's death, the story of Bras-Coupé recurs as a chorus to the drama as it unfolds. The episode reveals the real violence (to the oppressed and the oppressors) that exists alongside the apparently well-ordered New Orleans caste society and demonstrates how intimately related are all classes of that system in terms of actions and consequences. Over the entire society, in spite of its apparent gaiety, hangs the pall of slavery, an unmitigated evil, which will exact its measure of guilt and suffering for generations to come. In Cable's careful construction of a Creole-English dialect, Honoré describes the shadow that slavery had cast on the South: "I am amaaze at the length, the blackness of that shadow!. It is the Nemesis w'ich, instead of coming afteh, glides along by the side of this morhal, political, commercial, social mistake. It blanches, my-de'-seh, ow whole civilization! It drhags us a centurhy behind the rhes' of the world!" (219)

In Cable's view, the cultural confrontation that took place in New Orleans between Creoles and Americans and between blacks, Creoles of color, and whites resulted in a merging of cultures rather than in the domination of a weaker culture by a stronger. In his pairing of parallel and contrasting characters, he constantly demonstrates the interdependence of the cultures. On the political level, there is the continuing dialectic of Frowenfeld and the white Honoré. As Ringe has pointed out, they both learn from each other, and not just Honoré from Frowenfeld.[39] Honoré steels himself to stand up for justice, not just to seek expediency; Frowenfeld gains tolerance and understanding, though he cannot help but play the role of judge since he is set up as the detached observer commenting on the community and its culture. On the cultural level, the dialectic must occur within the mind of the reader; it is not made explicit. But in addition to the antithetical doubles, Agricola and Bras-Coupé, there are other doubles: Honoré and Honoré, f.m.c., and Palmyre and Aurora, two brothers and two sisters, in a sense.

While there are many stories of quadroon women in post-Civil War literature, there are few of the male quadroon. Cable's characterization of Honoré, f.m.c., anticipates Faulkner's treatment of miscegenation in such characterizations as Charles Bon and Lucas Beauchamp, and Charles Chesnutt's Paul Marchand, f.m.c., in the unpublished novel of that name. While the two Honorés went to school together in Paris, and Honoré's father hoped at his death that the two brothers could somehow be reunited, it is obvious by their contrasting temperaments that they could never be more than financial partners. Honoré, f.m.c., is defined by narrow, limited environments throughout the novel—in contrast to the light, open, unencumbered natural settings which often surround the white Honoré. The sumptuous furnishings of his home have qualities of "immovable largeness and heaviness, lofty sobriety, abundance of finely wrought brass mounting, motionless richness of upholstery, much silent twinkle of pendulous crystal, a soft semi-obscurity. . .cool and cavernous" (434). Cut off from the mainstream of society despite his wealth and education, the man, like his home, is characterized by a certain nobility, which is, however, qualified by heaviness, sobriety, and paralysis. Honoré, f.m.c., will never be a leader of his people; his pent-up anger, frustrated love, and lack of will leave him without a sense of self-definition. "[Honoré] was like the sun's warmth wherever he went; and the other Honoré was like his shadow" (265). As William Bedford Clark notes, the common name of the two brothers suggests that "the whole question of Grandissime honor is tied to their mutual destinies,"[40] but the idealized union in the business Grandissimes Frères becomes moot when Honoré, f.m.c., later drowns himself in Paris, after having been rejected again by Palmyre, who loves his brother, Honoré *sang pur*.

Palmyre and Aurora are also antithetical doubles that forge a comment on the situation of the two Honorés. As children the women were almost sisters, the father having acquired the young slave quadroon as a companion to his daughter. When they were older he sent Palmyre away because of her increasing domination over Aurora and, it is suggested, her skill with voodoo. Thus in this quadroon-white pair, the Negro is the stronger of the two. The sisterly relation between Palmyre and Aurora exists in spite of the opposite temperaments of the two and the extremely different ways they are viewed by society. The contrasts in their characters are made clearer by the opposing, though parallel, environments with which they are associated. Palmyre is described as "this poisonous blossom of crime" (189), while Aurora is "the red, red, full-blown, faultless joy of the garden" (84). Although Aurora is extremely superstitious and consults Palmyre, as voodoo priestess, on matters pertaining to love and money, she is always associated with the beneficent side of nature. Her home, though modest, is well-ordered with bits of crystal and silver and is awash in light and warmth: "The brass work, of which there is much, is brilliantly burnished, and the front room is bright and cheery" (84). When Frowenfeld visits Aurora and Clotilde, there is a bright fire in the fireplace.

While Palmyre's home is, on the exterior, anyway, similar to Aurora's, the atmospheres and interior details are direct opposites. Palmyre's home is "merely neat" (95); there are no pictures on the wall, no bits of crystal and silver; the furniture is Creole-made, not imported. While Aurora's front room is brightened by a portrait of Our Lady of Many Sorrows, Palmyre's is marked by one singular piece of furniture: "a small table of dark mahogany supported on the upward-writhing images of three scaly serpents" (96). There is something icy and inhuman about Palmyre's home, just as there is about her personality. When Frowenfeld visits Palmyre to check on her wounds, he goes to the fire to warm himself, but instead of receiving warmth, he thinks about the fire of the Judgment Day: "What ranks and companies would have to stand up in the Great Day with her and answer as accessory before the fact!" (189). Cable's portrait of Palmyre as the Creole woman-of-color is unusual in this work. She is neither long-suffering nor a nurse or mother-figure, as are Madame John (of "'Tite Poulette") and Madame Delphine. Instead, "this monument of the shame of two races . . . this answerable white man's accuser—this would-be murderess" is willful, vengeful, unusually sexual, for Cable's writings, and has a terrible longing for power (189). Voodoo gives her some of the power that she craves, for Palmyre Philosophe is a skillful hairdresser but is known best as a practitioner of "the less baleful rites of the voudous" (81).

Cable uses voodoo, like the carefully delineated pairings of characters, to demonstrate how inextricable the African and white cultures were in New Orleans.[41] The African and Santo Domingan religious practices held a definite sway over the everyday life of many New Orleanians. In the novel the legendary account of Bras-Coupé's voodoo powers is related as a realistic event. Bras-Coupé's curse on his master's plantation ends up with the ruin of the plantation and the death of Don José Martinez. Palmyre's powers as a voodoo priestess lead Agricola to manumit her because of his fear, not his sense of humanity. Her plan to take out her vengeance on Agricola by planting charms

in his home leads to the most brutal incident in the novel, the gratuitous murder of Clemence, the black *marchande de calas.* In Cable's day there were
numerous such senseless lynchings of blacks, and the numbers were increasing steadily, leading some historians to call the 1880s and 1890s the nadir in
race relations.[42] Cable attempted to make his contemporaries see what fear and
hate could lead them to by disguising his message in the dress and habits of
another time. If his readers accepted the prevailing idea of history as organic
and progress as a certainty, they would learn from past mistakes.

Cable did not realize, however, just how powerful was the related discourse
of the Social Darwinists, which accounted the white race as superior and the
black as primitive, the missing link, in the evolution from primates to humans.
At the 1872 New Orleans Mardi Gras, in fact, the theme and costume motif
was the Missing Link.[43]

After *The Grandissimes* and *Madame Delphine* (1881), Cable, for all practical purposes, was forced by the strength of public opinion in New Orleans
and throughout the South to give up the fight for Negro rights in fiction. As
Arlin Turner and Louis D. Rubin have explained in their biographies and articles, northerners, foremost among them William Dean Howells, applauded
the realistic portrait of Louisiana Creoles and the detailed picture of the New
Orleans environment. However, as Cable became "the fashion of the moment"
in the Northeast, meeting William Dean Howells, Oliver Wendell Holmes,
John Greenleaf Whittier, Matthew Arnold, and Mark Twain in New England,
his situation in the South became increasingly violent. Creoles in New Orleans
castigated him. Some would even spit in the street when his name was mentioned.[44] As a result, Cable turned his attention to social reform. He continued
his campaign for reform of prisons and asylums and continued to write and
make speeches on the Negro Cause, which he spoke about at the University of
Alabama on June 18, 1884. But in his fiction he moved away from the problem of race.

Doctor Sevier

In September 1884 *Dr. Sevier* was published by Osgood. Not primarily a Creole story, Cable emphasized in this novel the need for social reform, and the
impact of European immigrants and northerners on the New Orleans culture,
as he had researched it for his census report and his history, *The Creoles of
Louisiana* (1883).

The New Orleans of *Doctor Sevier* is the city that Cable knew in his
youth—the city near the warehouses on Tchoupitoulas Street on the river,
where he had watched the commercial activity of flatboatmen, ships, and
barges of cotton coming in and out. In the 1840s and 1850s New Orleans was
in the midst of a cotton boom; it had the greatest slave market in the country,

eighty ballrooms for dancing, and the fabulous Metairie racing track (which later became the Metairie cemeteries). Cable had become a bookkeeper at the age of fourteen when his father died, and he knew very well the seasonal vicissitudes of that business, as the disinherited John Richling discovers after arriving in New Orleans with his young wife, Mary. Cable avoids almost completely the discussion of race in *Doctor Sevier*; Zenobia, the quadroon landlady of the first apartment that the Richlings rent, is the only person of color in the novel. Instead, Cable centered the novel on the social problems of the metropolis in the Gilded Age—immigration and overcrowding, poor prisons, hospitals, and asylum facilities, underemployment, epidemics caused by poor sanitary conditions. The latter were all too clearly based in fact. The 1853 yellow fever epidemic had, for example, left eleven thousand New Orleanians dead;[45] one-third of them were Irish immigrants, who, along with immigrants from Germany, Italy, and Latin America had swarmed to New Orleans during the 1830s and 1840s, making it the fourth largest city in the United States: "Immigrants and Americans found in New Orleans an almost ideal combination of the New and Old Worlds—vigorous crude expansionism and the American myth of instant wealth versus a cosmopolitan, cultured way of life."[46] The 1878 yellow fever epidemic had left 4,046 persons dead. By the 1880s when Cable led reform, especially in the areas of health, asylums, and prisons, New Orleans had the reputation as "a harbor of pestilence whose officials could not be trusted to tell the truth about disease in the city."[47]

The Gilded Age was also a time of crime and violence for New Orleans. Between 1880 and 1887 there were numerous strikes, as organized labor struggled to become a reality; vigilante groups defied law enforcement, as could be seen in the notorious assassination of Police Chief David C. Hennessy in October 1890 and the mob-led executions which followed; and the Louisiana Lottery became a center of controversy as corrupter of businesses and government.[48]

Stemming from his work with the prisons and asylums, Cable argues in *Doctor Sevier* that wealthy people, such as Doctor Sevier, have a moral responsibility to help the poor (in this case, John and Mary Richling), in spite of the prevailing counter-arguments of the advocates of Social Darwinism. In other words, Cable agreed with the main tenets of Andrew Carnegie's "The Gospel of Wealth," that although the law of competition "is best for the race, because it insures the survival of the fittest in every department," the wealthy person must also become "trustee and agent for his poorer brethren, bringing to their service his superior wisdom, experience, and ability to administer, doing of them better than they would or could do for themselves."[49]

More important than the lessons learned by Doctor Sevier and John Richling, who become the "double centers" of the novel, *Doctor Sevier* gives us a glimpse into the kinds of social discourse taking place in Cable's time. As industrialization made its impact on the New South, New Orleans, like other big cities of the United States, showed the effects of social change. The new southern industrialists were forced to keep up with a competitive national spirit. John, a member of the old southern gentility (of Virginia) was unmotivated to operate successfully in the new environment of the South until he took a job with the German immigrant Reisen. The immigrants—Reisen, Raphael Ristofalo (Italian) and Kate Riley (Irish)—are the ones who bring new energy to the old city. Cable painstakingly reproduces the language of the German, Italian, Irish, as well as Creole New Orleanians. Their encounters and interaction represent social change taking place in New Orleans and other metropolises across the nation during the 1850s and 1860s.

As a humanist, Cable questioned the ruthlessness of capitalists and attempted to persuade Americans of the necessity for social change. He chose John Richling, a member of the aristocracy, the landed gentry, along with Mary, his wife and a member of the northern working poor, to be his protagonists in this novel, for he knew that they would more easily win the sympathy of his readers than a black, an immigrant, or a poor white in similar conditions. If the agrarian Richling was so incapacitated by the new industrialism, every man then surely ran such a risk. A great democracy, Cable argued, should make room for the rich and the poor, the old, the established classes and the new, men and women, in its overall mission.

In his writing, then, Cable continued his dialectic on the necessity for social change, but he expressed his thoughts on race in essays, speeches, and his Open Letter Club.[50] Writing to the Reverend R. C. Hitchcock, A.M., president of Straight University, Cable stated the plan of the Open Letter Club: "It was a group of citizens mainly resident in the South operating not by meetings but through the mails, and designed to supply the widely felt need of some well known medium through which information of every sort and from every direction, bearing upon the South, can be interchanged, in order for the promotion of the South's best interests, moral, intellectual and material."[51] In January 1885, his essay "The Freedman's Case in Equity" was published in *Century* magazine, and in September of that year, *Century* published "The Silent South." Southern editors, including Henry W. Grady of *The Atlanta Constitution* and the New Orleans historian Charles Gayarré, attacked Cable vehemently for his opinions and motives concerning the race question. After writing two more essays on the subject of black New Orleans culture, "The Dance in Place Congo" (published in *Century* in February 1886) and "Creole Slave Songs" (*Century,* April 1886), Cable left New Orleans and moved with his family to Northampton, Massachusetts. Although he wrote about Louisiana in *Bonaventure* (1888), *Strange True Stories of Louisiana* (1889), *Lovers of Louisiana* (1918), and *The Flower of the Chapdelaines* (1918), he expressed his thoughts about race only in letters, essays, and speeches after leaving New Orleans and the South.

In *Old Creole Days, The Grandissimes,* and *Doctor Sevier,* however, Cable established the patterns of dialectic that would define the fictional representation of New Orleans in much of the literature that would follow: the city's fusion of cultures—African, Creole, and Anglo-Saxon; the beauty and violence of both that culture and the landscape; the cosmopolitanism and provincialism of its population and mores; and the influence of Catholicism and voodoo. Cable, at once an outsider and an insider in New Orleans, had set forth publicly the parameters of the dialogue to follow. Cable had popularized for a larger American audience the image of "romantic old New Orleans." His picture of Creoles, voodoo, the Baratarians, the quadroon balls and *plaçage* arrangements, the mysterious gardens of the Vieux Carré, the natural disasters, the duels would continue to capture the minds of writers. More importantly, he had pointed out that the romantic image of New Orleans was due to the linkages of several cultures and that culture was dominant over societal laws or codes. Future writers would continue the dialogue over the definition of Creole and race and the power of the landscape and the culture over the psychology and behavior of its inhabitants.

Charles Chesnutt's "Paul Marchand, F.M.C.": A Last Word on "The Negro Question"

Since Charles Waddell Chesnutt's fiction dealt largely with characters of mixed racial ancestry, he must have been particularly interested in reading about the New Orleans Creoles of color in the histories and stories of George Washington Cable and Grace King. In his essay, "The Future American," Chesnutt wrote, "The Creole stories of Mr. Cable and other writers were not mere figments of the imagination; the beautiful octoroon was a corporeal fact; it is more than likely that she had brothers of the same complexion, though curiously enough the male octoroon has cut no figure in fiction, except in the case of the melancholy Honoré Grandissime, f.m.c."[52] Chesnutt believed that Cable both generally omitted the male octoroon from his fiction and emphasized the romantic features of racial contacts in Louisiana; like Albion Tourgée, Chesnutt wrote, Cable tended to create portraits of the tragic mulatto, who was "tainted" by a drop of black blood.[53]

While most of Chesnutt's stories and novels are set in the southern rural communities of North Carolina, which he knew as a child and young teacher, or Ohio, where he lived for the greater part of his life, one of his six unpublished novels, "Paul Marchand, F.M.C.," takes place in New Orleans. It is a

Photograph by Edmondson

CHARLES WADDELL CHESNUTT
NOVELIST

Charles Waddell Chesnutt. Courtesy of the Photographs and Prints Division; Schomburg Center for Research in Black Culture; the New York Public Library; Astor, Lenox and Tilden Foundations.

historical novel, whose purpose is "warning" or "admonishing" the public so that present and future race relations in the South might be improved.[54]

Chesnutt wrote "Paul Marchand, F.M.C." around 1928.[55] A letter from Chesnutt to Harry C. Block of Alfred Knopf, dated June 8, 1928, indicates that Chesnutt was working on a new novel, but he advised Block, "It is entirely agreeable to me that you keep the manuscript of 'Paul Marchand' as you suggest in your letter."[56] Unfortunately, because "Paul Marchand" was never published, Chesnutt's chance to introduce a New Orleans male Creole of color to fiction was unrealized, although in the course of the novel, we find that Paul is really white. "Paul Marchand, F.M.C." seems to be his last fictional word on the continuing debate about the definition and importance of race in the United States. The novel's format is primarily a legal argument in which the illogicality of racial distinctions is made apparent through a series of events. The characterization, setting, and plot are all subordinate to the ideological argument.

The discussion of race was one of the most prominent topics of social discourse during the late nineteenth and early twentieth centuries, and Chesnutt participated in the discourse both through fiction and nonfiction. The discussion of the "Negro" question or the "Southern" question took place in most of the country's major magazines when Chesnutt's "The Goophered Grapevine" was published in August 1887 and "Po' Sandy" in May 1888, both in *The Atlantic Monthly*. The publication of these stories led to a correspondence between Chesnutt and George Washington Cable, which was to bring Chesnutt into the arena of public discussion on the race question. Cable wrote Chesnutt to congratulate him on his work after the publication of "Po' Sandy" and also enclosed several pamphlets issued by the Open Letter Club.[57] Immediately prior to Cable's letter to Chesnutt, an article on "Race Antagonism" by Senator James Eustis had been published in the *Forum* (October 1888), and a reply by Atticus Green Haygood, of Georgia, had been published in the *Independent* (November 8, 1888); both were distributed by the Open Letter Club in pamphlet form.[58] Cable and Chesnutt continued to correspond during the decade; the last letter between them in the Chesnutt Collection at Fisk University is dated February 20, 1897. Chesnutt advised Cable on matters of race, suggested names and issues for the Open Letter Club, and did research into such areas of concern as the election laws in southern states, the distribution of southern school funds, and the work of county governments in the South. Cable read and commented on Chesnutt's writing and attempted to help him get articles and novels published.[59]

While Cable and Chesnutt agreed in large part about the unfair treatment of blacks in education, the courts, the electoral system, and the importance of getting rid of the whole caste system of the South, positions reflected in Cable's essays and fiction during the 1870s, 1880s, and 1890s showed that their attitudes toward race diverged in at least one significant way. Cable consistently argued that there could be civil and political equality between the races without social equality. He believed that the fear of social relation with blacks and the possibility of legally recognized miscegenation were the bugbears that led many southern whites to support segregation and disfranchisement. Thus he attempted to appease this southern element of the population with such statements as "we may reach the moon someday, not social equality,"[60] even though he knew also that irrational racial distinctions were made "to preserve the old arbitrary supremacy of the master class over the menial without regard to the decency or indecency of appearance or manners in either the white individual or the colored."[61]

Ironically, in fact, Cable's crusade for Negro rights came to an end shortly after vociferous attacks on him in the editorial columns of southern newspapers, occasioned when he dined with his black host and hostess, Mr. and Mrs. J. C. Napier, in their Nashville, Tennessee, home after they had arranged his meeting with black leaders there. An editorial in the *Nashville Daily American* voiced the opinion of many southerners: "In the South a man must choose between white and black, and Mr. Cable has chosen."[62] The furor over the Napier incident brought the already financially damaged Open Letter Club to an end. After the address, "The Southern Struggle for Pure Government" (1890), his book *The Negro Question* (1890), and two more essays on the Negro in the South ("Does the Negro Pay for His Education?" (1892) and "Education for the Common People in the South" (1892), Cable ceased to write on the civil rights question.[63]

Chesnutt, by contrast, believed not only in the necessity for social equality but also that the ultimate answer to the problem of race relations in the United States was the amalgamation of the races, or racial fusion. His idea concurs with that of Alexis de Tocqueville, who wrote in 1830 that the only hope for sound race relations in the United States in the future was that "the Negroes and the whites must either wholly part or wholly mingle."[64] According to Chesnutt, the phenomenon had actually been occurring slowly and obscurely for over three hundred years. "Slavery was a rich soil for the production of a mixed race, and one need only read the literature and laws of the past two generations to see how steadily, albeit slowly and insidiously, the stream of dark blood has insinuated itself into the veins of the dominant . . . race."[65]

Chesnutt's idea of racial fusion as an answer to the race problem appears in many of his essays and lies behind much of the fiction. He suggests the idea in one of his first essays on the race problem, "An Insider's View of the Negro Question." Written as a complement to Cable's essay, "The Negro Question in the United States" (published in the *London Contemporary Review*, the *New York Tribune*, and the *Chicago Inter-Ocean* in 1888), "An Insider's View" was edited by Cable and revised several times but was never published. Chesnutt sent the manuscript to Cable on January 10, 1889, welcomed Cable's criticisms of it, and sent him three copies of "The Negro's Answer to the Negro Question"; on January 30, 1889, Cable sent back the manuscript with cuts of nearly five thousand words and suggested the title "The Negro's Review of the Negro Question" or "The Negro's Answer to the Negro Question." On February 12, 1889, the article was turned down by the *Forum,* and Cable suggested the *Century,* February 22, 1889; on March 4, 1889, Chesnutt wrote that the *North American Review* had also turned down the manuscript. Chesnutt sent Cable a rejection by Richard Watson Gilder of *Century* on March 13, 1889. Gilder said in a letter to Cable of that date, "Mr. Chesnutt's paper,— 'The Negro's Answer to the Negro Question,' is a timely political paper—so timely and so political—in fact so partisan—that we cannot handle it. It should appear at once somewhere."[66] In the essay Chesnutt pointed out that "in the united and aggressive public opinion of the North the Negro sees his chief hope for the speedy and peaceful recognition of his public rights at the South." He also stressed that blacks would insist upon their rights, and would, "if need be, die in the attempt to exercise them, and in defense of them." Also, blacks did not seek out assimilation of the races, but did not believe in any theory of race antagonism which would prevent the races from assimilating. On May 30, 1889, the *Independent* published "What Is a White Man?"; the essay incorporated some of the ideas of Chesnutt's earlier paper.[67]

Chesnutt defined his use of the term *race* in his three-part essay, "The Future American": "I use the word 'race' here in its popular sense—that of a people who look substantially alike, and are moulded by the same culture and dominated by the same ideals."[68] Like W. E. B. DuBois, who was also at the time writing on the definition of race, Chesnutt believed that there was no scientific basis for racial distinctions, but that race was determined by culture and common "ideals."[69] In his essay "The Future American: A Stream of Dark Blood" Chesnutt gives his clearest projection of the future ethnic type of the American people: "It is. . .in the three broad types—white, black and Indian— that the future American race will find the material for its formation. Any dream of a pure white race, of the Anglo-Saxon type, for the United States, may as well be abandoned as impossible, even if desirable." In appearance, the white race would predominate in most areas of the United States; occasionally there would be an obvious trace of the black ancestor, but "no one would care, for all would be tarred with the same stick."[70]

Chesnutt explores these ideas about racial melding in "Paul Marchand, F.M.C." Here he deals with the irrationality of racial distinctions in the complex, multicultural New Orleans community, where the status of Creoles of color made division according to the color line virtually impossible and where debates led to the major legal challenges to segregation in the late nineteenth century, the most well-known case being *Plessy v. Ferguson,* which originated in New Orleans. The Comité des Citoyens (Citizens Committee), a group of civic-minded Creoles of color, brought the case to court in opposition to the state statute which forbade the "mixing of races" in conveyances traveling from one place to another within the state. The loss of this case in the United States Supreme Court in 1896 officially began the reign of "separate but equal" legislation in the South.[71]

"Paul Marchand, F.M.C." takes place in the New Orleans of 1821. However, like Cable, Chesnutt mentions many parallels between the situation of that era and the time of the writing. The narrator describes the strict social hierarchy of the city in that period: (1) the Americans, who were a class apart, (2) the Creoles, who were the elite, but who were also losing commercial power to the Americans, (3) the *gens de couleur,* who were often persons of means, well-educated but denied civil and social equality, and (4) the black slaves, "whose arduous and unrequited toil, upon the broad, deep-soiled plantations of indigo, rice, cotton and sugar cane, furnished the wherewithal to maintain the wealth and luxury of the capital."[72] Similarly, in Chesnutt's day, blacks still provided the basis of the South's agricultural community, but were subject to an ever-increasing limitation of the rights as citizens granted to them during Reconstruction. The major parallel that Chesnutt wants his reader to draw is expressed by Paul Marchand, who tells his family that he cannot turn from being a Negro to being white overnight because of a legal document. "Race consciousness," he says, "is not a matter of blood alone, but is in large part the product of education and environment. It is social rather than personal" (171).

The unpublished novel is a sophisticated tour de force. Paul Marchand, a free man of color (f.m.c.), has been raised by a quadroon mother with funds provided by a benefactor through the lawyer, M. Renard. He has studied in Paris, read Thomas Paine's *Rights of Man,* and has become an accomplished fencer, before returning to New Orleans. Although he is light-complexioned enough to pass for white and with the cooperation of family members and friends could have done so fairly easily, even in New Orleans, he decides (like Chesnutt) to define his race even more clearly by marrying a darker woman, still of the quadroon caste, who also has a significant dowry from her white father.[73] Although Paul is well off as a family and business man, he still chafes under the restrictions of the New Orleans caste system, which has grown more unbearable under American rule and increasing domination, for the Spanish and French had always had more regard for the *gens de couleur.*

After several insults from whites, Paul has decided to return to France with his family, but he is thrown into the *calaboza* (jail) for entering a quadroon ball, the balls being restricted to white men and quadroon women. Freed by his lawyer, he learns that the old man, Pierre Beaurepas, wealthiest man in New Orleans, has died and left him as heir and has recognized him as his white, legitimate son. The five nephews of Pierre Beaurepas, all refugees from Santo Domingo during the Revolution, had each expected to be named heir; thrown

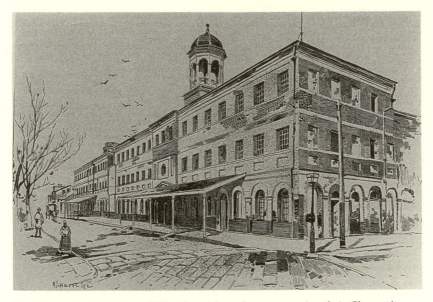

The Orleans Parish Jail, ca. 1880s. The calaboza *features prominently in Chesnutt's
"Paul Marchand, F.M.C." and Cable's* Doctor Sevier. *Courtesy The Historic New
Orleans Collection, Museum/Research Center, Acc. No. 1974.25.3.241.*

into a frenzy, they can nonetheless do little but submit to the word of the law.
They offer to join hands with Paul, especially since all of them have borrowed
money from their uncle, and are now indebted to his heir. However, before
Paul will shake hands with them, he says he must uphold the family honor and
its motto, "Coup pour Coup" ("Blow for Blow"), by challenging each of them
that has insulted him in any way to a duel; he has kept a careful written record
of such matters.

The dilemma that Paul is thrown into is made more complex by the fact of
his marriage to the quadroon, Julie. Now that his marriage is illegal under the
laws of Louisiana and his children illegitimate, he is free to marry the beautiful white Josephine Morales; Pierre Beaurepas had decreed her to be the wife
of his heir in order to save her family's plantation, Trois Pigeons, because her
father, Don José Morales, had once saved his life on the battlefield. The temp-
tation is great for Paul to accept a life completely in the white world. In the
meantime, as Paul looks through his father's papers, he notices a letter from
Beaurepas's sister-in-law in Santo Domingo during the Revolution, which
states that her four sons and one daughter will soon arrive at his home with her
slave Zabet. She fears what will happen to her youngest—the daughter—who
is frail. Since no daughter arrived in New Orleans, Paul demands that Zabet, a

marchande de calas like Clemence in *The Grandissimes,* tell him who the fifth, imposter "son" is; very reluctantly, Zabet admits that the fifth child is really a Negro, the child of a union between her daughter and Pierre's brother. This fortuitous circumstance is what Chesnutt calls "The Black Drop" (chapter 11). The narrator never says explicitly who the black drop is, but all clues point to Philippe, the youngest and most worthy of the nephews, the only one respected by either Paul Marchand or his father Pierre.

In the end Paul decides to reject the role offered him as head of the family and move with his immediate family to France, "where men are judged by their worth and not by their color, where in all honor my wife can be my wife and my children my children and I need not be ashamed of them nor they afraid of me" (172). He then frees the slaves and transfers the property to Philippe, whom he has chosen to be his successor. Before leaving, Paul says that he feels the five of them have a right to know that one of them is not white, and asks them if they wish to know that person's identity. The immediate consensus is that they do not wish to know, and "the black drop" remains a secret, to all except the reader, the narrator, and Paul, who realize that the head of the wealthy Creole family is a free man of color, while the man who was formally a free man of color (Paul) is now white.

The plot of "Paul Marchand" demonstrates the important role that law plays in the story as organizing theme or leitmotif. The theme of law recurs in the works of Chesnutt, e.g., *The House Behind the Cedars* and *The Marrow of Tradition.* Chesnutt himself was a trained lawyer, a member of the Ohio Bar, and a legal stenographer who founded his own legal stenographic service in Cleveland, Ohio, in 1890. The theme also reflects, however, the significance of the courts in determining the path that race relations would take in the United States at the turn of the century, beginning with the *Plessy v. Ferguson* case, which was decided by the United States Supreme Court in 1896. In the same year that Chesnutt wrote "Paul Marchand," for example, Edward Larocque Tinker published the novel *Toucoutou,* based on a well-known lawsuit that took place in New Orleans shortly before the Civil War. The suit was brought by a young woman against a neighbor who had publicly accused her of having Negro ancestry. She claimed to be white, and the case was brought before the Louisiana Supreme Court, where the young woman, nicknamed "Toucoutou," lost her appeal. Joseph Beaumont, a Creole of color and a poet, wrote satirical songs about the case, generally expressing the disgust of the people of color at what they perceived as the attempt of the young woman to pass for white.[74]

Chesnutt knew the New Orleans culture and landscape primarily through the writings of Cable and Grace King; he acknowledges in the foreword of "Paul Marchand" that "If there was not a Paul Marchand case in New Orleans, there might well have been, for all the elements of such a drama were present, as is clearly set out in the careful studies of life in the old Creole city, by Miss Grace King and Mr. George W. Cable, which are available for the student or the general reader—the author has made free reference to them—as well as in the more obscure records and chronicles from which they drew their informa- tion." As Sylvia Render points out, using such second-hand material in his fic- tion was unusual for Chesnutt.[75] Thus, while the characterizations in "Paul Marchand" are rich in ambivalence, especially concerning racial identity and motivations, they are also derivative of, and a comment on, Cable's and King's fiction.

Paul Marchand, for example, can be viewed as a combination of the two Honoré Grandissimes. Unlike the passive and melancholy Honoré, f.m.c., Paul Marchand keeps a record of the wrongs that he encounters, as though he fore- sees that he will one day have the opportunity of righting them. Cable portrays Honoré, f.m.c., as "an accusation . . . against that 'caste' which shuts him up within its narrow and almost solitary limits!"[76] The restrictions on his social and business life have made him virtually ineffectual, not even capable of win- ning the love of the quadroon Palmyre, who loves the white Honoré. In con- trast, Paul Marchand is a natural leader, and in his marriage and career choices, he listens to reason rather than to passion. As the white Honoré rights two wrongs by restoring Aurora's land to her and going into business with his half- brother, Paul Marchand's role is also the righter of wrongs. After carrying out the duels with his cousins to redeem his honor, he leaves the United States in order to live a life integrated socially and politically. While this decision to go to France is perhaps the only resolution that Chesnutt could work out given the terms of the moral debate, it is not the resolution that he espoused for blacks in his essays. In "An Insider's View of the Negro Question," for example, he argued that colonization of blacks in Africa or some other part of the world was not the answer; "by the unrequited toil of two centuries they have helped to make the country what it is, and they have a right to enjoy such advantages as a well-developed civilization may offer them."[77]

Just as Chesnutt's creation of Paul Marchand can be viewed as a criticism of Cable's portrait of the ineffectual quadroon male, so do his portraits of Julie, Paul's quadroon wife, and her sister Lizette comment on Cable's representa- tions of quadroon women by de-emphasizing the earlier writer's sentimental treatment of such characters as 'Tite Poulette and Olive, daughter of Madame Delphine. Cable apparently absolves the daughters of sin, while tainting their mothers with the society's sin; Chesnutt does not omit the charge of sinfulness from the lives of his quadroon women, although he carefully saves Julie from such circumstances; Grace King would slander all women of color with the charge of excessive sensuality. Chesnutt attempts to de-sentimentalize his qua- droon women by portraying them in terms of the practical circumstances of their everyday lives.

In "Paul Marchand, F.M.C." Chesnutt attempts to persuade his readers, much as Cable had done in *The Grandissimes,* of the illogical nature of race prejudice. As Chesnutt had said in an unpublished address to the Bethel Literary and Historical Association, "History is instructive, and may warn or admonish; but to this quality literature adds the faculty of persuasion, by which men's hearts are reached, the springs of action touched, and the currents of life directed."[78] In addition, he would correct some of the errors of Cable's portraiture of blacks of mixed ancestry. Unfortunately, he could not succeed in either objective because contemporary editors were not interested in publishing his legalistic fictional discourse about the nature of race. In 1928 the reading audience was much more interested in the idea of the New Negro as Alain Locke and other participants of the Harlem Renaissance defined and illustrated the concept. In his essay "Post-Bellum, Pre-Harlem," published in *The Crisis* in June 1931, Chesnutt, speaking as a veteran black American writer, commented on this new movement. He had written during a time, he said, when his race was never mentioned in announcing and advertising his books, a time very different from the present when the Negro was in vogue:

> The development of Harlem, with its large colored population in all shades, from ivory to ebony, of all degrees of culture, from doctors of philosophy to the lowest grade of illiteracy; its morals ranging from the highest to the most debased; with the vivid life of its cabarets, dance halls, and theatres; with its ambitious business and professional men, its actors, singers, novelists and poets, its aspirations and demands for equality—without which any people would merit only contempt—presented a new field for literary exploration which of recent years has been cultivated assiduously.[79]

While Chesnutt did not participate in this new field of literary exploration, he had left a legacy of his own.

In Chesnutt's "outsider's view" of New Orleans, but "insider's view" of the Negro Question, he further solidifies the myth of New Orleans as a city where the myth of race is particularly illusory. Thus, the opposition of reality/illusion in regard to race can be viewed as a voice responding to Cable in the continuing dialogue initiated by Cable's representation of New Orleans. As "Paul Marchand, F.M.C." remains unpublished and effectively silenced, as are several of the texts to be discussed in this study, the dialogue takes on a new dimension: it becomes hypothetical in respect to our mental reconstructions of the turn of the last century. But the dialogue continues as these texts are finally brought into the literary discourse.

THREE

W

Defining Race, Gender, and the Myth:
King, Chopin, and Dunbar-Nelson

The Louisiana Creole "mother-woman" described by Kate Chopin in *The Awakening* (1899) was apparently still the ideal in 1890s New Orleans, but as Larzer Ziff has noted, the other popular image of the time, as described by Henry James in *The Bostonians,* was the intellectual woman and social reformer.[1] American women of the 1890s were called upon to be managers of the home, preservers of the culture, and careerists. Writers in local newspapers and such national magazines as *Century,* the *Atlantic Monthly, Harper's,* and *Lippincott's* hotly contested the issues of women's rights and the conflict between home and workplace for women. Many authors also debated the issues in novels, like *Macaria* by Augusta Jane Evans.[2]

The turn of the century has also come to be known as the Women's Club Era for both black and white women. The campaign for women's suffrage, temperance, and social reform in prisons, asylums, and education—and against lynching—brought women together across the nation. White and black women in New Orleans worked together in certain programs for reform in the courts, the schools, and asylums. For instance, in New Orleans during the 1890s the Episcopal Church Women and the Era Club cooperated with Frances Joseph-Gaudet, a black woman, to establish the juvenile court system and a school for blacks (Gaudet School).[3]

Frances E. W. Harper, black poet and activist, delivered several speeches in New Orleans in April 1871 about Negro and women's rights and about the passage of the Fifteenth Amendment, which would grant suffrage to black men;

Richardson Memorial Building of the Gaudet School. Founded as the Colored Industrial and Normal School in 1902 by the African-American reform leader Frances Joseph-Gaudet, the school was at first both an orphanage and an academic institution. Courtesy of Xavier University Archives and Special Collections, New Orleans.

her poem on the Fifteenth Amendment was printed in the black newspaper, *The Louisianian.*[4] The 1890s, which saw the development of such women's rights groups as the National American Woman Suffrage Association (NAWSA) in 1890 and the National Association of Colored Women (NACW) in 1896, also saw a split between black and white women's organizations over the matter of the fifteenth Amendment. The southern-based Woman Suffrage Conference (WSC), organized in New Orleans by Kate Gordon, rejected the idea of federal enfranchisement in favor of state's rights. The white southern women of WSC, in effect, wanted to continue the disfranchisement of black men and women while enfranchising white women through actions of state legislatures, not through federal action.[5] In 1903 NAWSA held its national convention in New Orleans. Susan B. Anthony and many others signed a letter published in the New Orleans *Times-Democrat* assuring their southern supporters that NAWSA believed in state's rights and "that the race question was irrelevant to its purposes."[6]

Entering the dialogue on the Woman Question and the Negro Question during the 1890s, Grace King, Kate Chopin, and Alice Dunbar-Nelson add images to the myth of New Orleans which provide counterpoint to male writers of the post-Civil War city. There is an *implied,* sometimes *explicit,* dialogue among the three writers and with George Washington Cable and Charles Chesnutt. Like Cable and Chesnutt, the women writers re-created the New Orleans environment—Creoles, miscegenation, racial stereotypes, dialects, culture conflicts between races and immigrant ethnic groups. In many of their stories, King, Chopin, and Dunbar-Nelson also used the city to confront women's social issues: the restrictions of gender roles, especially as these influenced marriage and divorce, career, social networking, and motherhood.

Grace King

Grace King's first published story, "Monsieur Motte," which appeared in 1886, was in effect an answer to a challenge from Richard Watson Gilder, editor of the *Century.* When she had attempted to explain that the Creoles of New Orleans were hostile to George Washington Cable because he "proclaimed his preference for colored people over white and assumed the inevitable superiority . . . of the quadroons over the Creoles," Gilder responded, "If Cable is so false to you, why do not some of you write better?"[7] Like the later fiction of Chesnutt, King's stories were written in part to correct what she considered the inaccurate portrayal of Creoles in Cable's works, though from quite another perspective. She considered herself a realist, who wrote from her own experience about a romantic city. She wrote to Fred Lewis Pattee in 1915: "I am a realist à la mode de Nouvelle Orleans. I have never written a line that was not realistic—but our life, our circumstances, the heroism of the men & women that surrounded my early horizon—all that was romantic."[8] Grace King's realism was, nevertheless, as all realistic writing is, a product of her perceptions as influenced by her particular social, cultural, and personal identity. Her realistic stance must be viewed in terms of her position as a white southern woman in late nineteenth- and early twentieth-century America, a Protestant trained in French Catholic schools, who championed the cause of the Creole in New Orleans.[9]

Like George Washington Cable, King worked with the romantic materials of Louisiana history to create fiction and history. She was the first woman to write histories of the South; in her *New Orleans: The Place and the People* (1895) she portrayed the city as "the most feminine of women, always using the standard of feminine distinction," a city "of blood and distinction, 'grande dame,' and when occasions demand, grande dame en grande tenue."[10] In King's view, the *filles à la casette* ("an interesting lot of sixty [young women], who, intended as wives only for young men of established character and means, were of authenticated spotless regulation"), held sway over the region's future character, not the prostitutes and other disreputables, also sent from

Grace King. Courtesy The Historic New Orleans Collection, Museum/Research Center, Acc. No. 1974.25.27.214.

France to be wives of the early French settlers of Louisiana.[11] The rebellion of New Orleans's women of the Confederacy during the Union takeover of the city during the Civil War also contributed to King's image of New Orleans as a Parisian grande dame. The Union leader, General Benjamin ("Beast") Butler, King notes in her New Orleans history, hung a banner on his office wall declaring that "The venom of the she-adder is as dangerous as that of the he-adder"; he later passed his "Woman Order," which decreed that "when any female shall by mere gesture or movement, insult, or show contempt for any officers of the United States, she shall be regarded and held liable to be treated as a woman about town plying her avocation."[12] Notes Helen Taylor, "The ladies of New Orleans were certainly exhilarated to challenge notions of femininity that conflicted with their vocal loyalty to the Confederate cause."[13] In the white women's defiance of Butler, King found further justification for her identification of the city with woman's strength of character.

Literary critics have come to focus on the feminist poetics of Grace King, who, as Clara Juncker sees it, has "claimed for herself a female text, written, read and lived by a community of women"; she defines the feminist characteristics of King's prose as (1) her disregard for plot, with an insistence on "the plotless world of reality," (2) her autobiographical impulse, (3) her use of the oral tradition, including repetitious voices and circular sentence structure, along with an element of double entendre, (4) her experimentation with musical forms in her texts.[14] Indeed, Anne Goodwyn Jones observes, "The lives of women, not the defense of Creoles, is King's true subject."[15] However, the defense of Creoles and the old southern order were King's stated goals, and in many of her stories her ideologies color all of her other interests, even her feminism.

In the introduction to *Balcony Stories,* King describes her style of writing; the stories were, she said, "experiences, reminiscences, episodes, picked up as only women know how to pick them up from other women's lives . . . and told as only women know how to relate them."[16] Many of the stories are fashioned as oral texts in which the women speak for themselves. The style of narration, then, is persuasive in its very assumption of the air of confidentiality and sincerity. The prevailing theme in much of her writing is the impoverished aristocracy of the post-Civil War South. In all of her stories the women are much more prepared to face the hardships and humiliation brought about by the social change than men, who are caught up so fully in their abstract codes of honor and pride that they are blind to the obvious truths that surround them. In such stories as "Mimi's Marriage," "A Drama of Three," "La Grande Demoiselle," and "The Old Lady's Restoration," King portrays characters devastated by the changes of fortune brought about by the war. The narrator of "The Old Lady's Restoration" says of New Orleans: "Each city has its own roads to certain ends, its ways of Calvary, so to speak. In New Orleans the victim seems ever to walk down Royal Street and up Chartres, or vice versa. One would infer so, at least, from the shops and windows of those thoroughfares. Old furniture, cut glass, pictures, books, jewelry, lace, china—the fleece (sometimes the flesh still sticking to it) left on the brambles by the driven herd" (180). King, along with Chopin and Dunbar-Nelson, worked to reshape the southern patriarchal myths of women as fragile creatures, the nurturing forces in the

household, therefore unable to leave the home for careers. Their ideal southern woman was independent, innovative, sometimes even the breadwinner.

While it is true that King contributed significantly to the feminist discourse
of her time and our own, she also had her professed major intention—to correct Cable's portrayal of white Creoles and of blacks and to uphold the ideals
of the Old South. In this effort, her vision is shaped by the prominent discourse
on race at the turn of the century. As one might expect, even in her best stories
dealing with race and gender—"Bonne Maman" (1886), "Madrilène" (1890),
and "The Little Convent Girl" (1893)—her ideology, in Geertz's definition, "a
patterned reaction to the patterned strains of a social role," overshadows her
imagination.[17] As a result, her characterizations of blacks, especially of black
women, though suggestive, remain incomplete, and her hints that racial classifications are irrational and cultural linkages are the only verity, remain con-
fused.

One of King's most thought-provoking considerations of race and gender,
"Bonne Maman" was published in the July 1886 issue of *Harper's New
Monthly Magazine*; a slightly altered version was later published in *Tales of a
Time and Place* (1892).[18] The story takes place in a section of New Orleans
known as "Back-of-town," which at the time of the narrative (shortly after Reconstruction) exemplified what King calls "a fluid society," like the changing
neighborhoods described in *Dr. Sevier*.[19] The sounds of the neighborhood—
lively with the playing of children of many nationalities, the passing organ-
grinders, the often passionate music from the whorehouse and bar—contrast
significantly with the interior of the house inhabited by Bonne Maman; the
primary sound there is the feeble voice of Bonne Maman conversing with
Claire, her granddaughter, about the past, the old plantation, the slave, Aza,
who had been given to her as a child, and her other loved possessions. Their
house, on a triangle of land jutting out onto the sidewalk, is hedged in by or-
ange trees, just as its inhabitants are isolated from the community by race,
class, and attitude. "Bonne Maman" is part of the ongoing dialogue about
black-white, female-male, and class relations that New Orleans increasingly
frames in nineteenth-century fiction. The *heteroglossia* of the narrative, or in
Bakhtinian terms, "the diversity of individual voices, artistically organized,"
is presented as a musical construction; notes of discord are sometimes inten-
tional; others were probably not apparent to most nineteenth-century readers.[20]

The conversation that Bonne Maman carries on with her granddaughter is
all about the past; she remembers the green worktable that she received as a
wedding present and longs to see it and the souvenirs inside. "You see," she
says, "so much would come back to me if I could see my little table. I think
sometimes, mon enfant, that the loss of our souvenirs is the worst loss of all
for us women. . . . Ah, mon Dieu! one can get reconciled to changes in life, but
one cannot get reconciled to changes in one's self. Even when they [the souve-

nirs] are crumbling to dust they are fresher than we women are at the end" (83). The souvenirs are reminders of the old self, a comfort that the self is a continuum. Claire, the granddaughter, hears the grandmother's babbling mono-logue, but she does not really listen. She has her own interior reminiscences, about the convent and what was expected of her in spite of the Civil War, then her only interest. Even then her mind is on the "real" world, the world of the streets and people and life. The grandmother considers the city detestable and her decision to live there is simply a part of her "retaliation against fate," her self-sacrifice, but Claire thinks the city is full of life and gaiety. "It is so good to go on the street, bonne maman. It makes one feel so gay, so fresh, so strong" (90). She longs to know people and to follow the music that she hears nightly coming from the bar. Claire is growing up, "throwing out woman tendrils in all directions," and the narrator's language, as in the description of the music, suggests that Claire's ability to understand the city and the music is necessary to understanding herself on the deeper levels: "When I hear music like that, bonne maman, it is as if my blood would come out of my veins and dance right there before me. . . . I want so much to get up and follow it, out, out wherever it is, until I come to the place where it is, fresh and sweet and clear from the piano, and then dance, dance, dance until I cannot dance one step more" (91).

The music from the piano is balanced by the murmuring conversations that go on in the evening from one group to another as people sit on their porches. As in Cable's descriptions of the Place d'Armes in *The Grandissimes,* the com-munity enters the story through the conversations: "The women united their heads for female comment" (94), while the men with their cigarettes listened silently and wistfully to the merrymaking. The community also enters the story through the children as they peep through knotholes or race down the streets, and through the custom of visiting the home of a person who has died. When Bonne Maman dies during the night, black crepe is put on the green doors of the cottages, and everyone stops by on the way home from mass to pay their respects: "It is an old-fashioned creole city, with a pompous funereal etiquette, where no dispensation is sought or given for the visit commanded by the crape scarf" (103).

One of the persons to stop by is Aza, Bonne Maman's former slave who is now the quadroon owner of the nearby brothel, whose music Claire hears ev-ery night. The most jarring notes in King's discourse come through in the de-scription of Aza, whom Bush calls the story's "most interesting character."[21] But her characterization is unsuccessful because in King's attempt to bring to-gether her ideas about race, class, and gender, as in her description of Marcelite (Monsieur Motte), she is unwilling to develop the character fully. Just as Bonne Maman never understood Aza, who was given to her when the slave was only a day old, so that the child Bonne Maman saw her as a live doll, King is not able to conceive clearly of the quadroon's complexities. We see

Aza as a proud businesswoman who considers herself infinitely above the class of Betsie, the old black ragpicker whom Aza encounters tending Bonne Maman's body. The author, however, deflates Aza by contrasting the superior virtue of Betsie, who had stopped often to help Bonne Maman and Claire, with Aza's life of vice.

King uses the characters Aza and Betsie to represent the awkward incidence in the post-Civil War South of whites' dependence on blacks. These two black women serve as more than a mere foil for each other in "Bonne Maman." King dramatizes the dependence of the grandmother and Claire on Betsie for daily services and friendship, and Claire relies on Aza for a reunion with the relatives after Bonne Maman's death. In addition, Claire depends on the black women she sews for. The dependence of whites on blacks was a common theme of King's fiction, although it was usually hidden from whites by blacks, as in "A Drama of Three" and "Monsieur Motte"; in "Bonne Maman" King goes a step further, however. The grandmother and Claire actually acknowledge their dependence. But then, King had written to Charles Warner on November 22, 1885 that a "Southerner and a white person is not ashamed to acknowledge a dependence on negroes, nor to proclaim the love that exists between the two races, a love which in the end will destroy all differences in color; or rather I had better say—that love is the only thing which can do it."[22]

Aza has developed a successful life completely apart from the life of the past with Bonne Maman, and so her service in the story is out of respect for the woman who had raised her almost as a child. In order to conserve the myth of the Old South and caste, to which she had dedicated herself in her work, King compensates for this attempt at a "realistic" description of Reconstruction New Orleans by her excessive portrayal of Aza's nature as passionate and animalistic. Indeed, King herself, or her editors, must have recognized the excess, for in her second version of the story, she deleted much of the original description of Aza. In the original story, for example, the Aza who enters the cottage where the body of Bonne Maman lies in state is one whose sensual life has dulled her features and her thoughts. "She felt it beginning to move in her, the subtle current of an untamed savagery, the precursor of desires swelling on irresistibly to satiety, and she waited until her hot blood was flush for the cannibalistic gloating which no civilization could refine from her."[23] The lines were omitted from the 1892 edition.

The most jarring chords of the story are not the "loud, coarse, passionate" piano music which seems to intrude upon the peaceful harmony of the grandmother's cottage or the loud complaints of the black woman who had come to pick up a gown Claire was making; they are the exaggerated association of black womanhood with sexuality and uncontrollable passion, an association common in nineteenth- and early twentieth-century literature and discourse. The myth of the black slave woman's insatiable desires, as an explanation for the obvious sexual relations between white plantation owners and black slave women, did not end with emancipation. As Deborah E. McDowell has documented, not only fictional accounts but newspaper stories and letters popularized the myth, so much so that an important part of the Black Women's Club Movement's agenda was the myth's correction.[24]

King, or her editors, also saw fit to add a line at the end of the 1892 version of the story: "The piano had already commenced its dances." The last sentence of the later version assures the reader that Aza's returning to Bonne Maman's cottage in her "slavish dress" and marching at the end of the funeral procession with "a retinue of old slaves" was extravagant even in this sentimental southern literature of loyal slaves and devoted masters. Aza would return to her life after the funeral as the prosperous madame of a bar and house of prostitution. The changes that King made in her short story reflect her ambivalence about the changing role of blacks and whites in the post-Reconstruction South.

In "Madrilène; or, the Festival of the Dead," King creates an imaginative representation of New Orleans racial history that approaches the surrealistic. The short story was first published in the June to November 1890 issue of *Harper's* and reprinted in *Tales of a Time and Place*. It is a story not only of race relations and King's imagined life of Creoles of color, but also of voodoo and the New Orleans customs associated with the dead. The story takes place in two New Orleans cemeteries, one for the white population and one for "the colored," and in the yard of a Creole of color. It is October 31, All Hallow's Eve, the day and evening before All Saints' Day, or La Toussaint (November 1). The cemeteries are brimming with people whitewashing and scrubbing the tombs and buying wreaths and flowers to decorate them.[25]

Madrilène, or Marie Madeleine, has been brought up as a quadroon, as the niece and servant of Madame Lais, who has told everyone except the doctor and Monsieur Sacerdote, the sexton of the white cemetery, that the girl is the daughter of her dead sister, Rosemond Delaunay. Madrilène works in the cemetery, helping Monsieur Sacerdote, the octogenarian sexton, with burial preparations because she has long dreamed of dying, being buried in one of the white graves, and on resurrection day being reborn white in heaven: "We resurrect white, do we not, Monsieur Sacerdote? I would not be found out otherwise. All white—white limbs, white faces, white wings, white clothes. Not yellow— not black corpses rising with their white bands" (138).

The story is King's nightmare vision of the world of blacks: "a race creeping down or is it creeping up the scale? A patois race" (144), a world which in "Bonne Maman" she could only imagine from afar in her depiction of Aza, and in "Bayou l'Ombre" she admitted failure to fathom: "that opaque black skin which hid so well the secrets of life."[26] King's description of the quadroons and their boardinghouse contrasts dramatically with the Creole boardinghouses in Cable's fiction, which were always considered the cleanest and

The St. Roch Cemetery of New Orleans. Interment in the ground was once forbidden in New Orleans because of the city's altitude (below sea level), and burials were all in tombs built above ground or in high brick walls. The cemeteries became known as "cities of the dead." Courtesy The Historic New Orleans Collection, Museum/Research Center, Acc. No. 1974.25.6.419.

most respectable of inexpensive places to stay. Everything about Madame Lais's house is disreputable ("The appearance of the first of such placards [Chambres garnis] is the appearance of a first taint spot in the value of property in a locality—a symptom of corruption" [156]). The woman herself is attractive, but only by suggestion; one first has to notice the contrast of the yellow neck and soft, fat face, "thickly dusted with white powder," with her loose white gown (158). Into this place of corruption the innocent Madrilène is thrown, suffocating by her position as servant for these Creoles of color: "Madame Lais behind and Madame Lais before her, and all about her the Africanized wall of Madame Lais's children and grandchildren."

The mental image of entrapment becomes a reality on the night of All Hallow's Eve when Madrilène returns home to find Madame Lais hysterical over the voodoo curse that Zizi Mouton has just laid on the house. Further, Madame Lais's daughter Palmyre (cf. Palmyre, the quadroon voodoo priestess of *The Grandissimes,* also a passionate, vengeful woman of color) is screaming for revenge on Madrilène for having laid hands on her son when the son's monkey, which he bore on a leash in the cemetery, had tormented a white child there preparing for the festivities of All Saints' Day.[27] Palmyre's threats of violence increase as the neighbors laugh and jeer; caught between the roisterers in the street and Palmyre threatening to kill her in the yard, Madrilène moves toward the house. Attacked by Palmyre, she screams out, "Help! help! Negroes are murdering a white girl in here! Help! help!"

Crowds come into the yard; a stranger, who has appeared earlier in the cemetery and then at Madame Lais's to inquire about rooms, holds the wounded girl; policemen demand to know the truth, and Madame Lais finally confesses that the girl was really the white daughter of a white boarder who had died at her house. Was the stranger, who has now disappeared, the ghost of the dead father? This is suggested, though never made clear. But Madrilène has died and has moved on to the Resurrection Day of her dream. And Zizi Mouton screams in delight that she has paid Madame Lais for earlier slights; she has gotten her revenge: "*Ah, Lais, coquine, ta pe paye, chère.*" (179) She had loved the white father of Madrilène, but had lost him to Madame Lais.

What a bizarre rejoinder to Cable's *Madame Delphine* and "'Tite Poulette"! The girl brought up as a quadroon is really white; but so was 'Tite Poulette. Yes, but 'Tite Poulette was brought up like a little angel by her quadroon "mother," and Madame John, once beautiful and always faithful to M. John, had raised the child only because she gave the dying father/boarder a vow that she would do so. She produces the papers to acknowledge the child's whiteness when the love of Kristian. Koppig must be saved. Cable's empathy for the quadroons of "'Tite Poulette," *Madame Delphine,* and *The Grandissimes* is counteracted by King's disdain for the ethnic group, whose main attribute seems to be sexual deviance and a desire to lord it over those beneath them socially. And, moreover, the "patois race" of Madame Lais traps and destroys the white Madrilène.

"The Little Convent Girl" (1893)[28] is a typical story of the tragedy of mixed blood and is more of a parallel to Cable's "'Tite Poulette" and *Madame Delphine*; still, it goes beyond King's earlier stories to explore the deeper mysteries of the self. Here the quadroon mother is veritably ignored; the emphasis is almost totally on the eighteen-year-old daughter, an ideal convent girl—demure, disciplined, unemotional—who is travelling from the convent school in Cincinnati to visit her mother for the first time. Her father, whom she always visited in the past, has just died. The narrative point of view is that of a passenger on the ship who observes the girl and the captain. Until the end of the story, the only clues that she is not white are that her hair has a tendency to be curly and her complexion is sallow. The mother is not described at all; we simply hear the ship's crew whisper in shock, "Colored," when she boards. The resolution of the story—the girl's suicide by jumping overboard, rather than attempting to deal with the dilemma of her birth—emphasizes the girl's fascination with the captain's story of the great river which, he said, flowed directly under the Mississippi. Robert Bush has pointed out that the "buried river image suggests the unconscious, the almost impenetrable mystery of ourselves. . . . [The convent girl] is the most passive of creatures except in the final fact of drowning herself—a profounder action than perhaps any of the other characters is capable of."[29] Anne Goodwyn Jones in *Tomorrow Is Another Day* considers the story to be "a nearly perfect allegory of the life behind the southern lady's authorial mask" (121). True to the nature of allegory, the little convent girl has little three-dimensional reality; she is a martyr, not as pathetic as Madrilène, but as pure as the white Claire Blanche of "Bonne Maman." How can the girl be classified as "colored" in Grace King's terms? Or is being an octoroon radically different from being a quadroon? Jones suggests that "although the story's surface plot has to do with a girl's first knowledge that her mother is black, its thematic center has to do with that girl's aborted journey to self. The little convent girl's black mother represents her hidden self, a double that she represses in herself, by straightening her curls."[30] The girl's black mother represents her hidden self, just as Claire Blanche feels drawn to the music of Aza because it seems to represent something in her own nature. Further, Madrilène, the white girl mistakenly considered to be black, is unable to survive in the world, inexplicable to the narrator, of the Creoles of color. King's ideologies of allegiance to the Old South—black loyalty and white superiority—often ran counter to what her images signified. The images expressed instead the fusion of racial cultures that Cable revealed and the potential loss of racial distinctions that Chesnutt longed for.

Kate Chopin

Kate Chopin, a native of St. Louis, came to know New Orleans as the young wife of Oscar Chopin, a Creole cotton broker who was increasingly successful for the nine years that he and Kate lived in the city (1870–79), moving to consecutively larger homes, from Magazine Street, to Pitt and Constantinople, and finally to Louisiana Avenue. Emily Toth notes that Chopin loved to explore New Orleans by taking solitary walks, an unconventional habit for an upper-class nineteenth-century woman; she would often take the mule-train to the end of the line, and explore City Park and the cemeteries.[31] Chopin's observations of the Creoles, the Creoles of color, the Place Congo, and the activities in the French Market made impressions which would be expressed in her New Orleans short stories and *The Awakening*. The 1870s in New Orleans was a time of racial and economic turmoil, as has already been discussed in chapter 2. While the Chopins lived there, Oscar became a member of the White League, a military organization which fought against the Republican Party and the black politicians following the Reconstruction. Oscar took part in the Battle of Canal Street, later known as the "Battle of Liberty Place," during which sixteen of the White League were killed and forty-five wounded and eleven of the Metropolitan Police were killed, with sixty wounded.[32] Chopin does not describe such political battles over race, but in her New Orleans fiction, she demonstrates an awareness of the period's racial climate. In 1878-79 the cotton yields were poor, and Oscar's brokerage business failed; during the winter

Kate Chopin. Courtesy of the Missouri Historical Society, St. Louis, Missouri.

of 1879 the Chopins moved to Cloutierville, Louisiana, in Natchitoches Parish in northwest Louisiana, where Oscar's family owned an estate; just three years later, however, Oscar died of malaria.

While Natchitoches Parish was the prevailing setting in the short stories that made Chopin popular in her own time, New Orleans provided a counterpoint to rural Natchitoches in many of them. The city was a place of intellectual stimulation and cultural sophistication, yet also of social stratification and rigorous traditions and social practices. In *The Awakening,* as in the earlier short stories "In and Out of Old Natchitoches" and "Athénaïse," the psychological and sexual awakening which begins on Grand Isle or in Natchitoches Parish comes to fruition in New Orleans and reaches its greatest point of complexity there; in each story a young woman from a rural area comes to a confrontation with herself and society's conception of her. New Orleans was for Kate Chopin, as it was for Grace King and George W. Cable, the site of social change. But Chopin's interest is always primarily the internal world of her women characters as they search for a voice and space for themselves apart from society's agreed upon social roles. Her depiction of black characters contributes primarily to her painting of a realistic social milieu. In that interest, she populates her fiction with people of various races or nationalities and classes. In such short stories as "Nég Créol" and "La Belle Zoraïde," however, she goes further to make the black characters the consciences of the stories.

"La Belle Zoraïde" employs a frame story. The point of view is that of the black Manna-Loulou, who tells stories to the young white Madame Delisle, her mistress, to put her to sleep each night while her husband is away at war in the Confederacy. She always tells her stories in "the soft Creole Patois, whose music and charm no English words can convey" (304). In "La Belle Zoraïde" and its companion piece, "A Lady of Bayou St. John," written a month earlier, Chopin sets up parallels between the Creole slave Zoraïde, whose thwarted love for the handsome black slave Mézor leaves her insane, and the young white widow Madame Delisle, who turns away from her unsanctioned passion for the white Sepincourt when her husband is killed in the war.[33] By using Manna-Loulou as narrator, Chopin feels free to describe the noble and sensuous form of Mézor, so rarely handled in American literature of the period, "the stately movements of his splendid body swaying and quivering through the figures of the dance" (304), the Bamboula, in Congo Square.[34] As Joyce Coyne Dyer has pointed out, this choice of narrator also allows Chopin to distance herself from the description of Mézor and the passions of Zoraïde.[35] The reader, like Madame Delisle, is captivated by Zoraïde and Mézor and the injustice of Madame Delariviere, Zoraïde's mistress, who has Mézor sent away, and the baby that Zoraïde later delivers, declared dead. In fact, Madame Delisle tells Manna-Loulou in the same Creole patois, which they both speak, "Ah, la pauv' piti, Man Loulou. La pauv' piti! Mieux li mouri!" ["Better that she had died!"] (308).

Another of Chopin's stories which explored the complexity of color and race is "Nég Créol," written in April 1896 and published in *A Night in Acadie.* This picture of New Orleans, with its world of poverty as exemplified by the life of the old Creole of color, Nég, and the poor, once aristocratic, Mamzelle Algaé Boisduré, is a striking contrast to the well-to-do world of *The Awakening* and Edna Pontellier. It is more comparable to the environment populated

The Bamboula. Among the dances performed by the slaves in Congo Square were the bamboula, *the* babouille, *the* counjaille, *and the* calinda. *Courtesy The Historic New Orleans Collection, Museum/Research Center, Acc. No. 1974.25.23.54.*

by the various immigrant groups portrayed by George W. Cable in *Doctor Sevier*, Grace King in "Madrilène," and Alice Dunbar-Nelson in "Mr. Baptiste." The French Market where Nég hustles for a living—cleaning stalls, scaling fish, and doing other odd jobs, accepting any little thing in return: a cup of sugar, a stick of butter, a bag of shrimp, a soupbone—includes Choctaws, Italians, Irish, Hebrews, and Gascons, as butchers, fishmongers, and other vendors. Nég is a survivor in this "fluid society"; generally dismissed by his associates, he is known variously as Chicot, Nég, or Maringouin, but he holds on tenaciously to a world of the "remote past," when he was named "César François Xavier" and his master was the young Jean Boisduré. Mamzelle Algaé Boisduré is the last surviving member of that family, and she lives, as Nég does, solidly in the past, holding on to her culture and pride. She depends on Nég, in fact, to bring food and other essentials in his gunny sack, which he fills during the day. Nég refuses to pray to Mamzelle's "Bon Dieu," who has dealt both of them such a cruel fate; he prays instead to the Christian saints adopted by the Voodoos. Grace King had also written about whites who lived on the good will of blacks after Reconstruction, but she had not dealt

THE LOVE SONG.

Love Song. In addition to the satirical songs that the slaves often sang in Congo Square, there were also love songs. Courtesy The Historic New Orleans Collection, Museum/ Research Center, Acc. No. 1974.25.23.56.

with the black characters as the conscience of the story, through whose eyes and perceptions we see the other characters and events.

In *The Awakening,* however, the black characters form only a part of the local color background; they never enter the conscience of the novel. These characters include the quadroon nurse, who patiently follows the Pontellier boys always a few steps behind, sometimes "with a far-away, meditative air" (882), and whom Edna asks to sit for hours ("patient as a savage") as she tries her hand at painting (939). The Ratignolles also have a Creole servant—Cité— with whom Adèle speaks French and seems to be on good terms. Victor Lebrun, the careless brother of Robert, does not, as we might expect, adhere to the protocol for servants and their employers: he and his black servant have an altercation when Victor opens the door for Edna, and the woman hesitates to take Victor's message to his mother announcing Edna's visit. Few blacks are named in the novel. Besides Adèle Ratignolle's servant, Cité, and Madame Pouponne (the mulatto landlady Edna meets while looking for Mademoiselle Reisz's residence), there is Catiche, the "mulatresse" owner of the restaurant in a garden out in the suburbs where Robert and Edna accidentally meet. The most memorable black character, however, is the little girl who works the treadles for Madame Lebrun as she sews at her machine in the Grand Isle cottage. "Madame Lebrun was busily engaged at the sewing-machine. A little black girl sat on the floor, and with her hands worked the treadle of the machine. The Creole woman does not take any chances which may be avoided of imperiling her health" (901). With amazingly small strokes, Chopin suggests the complex social codes of the Creole and American New Orleans culture in order to fill out the novel's textual density.

Diane Bauer writes that "at the heart of Mikhail Bakhtin's dialogic model of discourse is the notion that we engage in simultaneous cultural and personal dialogues." The cultural code determines Edna's cultural voice, which is forced to respond to the gender- and race-restrictive society in which she lives.[36] However, in *The Awakening* Chopin's major interest is never the "cultural voice" of Edna and her outside world except as it illuminates the growth of her interior, personal voice and vision. Sounds, colors, lines are of utmost importance in this impressionistic painting which she creates. The colors of black characters—black, griffe, mulatto, quadroon—and their positions in the hierarchical Creole world are more important than their different psychologies. Even though the seductive odors and voice of the sea of Grand Isle are gone, when Edna returns to New Orleans the personal voice continues to grow and to demand some means of expression. After Edna calls off her Tuesday evening social engagements, throws off her ring, and gives up much of the responsibility for supervising the work of the servants, Léonce tells Dr. Mandelet that his wife has gotten "some sort of notion in her head concerning the eternal rights of women." Dr. Mandelet immediately suspects that her behavior must have

The French Market. Choctaws were among the many groups who bought and sold their wares in the French Market of the late nineteenth and early twentieth centuries. Courtesy The Historic New Orleans Collection, Museum/Research Center, Acc. No. 1982.127.188.

been caused by love for another man; this would have been the most probable cause for a nineteenth-century woman's mood swings. When Dr. Mandelet sees Edna for the first time since their trip, he is more certain than ever. He sees her as a transformed woman; once listless, she "seemed palpitant with the forces of life. Her speech was warm and energetic. There was no repression in her glance or gesture. She reminds him of some beautiful, sleek animal waking up in the sun" (952). Victor Lebrun notices the change, too, when she stops at the house in search of Mademoiselle Reisz. After he and Edna playfully banter with each other, Victor remarks to his mother, "Ravishing! . . . The city atmosphere has improved her. Some way she doesn't seem like the same woman" (943).

Edna attempts to throw off her old life and ties when she leaves her husband's house and moves to her little "pigeon house." She sends the children to their grandparents in Iberville, has an affair with Arobin, and tells Robert that she is no longer and never again will be the possession of any man. Still, she feels compelled to go to the bedside of her friend Adèle when she goes into labor. Thus Edna may rebel against the ceaseless demands of nature which tie a woman down, but she herself cannot deny nature's pull. She goes back to Grand Isle and swims out into the ocean, swimming further out than any woman had ever done, as she had wanted to do when she and Robert went out with the other Creole guests on Grand Isle for their midnight swim. In that final swim she sees "a bird with a broken wing . . . beating the air above, reeling, fluttering, circling disabled down, down to the water" (999). The voices of her youth beckon: "She heard her father's voice and her sister Margaret's. She heard the barking of an old dog that was chained to the sycamore tree. The spurs of the cavalry officer clanged as he walked across the porch. There was the hum of bees, and the musky odor of pinks filled the air" (1000).

Chopin critics have repeatedly debated whether Edna's death in the ocean is a triumph or a failure. Diane Bauer sees Edna's suicide as a failure, for "despite Edna's attempts to articulate her objection to the definition of women assumed by the Creole culture and by the men she knows, she is eventually silenced. Her suicide represents both her newfound consciousness of her body and its desire and the limit beyond which, in her culture, she cannot go with that desire."[37]

The ending of *The Awakening* is foreshadowed in the endings of earlier Chopin stories involving young women who come to the city and are awakened to their personal voices and vision. Athénaïse in the short story of that title leaves her husband, Cazeau, in Natchitoches and runs off to New Orleans, where her brother, Monteclin, has arranged for her to stay in the boardinghouse of a quadroon woman, Sylvie. Athénaïse considers marriage "a trap set for the feet of unwary and unsuspecting girls" (434). Cazeau has compared forcing his wife to return home with him from her parents' to the catching of a runaway slave. Although a rough farmer, he still does not like having his wife think she is trapped by their marriage. In New Orleans, however, in spite of her long conversations with the intelligent journalist Gouvernail, who is also one of Sylvie's boarders, during their walks in the city, Athénaïse begins to miss the country. When she discovers she is pregnant, she feels liberated ("Her whole passionate nature was aroused as if by a miracle" [451]), and she immediately returns to Cazeau and Natchitoches.

Suzanne St. Denys Godolph in "In and Out of Natchitoches" is another young woman who ends her period of exploration in New Orleans to return to Natchitoches. Having left her home in Natchitoches because the newcomer, Laballière, a neighboring planter, has insisted on trying to integrate her school by enrolling a young Creole of color, Suzanne moves to New Orleans. In the city she spends her time with her former neighbor, Hector Santien, and the landlady whom he puts her up with, Maman Chavan. The two ladies walk about together, going to mass at the cathedral and out to the theater. The relationship between Hector and Suzanne is growing into a more sensual and romantic attachment when Laballière appears in the city and insists that she not be seen again in public with Hector Santien. It is a matter of her reputation; Hector has become a notorious New Orleans gambler. Because Hector will not deny that his reputation could damage her own, Suzanne leaves for Natchitoches and meets Laballière on the train, where they sit together: "It seemed as though the sheer force of his will would carry him to the goal of his wishes" (266).

While the three female protagonists all experience awakenings, with New Orleans as a catalyst, their responses to their heightened awareness differ markedly. Edna and Athénaïse, for example, react to their roles as mothers and what part those roles play in their conception of selfhood in completely opposite ways. Patricia Hopkins Lattin has observed that "one cannot but be jarred by the contrast between young Athénaïse's pleasure at her pregnancy and Edna's desperate attempt to save her 'self' from her children. Nothing is dated about this contrast. Even today, with birth-control information freely available and with the concept of equal rights growing in the workplace and home, women in real life and in fiction still struggle to reconcile their self-actualization with the inescapable biological reality that the human race can be perpetuated only by childbirth."[38]

We might also compare the responses of Athénaïse, Suzanne, and Edna to the city itself. Athénaïse runs to New Orleans to get away from her husband, but is not content with the liberation she finds there; it does not speak to her complete being. Suzanne escapes to the city to get away from Laballière and his insulting demand that she integrate her school. Yet even though she enjoys the city and begins a romance with her old neighbor, she returns to Natchitoches with Laballière when she feels that her "programmed" idea of respectability is at risk.[39] She feels subject to the stronger will of the male representative of her home environment. Edna Pontellier, on the other hand, feels her first sense of liberation at Grand Isle. That sense grows in New Orleans, where she attempts to rid herself of one restriction after another as the well-to-do wife of a prominent Creole businessman in order to find solitude and a sense of self-identity. But even in moving out of her husband's house to her own "pigeon house" and entertaining the cosmopolitan Arobin at will, she still cannot overcome the programming of her culture. "Kate Chopin must end Edna's story with suicide," Suzanne Jones concludes, "because of her own inherited notions. She cannot reconcile her own ambivalent feelings about the traditional view of woman's role in society with the modern view of the individual personality."[40] Thus "Athénaïse" and *The Awakening* represent two of Chopin's answers to the problem of a woman's liberation and discovery of self-identity. Chopin is not sure that the freedom from traditional mores the city symbolizes is the answer. None of the characters remain in the city and live lives true to their personal voices. Athénaïse and Suzanne St. Denys Godolph retreat to Natchitoches, while Edna retreats to Natchitoches and beyond: into solitude and death rather than express her own personal voice and vision in her limitless world.

Like Edna, whose "cultural voice" responded to the Creole life of New Orleans even though she was never a true part of it, Kate Chopin was interested in both the social community of New Orleans and Natchitoches and the interior world of her characters. While she discussed racial and other social themes in such stories as "La Belle Zoraïde," "Nég Créol," the earlier "Desirée's Baby," and her first novel, *At Fault,* Chopin for the most part left that arena to others; perhaps she felt that it was a sphere that Cable and King had just about exhausted.[41] Her sustaining interest was instead the development of the "personal voice," which had not been developed adequately, especially in women; unfortunately, that voice was one that society was not yet ready to hear. *The Awakening* was silenced for about sixty years until rediscovered by Cyrille Arnavon in 1953 and taken up as a major text of the feminist movement of the late twentieth century.

Alice Dunbar-Nelson

Proud, loyal, enamored of beauty, art, and festivity, superstitious even to the point of irrationality—these are the attributes of most of the Creole characters of Alice Dunbar-Nelson's *Violets and Other Tales* (1895) and *The Goodness of St. Rocque* (1899).[42] Nuns and praline women, Creole belles and beaux, rejected lovers and musicians, Mardi Gras Indians and fishermen—all are characters of the New Orleans environment, speaking in distinctive voices using their diverse dialects. In writing about them, Dunbar-Nelson was mining the same soil as George Washington Cable, but, as Vernon Loggins has noted, she "found types in New Orleans which her master [Cable] had neglected, and she treated them in sketches which are frail and at the same time redolent of a

Alice Dunbar-Nelson. Courtesy Ohio Historical Society, Columbus.

delicate sympathy."[43] Using the word *master* in this assessment to refer to Cable says much about the black male critical establishment's evaluation of Dunbar-Nelson, a black woman writer, and its presumption that she was subordinate to the prominent male white writer. The primary differences between

Dunbar-Nelson and Cable were that she dealt mainly with Creoles of color, which she cleverly disguised for her reading audience to be Creoles of any color, and her basic assumption was that the color distinctions meant little in terms of basic Creole attitudes. Like King and Chopin, the protagonists of most of her early stories were women, and in several of the sketches she explicitly dramatized current issues of women's rights.

Like Grace King, Dunbar-Nelson also wrote history. Her two-part study, "People of Color in Louisiana," which appeared in the *Journal of Negro History* (1916-17), was an attempt to clarify, to even a minor extent, the contribution of the *gens de couleur* to Louisiana history.[44] In this work she explained that there were certain difficulties inherent in defining the term *Creole*:

> The native white Louisianian will tell you that a Creole is a white man, whose ancestors contain some French or Spanish blood in their veins. But he will be disputed by others. . . . It appears that to a Caucasian, a Creole is a native of the lower parishes of Louisiana, in whose veins some traces of Spanish, West Indian or French blood runs. The Caucasian will shudder with horror at the idea of including a person of color in the definition, and the person of color will retort with his definition that a Creole is a native of Louisiana, in whose blood runs mixed strains of everything un-American, with the African strain slightly apparent.[45]

Dunbar-Nelson wrote her history of Louisiana's people of color to fill a gap she believed existed in the popular histories of New Orleans; the two accounts she most often referred to in her essay were Charles Gayarré's *History of Louisiana* and Grace King's *New Orleans: The Place and the People*.[46] She also refers to many lesser-known historical records, memoirs, and newspaper articles. Rodolphe Desdunes's *Nos Hommes et Notre Histoire* had just appeared in 1911, but in Montreal and in French; an English version would not appear until 1973.[47]

Thus Dunbar-Nelson felt compelled to retell the story that was so often maligned in the popular white histories, and her fascination with Louisiana's Creoles of color is apparent both in her history and in many of her stories. Yet whether or not she herself would be classified as a Creole is not readily apparent. According to a family history she outlined in a letter to her husband, Paul Laurence Dunbar, her mother (Patricia Wright) was born a slave in Opelousas, Louisiana, and as Gloria Hull points out, the identity of her father (Joseph Moore), generally acknowledged as a seaman, was questionable.[48] Born in New Orleans in 1875, Alice Ruth Moore lived at 56 1/2 Palmyra Street in uptown New Orleans.[49] She was an Episcopalian in her childhood, until being sent upstairs to sit in the separate Negro church gallery upset her so terribly that she gave up the church: "Many things will be forgiven by me in this world.

Rodolphe Desdunes, author of Nos Hommes, Notre Histoire *(1911), a history of* les gens de couleur libres, *free persons of color. Courtesy of Xavier University Archives and Special Collections, New Orleans.*

But the circumstances which destroyed my faith in Rich and Trapnell [pastors of St. Andrews Episcopal Church, New Orleans] and turned me from the Episcopalian Church will never be effaced from my mind."[50]

In the essay "Brass Ankles Speaks" Dunbar-Nelson describes her earliest recollections of life in her native city, "a far southern city, where complexion did, in a manner of speaking, determine one's social status."[51] In this essay and the fictional "Stones of the Village," she portrays the horrors and the terrible ambivalence that she felt about being a light-complexioned woman of color, where one was tempted to "pass" to get a job or to be treated respectfully in segregated situations, but often met rejection by other blacks, who called them "yaller niggers" and "Brass Ankles."

Alice Ruth Moore attended Straight College (now Dillard University), founded by the American Missionary Association in 1869 to educate blacks, but open to all regardless of race, creed, or color. As a Straight College graduate, she was among an impressive group of Negro elite, which included Louis A. Martinet, attorney for the Comité des Citoyens, who struggled for the rights of blacks to ride any streetcar in the *Plessy v. Ferguson* court case, and editor of *The Crusader* newspaper, as well as Rodolphe Lucien Desdunes, historian and author of *Nos Hommes, Notre Histoire* (1911). Moore was an active member of the New Orleans social community at a very young age, as elementary school teacher, journalist, and participant in the city's social and literary circles, especially in her work with the Delta Sigma Theta Sorority.

At twenty she published her first book, *Violets and Other Tales* (1895). Her early poetry caught the attention of Paul Laurence Dunbar, already a prominent American Negro poet, although only two years her senior. He noticed her picture and poem, probably in the *Boston Monthly Review* and fell in love, courting her through letters;[52] the first letter from Alice was mailed from Palmyra Street, May 7, 1895. In Dunbar's early letters he implored, "Please let me have your photo as soon as possible and don't consider me selfish for saying that I would rather not send you mine."[53] While much has been written about the color difference of Paul and Alice as one of her mother's major objections to the marriage, it is not clear from the correspondence that this was the primary issue. Mrs. Moore wrote to Paul on November 3, 1897 from West Medford, Massachusetts: "You have surprised me quite a lot as I thought you & my daughter were friends,—nothing more. I scarcely know what to say to you about this important matter. You are a perfect stranger to us, I do not know anything of you. . . . My daughter is young & for her to take such a serious step and perhaps regret it & be unhappy the remainder of life would be dreadful." Mrs. Moore's reluctance may have been due as much to her protectiveness and lack of knowledge about this suitor, a public figure known to her mainly through correspondence to her daughter. His color, the poetry of dialect that he was known for, his willingness to be a part of the minstrel tradition

Dillard University. Straight College merged with New Orleans University to become Dillard University in 1935. Courtesy The Historic New Orleans Collection, Museum/ Research Center, Acc. No. 1979.325.1927.

as displayed in his musical *Clorindy*[54]—these did not endear him to Alice's society-oriented, properly Victorian, southern family. On the other side, Mrs. Dunbar, who acknowledged being born a slave and earning her money as a laundry woman before Paul made money with his poetry and could set her up in a nice

Alice Ruth Moore, soon to become Mrs. Paul Laurence Dunbar. Courtesy of the Photographs and Prints Division; Schomburg Center for Research in Black Culture; the New York Public Library; Astor, Lenox and Tilden Foundations.

home in Washington, D.C., was not entirely happy with the prospective marriage, either. Paul answered Alice's question in a letter dated October 29, 1897:

Paul Laurence Dunbar. At the turn of the century, Dunbar was the most prominent African-American poet. Courtesy of the Photographs and Prints Division; Schomburg Center for Research in Black Culture; the New York Public Library; Astor, Lenox and Tilden Foundations.

"Is my mother pleased at the marriage? Well, dear, to tell the truth, she doesn't hanker after it, but she is reconciled and is prepared to love you. Before I left home she had begun to enter pretty heartily into my enthusiasm." In spite of the hesitancy of both mothers, Paul and Alice felt themselves ready financially and emotionally to marry on March 6, 1898.

Throughout the letters to Paul and in her early poems, short stories, and essays, all written primarily in New Orleans, the profile of Alice Ruth Moore reflects an ambitious, upwardly mobile, romantic young woman, light-complexioned, and of mixed ancestry, who adopted the lifestyles and values of the New Orleans Creoles of color, *les gens de couleur*. Like Grace King, she was brought up in the Creole tradition, but in her literature and general perspective she was an outsider looking in.

Paul Laurence Dunbar considered Alice's early stories comparable to those of George Washington Cable and Grace King. In a February 16, 1896 letter to Alice he wrote: "Your determination to contest Cable for his laurels is a commendable one. Why shouldn't you tell those pretty creole stories as well as he? You have the force, the fire and the artistic touch that is so delicate & so strong."

"Those pretty creole stories" were sometimes very violent, but they were the romantic (beautiful and tragic) tales that Americans loved to read during post-Reconstruction, especially when told with a woman's delicate touch. To make her stories marketable and to reflect her perception of life and the role of art, Dunbar-Nelson camouflaged the issue of race, even though conflicts surrounding race and gender are readily apparent to the later twentieth-century reader. Her protagonists are for the most part women who act silently and secretly, in the end accepting their isolation from the community in which they live. They reflect the dilemma of Alice Ruth Moore, the author of *Violets* and *The Goodness of St. Rocque,* who did not have, perhaps could not have, a voice in New Orleans literature which clearly identified her as a southern black woman. In the stories where she mentioned race at all, it is only indirectly by description—"dusky-eyed," "the small brown Hands" (Sister Josepha), the "wizened yellow woman," "dat light girl" (Claralie), or by place names, particularly of streets and neighborhoods, such as Rampart Street or "the lower Districts" in "A Carnival Jangle." When she raised issues of women's rights in her stories and poems, such as in the frequently anthologized "I Sit and Sew," her criticism focused on the plight of all women with no mention of the particular problems of the black woman. And her stand on women's issues in these early volumes is always ambivalent.

In the 1890s the story "Little Miss Sophie" would have been read as a typical story of "tragic heroism," a tale of a young woman whose lover had rejected her but who still loves and works to save him in his distress. To contemporary readers the story is another *Madame Delphine* or "'Tite Poulette," but Neale is an irresponsible Monsieur John and the quadroon Madame John (Sophie in this story) maintains the innocence of 'Tite Poulette, even after she has been rejected by her white lover. Dunbar-Nelson, in her muted way, was revising the image of the free woman of color, who was a major partner in the traditional *plaçage* arrangements.

The narrator of Dunbar-Nelson's story, who speaks from the perspective of a neighbor looking in on Miss Sophie's life, reflects Cable's style of narration, especially "'Sieur George" or "Jean ah-Poquelin" of *Old Creole Days*. Miss Sophie is praying in church when a wedding party arrives; she stays to enjoy the ceremony and finds that her lover of five years ago is about to be married. After the wedding, she overhears neighbors talking about the unfortunate circumstances of the young man, whose business has failed, and who cannot inherit his uncle's wealth because he does not have the family ring necessary for identification.

> "Well, you're all chumps. Why doesn't he get the ring from the owner?
>
> "Easily said—but—It seems that Neale had some little Creole love-affair some years ago and gave this ring to *his dusky-eyed fiancée* [my emphasis]. But you know how Neale is with his love-affairs, sent off and forgot the girl in a month." (147)

Having received the ring from Neale, Sophie had pawned it so she could attend to her father before his death. Now she resolves to raise enough money to recover the ring from the pawn shop in order to return it to her lover and save him from financial disaster. Everyone watches as she carries increasingly bigger black bundles of clothes to sew and skimps on fuel and food until she becomes a mere wraith. Her work had always been "her only hope of life" (141), but now the ring becomes even more the meaning of her life—so much so that when she finally recovers the ring on Christmas day, she dies with it "clasped between her fingers on her bosom" (154).

To any reader knowledgeable about New Orleans culture, the phrase "dusky-eyed" would signify that Sophie was a quadroon. Her young white lover has broken off their liaison; it is suggested that he has had several such affairs before his marriage. Dunbar-Nelson's ambivalence toward race is reflected in the theme of the story as well as the images, such as the use of the color white in the story, which is always associated with the good, pure, and innocent, while black personifies the protagonist's guilt. In the church, Miss Sophie is comforted by "the beneficent smile of the white-robed Madonna" (140); she herself is "a slight, black-robed figure" (143) leaning her head against the Virgin's altar. When she hears of Neale's loss of his business, she cannot bear to think of the sorrow of "the white-gowned bride." In death, Miss Sophie lies with the ring clasped between her fingers, on "a bosom white and cold, under a cold happy face" (152).

A slightly more explicit consideration of race and gender in New Orleans of the nineteenth century is expressed in the story "Sister Josepha," from *The*

Goodness of St. Rocque. This is the story of a young novice who had come to
the convent as an orphan fifteen years earlier, to become one of the many
"scraps of French and American civilization thrown together to develop a
seemingly inconsistent miniature world" (157–58). At the time of the narration, she is eighteen, having become a novice at sixteen, shortly after a couple
had desired to adopt her. She had refused their offer and "fled into the yard
like a frightened fawn" (158), however, because the husband had too obviously admired her physical charms: "She was fifteen, and almost fully ripened
into a glorious tropical beauty of the type that matures early. . . . It was doubtless intuition of the quick, vivacious sort which belonged to her blood that
served her" (159). The sensual imagery used to describe the attractive young
woman is unusually direct for Dunbar-Nelson; it is more in line with Kate
Chopin's descriptions of Edna Pontellier, as when she reminds Doctor
Mandelet of "some beautiful, sleek animal waking up in the sun."[55]

But by her eighteenth year Josepha has begun to question her decision. The
ceremonies held at the St. Louis Cathedral—the beautiful colors and lights—
as well as the intrusion of the outside world in the form of a young service-
man, who looks at Josepha tenderly, make her wonder again at her commitment to the convent, "this home of self-repression and retrospection" (168).
She decides to run away from the convent into the great city, perhaps to find
the young man again when, overhearing three older nuns whispering, she realizes that she is without identity, "no name but Camille, no nationality; no
friends; and her beauty" (170). finally, realizing that she knows neither *who*
she is nor *what* she is (black or white), she goes back into the convent and
vanishes "behind the heavy door" (172). The refuge into the convent when in
doubt about personal or racial identity or when troubled by the evils of the
mundane world was a resolution of many Creole tales, including Cable's
"'Sieur George," Grace King's "The Little Convent Girl," and Dunbar-
Nelson's "Odalie." The story, moreover, has a historical counterpart in the
form of Henriette Delille. Because of her reluctance to go the way of the rest
of her relatives—Creoles of color—and attend the quadroon balls, be selected
by a white man, and spend the rest of her life as his faithful mistress, she actually went much further. Not only did she flee to the convent; she established
an order for women-of-color, the Sisters of the Holy Family.[56]

In *Violets,* four sketches are specifically directed toward the dialogue on
the role of women in the home and in the world of work. In 1863, when one
would think that the attention of the public would have been focused on the
Civil War, Augusta Jane Evans published *Macaria,* and while she dedicated it
to the Army of the Confederacy, many who condemned her political ideas were
heartily in support of her concept of the role of wives as dedicated homemak-
ers. The New Orleans *Tribune* published an excerpt from the book in its religious column, entitled "'Married Belles'—What a Woman Says." Evans de-

Sister Henriette Delille, founder of the Sisters of the Holy Family. Courtesy of the Sisters of the Holy Family, New Orleans.

clared in the article that "women who so far forget their duties to their homes and husbands, and the respect due to public opinion, as to habitually seek for happiness in the mad whirl of so-called fashionable life, ignoring household obligations, should be driven from well-bred, refined circles, and hide their degradation at the firesides they have disgraced."[57] Many editors, both black and white, seemed intent on publicizing the opinions of women who supported the conventional idea that a woman's place was in the home, even in light of the changing trends in women's employment, a declining number of marriages, and an increasing divorce rate. In June 1894, for example, in the same issue of *Lippincott's* that included Paul Laurence Dunbar's novel *The Uncalled,* for example, Eleanor Whiting argued in "Woman's Work and Wages" that "women bettered themselves financially, legally, and socially by becoming in-direct wage-earners through marriage rather than direct wage-earners in the world of business."[58] Women in the workforce, she argued, would reduce wages for men, affect children adversely, and deprive the home of its "greatest source of well-being," the mother. The young Alice Ruth Moore jumped into the debate in her first volume with "A Story of Vengeance," "At Eventide," "The Woman," and "Violets." Dunbar-Nelson's attitude toward marriage as

Sisters of the Holy Family with lay Creoles of Color, New Orleans. Courtesy Xavier University of Louisiana Archives and Special Collections, New Orleans.

viewed in several of these early stories is often as negative as that of Grace King or Kate Chopin; for her characters, as for theirs, marriage often entailed the loss of a woman's dreams, especially the ambition for a career. Nevertheless, Dunbar-Nelson could not divorce herself from the conventional idea that women have an often irrational impulse to marry.

The volume *The Goodness of St. Rocque* was dedicated to "My best Comrade, My Husband, Paul Laurence Dunbar," as could be expected of a loving wife of the 1890s; Dunbar-Nelson separated from Dunbar in 1902, however. In the short stories, "The Decision" and "No Sacrifice" (only published in 1988), Dunbar-Nelson indirectly describes the "Bohemian" lifestyle she and Dunbar lived for four years, including his alcoholic excesses and romantic involvements. It is difficult to know how much material in these stories is autobiographical, for the narrator describes the husband (called Burt Courtland in "The Decision") as "this Greek god," with chestnut hair and warm coloring in his face; perhaps more honestly she describes the life of the two as a four-year "fitful dream of torment, disgust, terror, love, longing for release."[59] She moved (with her mother and sisters) to Wilmington, Delaware, and there dramatic changes in her lifestyle and her writing occurred. She became a prominent member of the Black Women's Club Movement and became active politically and socially, as teacher, lecturer, and journalist; her writing simultaneously became more overtly race-conscious, though not so clearly gender-conscious.[60]

In 1910 she secretly married a young male teacher and colleague at Howard High School, where she taught for eighteen years; Dunbar-Nelson later divorced him and married the journalist Robert Nelson in 1916.[61] During her years in Wilmington, until her death in 1935, she was actively involved in the Federation of Colored Women's Clubs, the League of Colored Republican Women, and the Delta Sigma Theta Sorority. At various times from 1915 to 1931 she campaigned for women's suffrage, worked with other women to found the Industrial School for Colored Girls in Marshalltown, Delaware, headed the Anti-Lynching Crusaders in Delaware, and was executive secretary for the American Friends Inter-Racial Peace Committee. She was a member of the delegation of prominent black citizens who presented racial concerns to President Harding at the White House in 1929. That delegation presented the case on behalf of sixty-one Negro soldiers who were sentenced to life imprisonment because of their participation in the Houston riot of 1917; nineteen had been executed by hanging. In 1930 we see in her diary that Dunbar-Nelson became emotionally and legally involved in devising a way of getting pardon for a young man named Russ. Russ had been sentenced to death for raping a white woman. When Dunbar-Nelson and others sympathetic to the cause lost the fight, she reflected: "The end of Theodore Russ. Poor chap. Life snuffed out at the end of a noose. I felt cross and bitter all day. . . . Went home feeling depressed to read how calmly Russ met his fate protesting his innocence. How I wish all those who sent him to his fate could swing alongside of him."[62]

From 1920 to 1922 she and Robert Nelson were co-editors of a progressive black newspaper, *The Advocate,* and Robert (Bobbo) edited the Elks' newspaper, the Washington *Eagle* from 1925 to 1930. In the 1920s and 1930s Dunbar-Nelson was a friend and critic of several of the leading figures of the Harlem Renaissance, including Jessie Fauset, Alain Locke, and Georgia Douglas Johnson.

The change in Dunbar-Nelson's attitude toward using racial themes in her literary works during her life in Wilmington, as journalist, literary critic, club woman, and writer, is apparent in several of her later stories. In "The Pearl in the Oyster" (published in *The Southern Workman* and *The Collected Works*) and "The Stones of the Village" she dealt with the themes of race and "passing" much more explicitly than in her earlier New Orleans stories.[63] In "The Stones of the Village," the light-complexioned Auguste Picou moves to "uptown" New Orleans in order to get away from his racial and family connections and attempts to enter the Irish-dominated political scene of New Orleans. He is rejected, however, and moves back "downtown," still hoping to win an election, this time in his old neighborhood. His family and friends, however, do not forget his earlier "defection" and have little pity when his party loses. He and his wife decide to leave for another city and then decide whether they will be white or black. The difficulty of publishing such stories is no doubt a major reason that she did not pursue such literary themes more aggressively. Hull has noted that when Dunbar-Nelson proposed enlarging "The Stones of the Village" into a novel, "Bliss Perry of the *Atlantic Monthly* discouraged her in 1900 by saying that the present American public disliked 'color-line' fiction.[64]

Much of Dunbar-Nelson's poetry also became more overtly race-conscious. "Throughout her writing career, she shared what Charles Dudley Warner called New Orleans's 'passion for flowers.' These flowers pervade the town, old women on the street corners sit behind banks of them, the florists' windows blush with them, friends despatch to each other great baskets of them. . . . In this passion for flowers you may read a prominent trait of the people. For myself I like to see a spot on this earth where beauty is enjoyed for itself and let to run to waste, but if ever the industrial spirit of the French-Italians should prevail along the littoral of Louisiana and Mississippi, the raising of flowers for the manufacture of perfumes would become a most profitable industry."[65]

In the poem "Violets," published in 1917, she writes a simple love poem, but the contrast that she creates is the same that Warner describes; her new lover has made her think again of wild violets as she once had: "I had not thought of violets of late, /The wild, shy kind that springs beneath your feet/In wistful April days." (2: 81). Her mind had left wild nature and the naive love of beauty for beauty's sake, and she had begun to think only of violets in florists' shops and corsages for parties: "And garish lights, and mincing little fops? And cabarets and songs, and deadening wine." (2: 81) Her lover has made her think again of "sweet real things"—wild violets "and the soul's forgotten gleam (2: 81-82)." Although written after Dunbar-Nelson left New Orleans, "Violets" reflects the themes and language of Dunbar-Nelson's earlier poetry.

"April Is on the Way," for which Dunbar-Nelson won an Honorable Mention in the *Opportunity* contest of 1927, does something quite different.[66] Its theme is lynching, a subject she would have once thought unsuitable for poetry. The speaker is a young man running from a mob of lynchers. The constant refrain is "April is on the way;" that is, spring has returned and there is hope of the Resurrection and an end to the young man's pain and suffering. But in his feverish imagination, the speaker asks: "(Was that a stark figure outstretched in the bare branches/Etched brown against the amethyst sky?)" (2: 89). His observation of a little boy lightly rolling a hoop down the road contrasts with his own bloody feet "clutched" by the earth's "fecund fingers." All about him nature gives hope of renewal but also warns; the speaker remembers "the infinite miracle of unfolding life in the brown February fields," but simultaneously hears the hounds baying. In "April Is on the Way" Dunbar-

Nelson seems at least to recognize the futility of trying to escape from the "real," which is both beautiful and terrible.

As a light-complexioned African-American woman in nineteenth-century New Orleans, Alice Dunbar-Nelson was a rarity as a writer and freethinker. Whether or not she was a Creole is unclear; nonetheless, she spoke from that perspective.[67] The distinction of being a Creole rather than a black gave her prestige. Her colleagues were predominantly the Creole male journalists of the newspapers published by the free men of color, *L'Union,* founded in 1862, which later became the *Tribune de la Nouvelle Orleans* and continued until 1869, followed by the *Louisianian* (1870-81) and the New Orleans *Crusader* (1890-97). Rodolphe L. Desdunes was her peer; Louis A. Martinet, lawyer, politician, journalist, was her elder. As an active society woman, violinist, teacher, and secretary, she probably knew many socially elite women of color as well, but they were not published writers. It is very unlikely that she would have known white New Orleans women writers like Grace King, Mollie E. Moore Davis, and Ruth McEnery Stewart, or the journalists Elizabeth Poitevant Nicholson (Pearl Rivers), editor and publisher of the *Daily Picayune,* and Elizabeth Gilmer (Dorothy Dix).

Alice Dunbar-Nelson wrote her coded stories of Creole life, while most Creole stories were told in oral discourse within the black community and thus remained unknown to largely white reading audiences. Ironically, the black male intellectual world in New Orleans, in which Dunbar-Nelson found most of her colleagues as a writer, apparently encouraged her exploration of feminist themes and led to the writing of such tales as "A Story of Vengeance," "The Woman," "At Eventide," and "Violets." With her departure from the closed patriarchal New Orleans culture and her entrance into the Northern Black Woman's Club movement and the Harlem Renaissance, Dunbar-Nelson became more outspoken, but her literature, although more overtly race-conscious, was often silent or ambivalent on the question of gender.

A knowledge of Dunbar-Nelson's works alters our reception of George Washington Cable, Grace King, and Kate Chopin. Dunbar-Nelson showed that George Washington Cable's pretty but tragic quadroons and octoroons, the landladies of neat, well-run boardinghouses, the nurses, prostitutes, and voodoo women, were not the only free women of color and that African women were not all vendors of pralines, flowers, and calas (rice cakes) who sold their words of wisdom with their wares. Unlike Chesnutt, unfortunately, Dunbar-Nelson thought it inappropriate, in her earlier stories, either for publishing purposes or because of her own ambivalences about race, even to mention color or race. As Gloria T. Hull has commented, "Dunbar-Nelson spent her life assiduously writing herself both into and out of her literary 'fictions,' using conventional concepts of form, genre, and propriety that . . . bound her to divisiveness and inarticulation."[68] However, even in her often incomplete forms, she added to the representation of race and gender in New Orleans. Dunbar-Nelson also shows that culture cuts across racial lines. The myth of New Orleans would not be complete without Dunbar-Nelson's "insider's view" of the quadroon mistress who works herself to death for a white lover who has rejected her (Little Miss Sophie), the novice who retreats into the church because she has no idea of her racial identity (Sister Josepha), the young man who tries to "pass" and go into Irish politics "uptown," but fails and moves again "downtown," only to meet rejection there as well (Auguste Picou). As Hélène Cixous describes women's writing, our discovery of Dunbar-Nelson's writing creates a new history, as "personal history blends together with the history of all women, as well as national and world history."[69]

FOUR

ய

The Double Dealer *Movement and New Orleans as Courtesan in Faulkner's* Mosquitoes *and* Absalom, Absalom!

In the two decades between world wars the French Quarter furnished "the kind of sensually pleasant and socially tolerant atmosphere" which artists also found in New York's Greenwich Village.[1] James K. Feibleman, a young poet at the time, said of the city that "the climate was mild, the heat comforting, and the pervasive smells were good; in particular the odor of roasting coffee drifting across Canal St. early in the morning. There were a few night clubs in the Quarter in those days, but mostly it was given over to an assortment of people moving quietly, rich people and poor, happy to be left alone just to be themselves."[2] Besides Feibleman, resident writers in the city included John McClure, Basil Thompson, Roark Bradford, E. P. O'Donnell, Lyle Saxon (who moved to New Orleans in 1916), and Hamilton Basso. Sherwood Anderson, Gertrude Stein, Erskine Caldwell, William Faulkner, John Dos Passos, Oliver La Farge, Sinclair Lewis, Thomas Wolfe, and several other writers wrote and joined in the intellectual life of the city during the twenties and thirties. New Orleans was fast becoming a culture capital in the South.[3]

Ironically, H. L. Mencken had lampooned the post-Reconstruction South a few years earlier in an essay, "The Sahara of the Bozart," in which he argued that "for all its size and all its wealth and all the 'progress' it babbles of, it is almost as sterile, artistically, intellectually, culturally, as the Sahara Desert. . . . The South has not only lost its old capacity for producing ideas; it has also taken on the worst intolerance of ignorance and stupidity."[4] Almost in answer to Mencken, the Fugitives, a group of poets including John Crowe Ransom, Donald Davidson, Allen Tate, and Vanderbilt University faculty members and students, began meeting in Nashville, Tennessee, in 1920, later publishing the little magazine, the *Fugitive* (1921-25).[5] In the same year a group of New Orleans intellectuals and writers founded the literary magazine, *The Double Dealer,* the first issue appearing in January 1921. Julius Weis Friend and Basil Thompson were the first editors; Albert Goldstein, Paul L. Godchaux, Jr., and John McClure were on the editorial board. The magazine's aims were to encourage new writers, or, as the editors explained:

> It is high time, we believe, for some doughty, clear-visioned penman to emerge from the sodden masses of Southern literature. We are sick to death of the treacly sentimentalities with which *our lady fictioneers* regale us [my emphasis]. The old traditions are no more. New peoples, customs prevail. The Confederacy has long since been dissolved. A storied realm of dreams . . . no longer exists. We have our 'Main Streets' here as elsewhere. . . . We mean to deal double, to show the other side, to throw open the back windows stuck in their sills from disuse, smutted over long since against even a dim beam's penetration.[6]

During its five-year history the magazine published the works of such notable American authors as Sherwood Anderson, Jean Toomer, Hart Crane, Edmund Wilson, Robert Penn Warren, Allen Tate, Donald Davidson, William Faulkner, and Ernest Hemingway. The last issue was published in May 1926.[7]

Sherwood Anderson, who had come to New Orleans in 1922, actively sought to draw other writers to the city and was at least partly responsible for attracting William Faulkner there. In the March 1922 issue of *The Double Dealer,* Anderson wrote an article, "New Orleans, *The Double-Dealer* and the Modern Movement in America," in which he attempted to define the modern movement and his attraction to the city of New Orleans. The modern movement, he said, was an effort to reopen the channels of individual expression at a time when standardization of life and thought was the norm. For young writers, Anderson claimed, New Orleans's *Double Dealer* magazine offered an alternative to the money-making magazines put out by the Hearsts, the Buttericks, the Curtises, the Munseys.[8]

In spite of their forward-looking interest in literary experimentation, however, the New Orleans intelligentsia of the *Double Dealer* magazine often concurred with many of the stereotypical race and gender views of the period. For example, a review of *Darkwater* by W. E. B. DuBois in the June 1921 issue pointed out that DuBois's "bitterness" was not typical of his race's attitudes, that he was alien to his own race and to the white race. "His values are not those of his people, his aspirations are not theirs, and his voice is scarcely audible above the voices of the cotton fields which sing the paean of the negro's joy in life."[9] Cohn alluded nostalgically to the conservative voice of the late Booker T. Washington. A review of Jean Toomer's *Cane* praised the lyricism and "the harmony of language and beauty of imagery" of Toomer, but not his "criticism of life," for he was "primarily an artist, a spectator of the human tragedy, free from bitterness, free from the sense of persecution, uplifted by a fine tolerance."[10] The reviewer of Langston Hughes's *The Weary Blues* praised the poet most for his jazz variations, sensuous rhythm, and lyric simplicity, and placed him far above most other younger American poets in terms of originality, but summarily concluded: "With this volume Langston Hughes takes his place with other poets of his race: Countee Cullen, Jean Toomer, Dunbar, and Claude McKay."[11]

The poem "Black Tambourine" by Hart Crane, published in the June 1921 issue, voices a deeper insight into the life of black artists. Similar in theme to William Faulkner's short story "Carcassonne," the persona reflects on the troubling relationship between art, life, and loneliness. He identifies the poet with the "black man," like Aesop, an ex-slave, but without even the identification of a "fox brush and sow ear."[12]

> *The interests of a black man in a cellar*
> *Mark an old judgment on the world.*
> *Gnats toss in the shadow of a bottle,*
> *And a roach spans a crevice in the floor.*
>
> *Aesop, driven to pondering, found*
> > *Heaven with the tortoise and the hare:*
> *Fox brush and sow ear top his grave,*
> > *And mingle incantations on the air.*
>
> *The black man, forlorn, in the cellar,*
> > *Wanders in some mid-kingdom, dark, that lies*
> *Between his tambourine, stuck on the wall,*
> > *And, in Africa, a carcass quick with flies.*

The black musician in the cellar is lost in a mid-kingdom, or the "Middle Passage," the mental and physical journey for the slave from Africa to America. Forgotten in America, he tries to hold on to his past—Africa—by holding on to his music (the tambourine), but he fears that the limits of his imagination will deaden his memories of Africa, making it eventually only "a carcass quick with flies." The interesting thing here is that Crane chose a *black* musician to be the center of his poem and pointed out that the black man's interests "mark an old judgment on the world." In the poem's later appearance in *White Buildings* (1926), the second line becomes "Mark tardy judgment on the world's closed door." Warner Berthoff views the revised line as "rendering . . . a specific and circumstantial indictment" against the condition of the black man;[13] both versions of the line, however, stress that the wretched condition of the black man, like that of the poet, is an indictment of society. Consciousness of blacks, particularly black artists, and their impact on American culture is clearly a part of the literature published in *The Double Dealer*.

Reviews of new books by black authors in *The Double Dealer* and the inclusion of poetry and fiction with themes of black life or by such blacks as Jean Toomer and Langston Hughes reflected the new national interest in the Negro. Alain Locke's *The New Negro* (1925), a manifesto of the Harlem Renaissance, was accompanied, in some cases preceded, by such nationally famous productions about blacks by white authors as T. S. Stribling's *Birthright* (1922), Julia Peterkin's *Black April* (1927) and *Scarlet Sister Mary* (1928), and DuBose Heyward's novel and play *Porgy* (1925, 1927). White New Orleans writers also showed their fascination with—if lacking a sensitivity to—black life, as is evident in Sherwood Anderson's *Dark Laughter* (1925), Edward Larocque Tinker's *Toucoutou* (1928), Roark Bradford's *Ol' Man Adam an' His Chillun* (1928) and *John Henry* (1931), and Lyle Saxon's *Children of Strangers* (1937). In most of the books by writers involved in the production of *The Double Dealer*, however, as in the magazine's articles and reviews, the refusal to come to terms with contemporary racial stereotypes severely limited the writers' imaginative range.[14]

Similarly, direct resistance to the modern woman and open resentment of male "dependence" reverberates throughout *The Double Dealer*. The New Orleans literati did have a number of consequential women artists among them: Grace King still reigned as literary *grande dame* in the French Quarter; Dorothy Dix, retired editor of the *Times-Picayune,* was still on good terms with the young writers; Elizabeth Prall Anderson, Sherwood Anderson's wife and former manager of the New York Doubleday bookstore, still inspired the young Faulkner and other writers of *The Double Dealer*. Caroline Durieux was a young artist associated with the group, and Flo Field would soon write the play *À la Creole,* produced in Philadelphia (1929) as *Mardi Gras.* Lillian Friend Marcus, sister of Julius Friend, a part of the literary coterie, would serve as inspiration for the character of the poet, Mrs. Eva Wiseman, in *Mosquitoes.* And Helen Baird, sister of Theodore Baird, writer for the *Picayune,* was the attractive young woman for whom Faulkner wrote poetry and on whom he based at least two characters of his novels, Pat Robyn (*Mosquitoes*) and Charlotte Rittenmeyer (*The Wild Palms*).[15]

This distinguished roll call notwithstanding, *The Double Dealer* included many scathing attacks on the "new woman" of the Jazz Age, the newly victorious suffragette. For example, in an editorial entitled "The Ephemeral Sex," the editor unashamedly declares that "as a creative artist woman is a complete

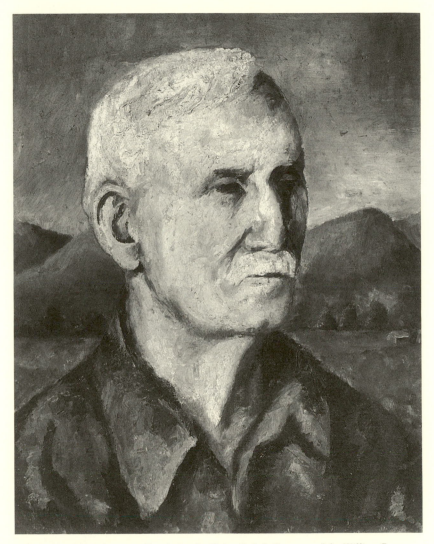

William Faulkner, from an oil painting by Helen Baird. Courtesy of the William B.
Wisdom Collection of William Faulkner, Manuscripts Department, Howard-Tilton
Memorial Library, Tulane University, New Orleans.

failure, a nonentity." Many successful artists, such as George Sand, George Eliot,
or Rosa Bonheur, he argues, were only "so-called women artists . . . fripperied
males, some of them minus even the fripperies."[16] In another editorial, "a burning question" is raised: Should women smoke? And the editor suggests that

men let them "happily follow the jet set."[17] Concern with the victory of the woman suffrage movement led to the editorial "The Dominant Petticoat" and the question of where women's new-found rights left men: "Shades of Mary Wolstonecraft [*sic*], 'women's rights' forsooth. They have the vote. Subtly they run the country. Our lives are mortgaged to them. They have already gone the bees one better, for we are not only used as repopulators like the drone, but we also play the role of the worker."[18]

Ambivalences about gender and race in *The Double Dealer* articles, a central theme of the Southern Renaissance and twentieth-century modernism generally, contribute also to the myth of New Orleans created by the period's most respected writer—William Faulkner.[19]

Faulkner was among the many writers who came to New Orleans in the 1920s, accepting Sherwood Anderson's invitation to join him in the "most cultural city" he had yet found in America, where "the crowds have a more leisurely stride, the negro life issues a perpetual challenge to the artists, sailors from many lands come up from the water's edge and idle on streetcorners, in the evening soft voices, speaking strange tongues, come drifting to you out of the street."[20]

Before Faulkner came to New Orleans, he had considered himself to be chiefly a poet, but during his stay in New Orleans, he made his first sustained attempt at writing prose fiction. His first prose writings were contributions to the January-February 1925 issue of *The Double Dealer,* including a three-thousand-word piece entitled "New Orleans," which comprised eleven sketches, spoken by eleven New Orleans characters—the wealthy Jew, the priest, Johnny (to Frankie), the sailor, the cobbler, the longshoreman, the cop, the beggar, the artist, Magdalen, and the tourist. The New Orleans characters are in some ways similar to Sherwood Anderson's "grotesques" of *Winesburg, Ohio*; each has suffered, but all have culled some meaning out of their pain. The last character—the tourist—does not speak of himself; he speaks of the city, and gives us one of New Orleans's most memorable images:

> *A courtesan, not old and yet no longer young, who shuns the sunlight*
> *that the illusion of her former glory be preserved. . . . She lives*
> *in an atmosphere of a bygone and more gracious age.*
> *And those whom she receives are few in number, and they come to her*
> *through an eternal twilight. . . . And those who are not of the*
> *elect must stand forever without her portals.*
> *New Orleans . . . a courtesan whose hold is strong upon the mature, to*
> *whose charm the young must respond. And all who leave her,*
> *seeking the virgin's unbrown, ungold hair and her blanched*
> *and icy breast where no lover has died, return to her when she*
> *smiles across her languid fan. . . .*
> *New Orleans.[21]*

Faulkner's choice of the word *courtesan* as an image of New Orleans has significant ideological associations.[22] Not only does he characterize New Orleans (particularly, the Vieux Carré, the city in most of his fiction) as a place of cabarets and easy access to prostitutes and alcohol during a time of professed Prohibition; but he also expresses respect for woman's experience over youthful, adventurous enterprise and questions his society's smug assuredness of woman's role as wife, mother, and paragon of community values. In his image of New Orleans as *courtesan,* he suggests the complexity of the term, which refers both to the woman of pleasure and to the woman of sophistication and tradition.[23]

Literary cities, as David Weimer notes, should be studied as metaphors, for these fictive cities are invented by the writers as an extension of their psyche.[24] The seductive courtesan image of New Orleans was also a part of Faulkner's psyche. It showed the importance to him of projecting a space that was not Puritanical, or ordered according to some stern religious code. New Orleans corresponded to that part of his psyche which demanded an older order, from "a bygone and more gracious age," which rewarded pleasure, leisure, and experience, not the new and untried.

Faulkner was introduced to New Orleans in the decade following the birth of jazz, the new African-American sound, which had already traveled to Saint Louis, Chicago, and New York. At cabarets in "the District"—where jazz was born as Creoles of color and uptown blacks got together on Rampart, Basin, and Perdido—and in the Vieux Carré and the Faubourg Marigny, jazz contributed a new perspective as well as music for the new generation of modernists.[25] Jelly Roll Morton, Buddy Bolden, King Oliver, Bunk Johnson, and Louis Armstrong developed as a close-knit body of jazz musicians at the turn of the century until World War I, when many left to go to St. Louis, Chicago, Detroit, and Los Angeles. The new Negro music traveled with them, but still kept the French Quarter "hot" as the *Double Dealer* artists met and discussed their ideas. New Orleans had closed down its famed Storyville district only eight years before Faulkner arrived, when the U.S. Army declared an entire neighborhood of legitimate prostitution too tempting for their soldiers who might be stationed in the city during World War I. Of course, prostitution still flourished, and Prohibition was virtually unheard of in the French Quarter.[26]

Carvel Collins writes that Roark Bradford, John McClure, and Faulkner often spent time together at "a cabaret in Franklin Street just off Canal, where the playing of the talented jazz clarinetist George ('Georgia Boy') Boyd especially delighted Faulkner." The threesome also frequented another café, which "the owner is said to have used as his business headquarters in directing much of the section's prostitution but which he ran with notable decorum—and considerable style, serving the best Roquefort sandwiches John McClure remembered ever having tasted."[27]

Jelly Roll Morton at piano, 1926. Courtesy of the Hogan Jazz Archive, Howard-Tilton Memorial Library, Tulane University, New Orleans.

Cabarets, jazz, and prostitution, as well as New Orleans's historical, virtually "mythical," tradition of interracial liaisons between white men and quadroon or octoroon women, all interact in Faulkner's image of New Orleans as courtesan. As Frederick Gwynn has shown, Faulkner is also indebted to T. S. Eliot,

Louis Armstrong and Lil at the Jones Home, 1931. At the school, formerly the Colored Waifs' Home for Boys, Armstrong first joined a brass band. Courtesy of the Hogan Jazz Archive, Howard-Tilton Memorial Library, Tulane University, New Orleans.

since Faulkner's image corresponds "with the courtesan in Part II of *The Waste Land* whose room features the perfumed smoke of candles, and with the aging Lady of the 'Portrait' who, 'among the smoke and fog, has saved candles in the darkened room.'"[28] Various aspects of Faulkner's courtesan image are delineated in *Mosquitoes* (1927), *Absalom, Absalom!* (1936), and *The Wild Palms* (1939).

In *Mosquitoes* the dialectic between the sculptor Gordon's (i.e., Faulkner's) ideal woman and the courtesan's immanent reality provides the central theme. Faulkner dedicated *Mosquitoes* to Helen Baird, a young woman whom he met in New Orleans in 1925, and maintained an attraction for over the years. He also presented the allegorical novelette *Mayday* and the poems *Helen: A Courtship* to her in handbound volumes. Joseph Blotner describes her as "an artist and sculptress who struck people as elfin or spritelike. Barely five feet tall, she had light blue eyes, a wide mouth, and dark hair and skin. To some she looked as dark as a gypsy. . . . She was quick, volatile and amusing, with a straight-

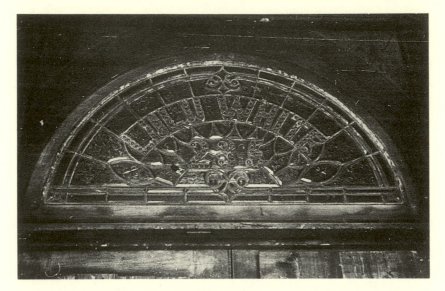

The door of Lulu White's fabulous house of prositution, Mahogany Hall, in Storyville.
Courtesy The Historic New Orleans Collection, Museum/Research Center, Acc. No.
1990.2.2.

forward manner . . . like people who did not care about convention, who had talent and something of her own devil-may-care manner."[29] Theirs was an aborted courtship, however; before *Mosquitoes* came out he read in the *Times-Picayune* of Helen's engagement to a New Orleans lawyer. Faulkner continued to associate New Orleans with Helen, however. He later wrote to her: "I hope to come to New Orleans before the winter is over. I dont hate it. I dont come back much because I had more fun there than I ever had and ever will have again anywhere now. I remember a sullen-eyed yellow-eyed belligerent humorless gal in a linen dress and sunburned bare legs sitting on Spratling's balcony and not thinking even a hell of a little bit of me that afternoon, maybe already decided not to. But damn letters anyway. I will come down as soon as I can."[30] Faulkner's characterization of Pat Robyn in *Mosquitoes,* the young, attractive, and rebellious niece of the art patron Mrs. Maurier—and Gordon's ideal—is obviously based largely on Helen Baird.[31]

Gordon sees Pat, with "her flat breast and belly, her boy's body . . . sexless, yet somehow vaguely troubling . . . like a calf or a colt," as the embodiment of his marble sculpture, to which he is just adding the finishing touches before he meets her.[32] Pat also sees a resemblance of herself in "the virginal breastless torso of a girl, headless, armless, legless in marble temporarily caught and hushed yet passionate still for escape" (3). Cleanth Brooks observes the influ-

Storyville was also known as Andersonville, after its financial and government patron, Tom Anderson, an oil businessman, state legislator, and owner of a café and house of prostitution. Courtesy The Historic New Orleans Collection, Museum/Research Center, Acc. No. 1990.2.2.

ences of Gautier's *Mlle. de Maupin* and Helen Baird on Faulkner's conception of the ideal woman in *Mosquitoes.* "*Mlle. de Maupin* has a special bearing on *Mosquitoes,* for in *Mosquitoes* the artist par excellence is a sculptor, and Gautier's hero insists that he regards women with a sculptor's eye and even affects to prefer a statue to a living woman."[33]

As Gordon cannot find sexual fulfillment in a cold, lifeless work of art, he finally has no choice but to renounce both Pat and the marble sculpture. When he returns to the Vieux Carré after having been deadlocked for three days on Mrs. Maurier's yacht on Lake Pontchartrain, he borrows a dollar from his friend, the Semitic man (based on Julius Friend), and enters a brothel.

> *The centaurs' hooves clash, storming shrill voices ride the storm like gusty birds, wild and passionate and sad.* (A door opened in the wall. Gordon entered and before the door closed again they saw him in a narrow passageway lift a woman from the shadow and raise her against the mad stars, smothering her squeal against his tall kiss.) *Then voices and sounds, shadows and echoes change form swirling, becoming the headless, armless, legless torso of a girl, motionless and virginal and passionately eternal before the shadows and echoes whirl away.* (282)

Faulkner describes Gordon's act of going to the prostitute in the rhetorical style and language of "Carcassonne." Gordon keeps his male image of the ideal woman intact while he realizes the limitations of his flesh. Pat also has to accept the limitations imposed on her by nature when she and the steward David West are almost eaten alive by the mosquitoes in the Mandeville swamp, on the first step of their projected journey from Mrs. Maurier's yacht to Europe and the Alps. The worrisome Louisiana mosquitoes constantly remind the New Orleans characters of their human limitations; ironically, like "the majesty of Fate," they "become contemptuous through ubiquity and sheer repetition" (epigraph, *Mosquitoes*).

Though Gordon goes to the prostitute, he only partially confronts the reality of the city, New Orleans, which, outside of his studio window, "brooded in a faintly tarnished languor like an aging yet still beautiful courtesan in a smokefilled room, avid yet weary too of ardent ways" (2); he still holds on to his image of the ideal woman. Henry Sutpen, Quentin Compson, and Mr. Compson of *Absalom, Absalom!* cannot accept their imagined New Orleans courtesan world even to that degree. In *Absalom, Absalom!* (1936) the courtesan image recurs, though in a much more complicated sense than in the earlier prose sketch, "New Orleans," and *Mosquitoes*.

The courtesan image is first described in *Absalom, Absalom!* when Henry Sutpen and Charles Bon visit New Orleans after Henry renounces his birthright, as Mr. Compson narrates to Quentin (chapter 4). Henry apparently finds his friendship with Bon and the suggested marriage between Bon and his sister Judith more important than fulfilling his father's "design"—of setting up a Sutpen dynasty in Yoknapatawpha. While New Orleans is not described explicitly as a courtesan in the novel, as it was in the "New Orleans" sketch and *Mosquitoes,* Mr. Compson's narration of Henry's visit to the city is dominated by the description of the quadroon ball and the octoroon's home. Bon's intent is to persuade Henry that his *plaçage* arrangement and his child by the octoroon will not conflict with his plan to marry Judith.

While Bon is sure that Henry will have no trouble accepting the knowledge that he has a mistress and intends to keep her after the marriage, he fears that Henry will not understand the peculiarities of "that city, foreign and paradoxical with its atmosphere at once fatal and languorous, at once feminine and steel-hard" (134), particularly that interracial relationship blessed by a "morganatic" ceremony.[34] Henry's Anglo-Saxon, Puritan upbringing in Yoknapatawpha had taught him that there were three divisions of women—"ladies, women, females—the virgins [ladies] whom gentlemen someday married, the *courtesans* [women] to whom they went on sabbaticals to the cities, the slave girls and women [females] upon whom that first caste rested and to whom in certain cases it doubtless owed the very fact of its virginity" (135; my emphasis). Doubtless, Henry understood that white men often had Negro mistresses; he

himself had a slave half-sister, Clytie. The contrast between Charles Bon and
Clytie, in fact, brings out the contrast between Faulkner's myth of the Creole
world and the miscegenation that occurred in Yoknapatawpha. The former was
a part of a world of lace and silk; the latter was the practical result of the out-
door, rural world of denim.[35]

Faulkner's Yoknapatawpha County, and the Old South generally, are associated with what he considered "masculine" virtues, and the city, particularly
New Orleans, with the "feminine." Masculine virtues include being true to a
particular code of conduct, or being punished for the diversion, for the world
of Yoknapatawpha is ruled by "a jealous and sadistic Jehovah." Masculine
means being unbending, "granite," even if the intolerance means that one is a
"yokel." The feminine virtues of the modern city mean cosmopolitanism, in-
tellect, tolerance, a quest for self and art, a questioning of religious truth. In
Faulkner's mind, New Orleans was a part of this feminine world, perhaps a
descendant of an older order than Christianity, dating back to a Hedonistic order, even before Apollo, more Dionysian, "whose denizens had created their
All-Powerful and His supporting hierarchy-chorus of beautiful saints and handsome angels in the image of their houses and personal ornaments and voluptuous lives" (134). Faulkner shows the influence of the modernists in his portrayal of New Orleans; this old, cosmopolitan city, like the moderns, rejects
the values of Christianity, and sees the human not as a rational animal "able to
understand and control his world, but a mysterious being subject to both internal and external forces that he cannot understand."[36]

The visit to New Orleans is Henry's initiation into sophistication. Bon has
to introduce him cautiously to the world of *plaçage* arrangements, "corrupting
Henry gradually into the purlieus of elegance . . . the architecture [of the city]
a little curious, a little femininely flamboyant and therefore to Henry opulent,
sensuous, sinful" (136). He must never consider the octoroon mistresses to be
whores, not even courtesans, argues Charles Bon, who here is very much the
voice of "the Good"; they were created and produced by white men, as were
the laws which defined race and the status of the various gradations of racial
mixture (142). They were "flowers" created by the combination of white blood
and the African "female principle . . . which existed queenly and complete, in
the hot equatorial groin of the world long before that white one of ours came
down from trees and lost its hair and bleached out."[37] According to Bon, via
the reporting of Mr. Compson, the octoroon may be "the only true chaste
women, not to say virgins, in America" (145).

Faulkner's story of the relationships between white men and quadroon or
octoroon women differs from the historical record in a number of significant
ways. Mr. Compson refers to the women of color as slaves or sees them as
being in danger of being taken into slavery, while historically, those who participated in the quadroon balls were free women of color, more accurately de-

picted by Cable's 'Tite Poulette, Madame John, Olive, and Madame Delphine. Faulkner's intent is to create a myth of New Orleans which is so different from Yoknapatawpha that Henry, Quentin, and the Compsons can never truly understand it, but are nevertheless enticed by its romance and irrationality. In portraying New Orleans settings and characters, Faulkner shows the influence of Aubrey Beardsley, the *fin-de-siècle* artist whom Faulkner admired from his early days as a poet and painter. In Faulkner's depiction of the situation of miscegenation in New Orleans, he employs Beardsley's ability to show the relationship between beauty, passion, and degradation.[38] He pictures the women at the quadroon ball as "a row of faces like a bazaar of flowers, the supreme apotheosis of chattelry, of human flesh bred of the two races for that sale—a corridor of doomed and tragic flower faces walled between the grim duenna row of old women and the elegant shapes of young men trim predatory and (at the moment) goatlike" (138). Somewhere between a flower- and a slave-market and a house of prostitution, the ball is reduced to a commercial enterprise, in which the women of color are the objects for sale. At Bon's burial at Sutpen's Hundred four years later, the octoroon appears again in

> the pageant, the scene, the act, entering upon the stage—the magnolia-faced woman a little plumper now, a woman created of by and for darkness whom the artist Beardsley might have dressed, in a soft flowing gown designed not to infer bereavement or widowhood but to dress some interlude of slumbrous and fatal insatiation, of passionate and inexorable hunger of the flesh, walking beneath a lace parasol and followed by a bright gigantic negress carrying a silk cushion and leading by the hand the little boy whom Beardsley might not only have dressed but drawn—a thin delicate child with a smooth ivory sexless face. . . . (242)

Cleanth Brooks emphasizes that the only real evidence we have to support the contention that Charles Bon himself was Sutpen's part-black son from his first marriage in Santo Domingo is that Quentin learns about Sutpen's first marriage from Rosa Coldfield. Rosa had heard from Henry that Sutpen had married and that he had killed Bon at the gate of Sutpen's Hundred, not to prevent the incestuous marriage between Bon and Judith but to prevent the interracial union.[39] The story of the former Santo Domingan wife of Charles Sutpen, Eulalia Bon, another woman of color, is slight and indirect. Due to Shreve's typically cynical additions to Quentin's narrative, as well as to Mr. Compson's narrative, the reader learns that Sutpen's first wife was the daughter of a wealthy Santo Domingan landowner, who was forced to leave her home and settle in New Orleans because of the Haitian Revolution. According to Quentin, she was a vengeful woman who planned the meeting of her son Charles Bon and his half-brother Henry and half-sister Judith; she even

planned the proposed marriage. Having been rejected by Sutpen because of
her black ancestry, she who once had been a part of Sutpen's design to gain
eminence and move from the social status of poor white to wealthy Santo
Domingan landowner, worked to destroy Sutpen's design as landed gentry in
Mississippi. It is never made clear how much Charles Bon, often described as
calculating and catlike, is conscious of her plan. But what the reader does know
is that Henry (as well as Judith, her mother, Ellen, and even Rosa) is as much
seduced by the glamor of the elegant young man from the city as the narrator
and Mr. Compson are tantalized by the figure of Bon's mistress, the octoroon,
and New Orleans.

Faulkner's tourist in the *Double Dealer* prose poem had suggested that the
young epicene modern woman must learn from the courtesan, New Orleans.
The theme appears again in *Mosquitoes,* though implicit, as represented by Pat
Robyn. In *Absalom, Absalom!* the courtesan image and the issue of racial identification are combined. Judith Sutpen certainly does not fit into the image of
the modern woman, who, like Pat Robyn or Helen Baird, must learn from the
courtesan; Judith, according to Mr. Compson, is "just the blank shape, the
empty vessel in which each of them [Bon and Henry] strove to preserve, not
the illusion of himself nor his illusion of the other but what each conceived the
other to believe him to be" (148). However, Judith is a felt presence in the
novel, one who learns from all around her. She receives the letter from Charles
Bon with his decision, "We have waited long enough" (162), and hands it over
to Mrs. Compson, so that Bon's role in the struggle that they are destined to
play will not be lost. She invites the octoroon mistress to Bon's burial and then
sends Clytie to bring the son of Bon and the octoroon, Charles Étienne St.
Valery Bon, back to Sutpen's Hundred when his mother dies. She and Clytie
hide Henry in the plantation house when he returns home for refuge after the
funeral. She helps Bon's son when he contacts yellow fever and dies herself in
the process. Even though she is one of Faulkner's voiceless women,[40] she manages to learn from all of the black characters, ironically accepting their reality
as a part of her own, or as she (in Mr. Compson's words) sums up the matter
of our interdependence as individuals:

> You get born and you try this and you dont know why only you keep
> on trying it and you are born at the same time with a lot of other
> people, all mixed up with them, like trying to, having to, move your
> arms and legs with strings only the same strings are hitched to all the
> other arms and legs and the others all trying and they dont know why
> either except that the strings are all in one another's way like five or
> six people all trying to make a rug on the same loom only each one
> wants to weave his own pattern into the rug; and it cant matter, you
> know that, or the Ones that set up the loom would have arranged
> things a little better. (157)

New Orleans, the sophisticated city of Faulkner's literary apprenticeship, is always associated in his fiction with *modernism*—new philosophical, literary, and artistic trends—and with the courtesan, who was herself of a sophisticated older culture. The "foreign and paradoxical" city was "at once feminine and steel-hard," qualities that were not necessarily polarities, as the contemporary discourse would have had it. The city's mores were not governed by a jealous and unforgiving Jehovah, and its racial ethics were paradoxical. New Orleans was dramatic counterpoint to Yoknapatawpha, the more typically southern experience, and would remain a riddle to be solved by Faulkner and his characters. Faulkner's Barthean "appropriation" of New Orleans's interracial and "feminine" culture adds to his myth of the South and to the evolving myth of New Orleans.

FIVE

ய

Shaping Patterns of Myth and Folklore: The Federal Writers' Projects

During the 1920s and 1930s Lyle Saxon was "Mr. New Orleans," a legend in his own right—spokesman for the Vieux Carré, southern aristocratic gentleman and host, heir to the Charles Gayarré-Grace King New Orleans literary *ancien régime,* reporter for the *Times-Picayune,* novelist and historian. From 1935 to 1942 he was director of the Louisiana Federal Writers' Project of the Works Progress Administration (WPA), which published the *New Orleans City Guide* (1938) and *Gumbo Ya-Ya* (1945).[1] Marcus Christian (1900–1976)—poet, folklorist, historian, director of the "Colored Project" of the Louisiana Federal Writers' Project of the WPA (1936–43) during Saxon's directorship, compiler of the unpublished "Black History of Louisiana"—was silent contributor to much of what was published by the project. In his published poetry and articles in newspapers, journals, and collections by Arna Bontemps and Sterling Brown, in his books, *Negro Soldiers in the Battle of New Orleans* (1955) and *Negro Ironworkers of Louisiana, 1718–1900* (1972), and in his numerous unpublished articles of research and poems, Marcus Christian elaborated on the multiculturalist theme of his 1968 poem, "I Am New Orleans." The explicit and implicit dialogue between Saxon and Christian dramatizes a national dialogue between black and white writers of the thirties, forties and fifties, and between two generations of black writers.[2] While Lyle Saxon, along with Roark Bradford and Robert Tallant, continued to contribute to the written myth of New Orleans and to publish books about the black experience, Marcus Christian revised the myth, supporting the new black aesthetic of Sterling Brown, Zora Neale Hurston, Langston Hughes, and Arna Bontemps, which drew on the folklore, music, language, and culture of the Negro folk.

*Lyle Saxon, Mr. Vieux Carré of the 1930s. Courtesy The Historic New Orleans
Collection, Museum/Research Center, Acc. No. 1983.215.75.*

Lyle Saxon

When Storyville was closed down in 1917, many feared that cabarets and
brothels would take over the French Quarter. "There was even, at one time,"
Lyle Saxon remarked, "a movement among a group of citizens to tear down
the entire Quarter, as a rat-infested slum not in keeping with their views as to
what a city should be."[3] As many fashionable persons left the Quarter, Lyle
Saxon's numerous *Times-Picayune* articles about the beauty and romance of
the Quarter attracted writers and artists to become residents, even before the
call of Sherwood Anderson in *The Double Dealer*. By 1922 Saxon had become "the official spokesman of Frenchtown" and its unofficial host from his
restored French Quarter home at 536 Royal Street.[4]

While acting as host of the Vieux Carré, however, William Faulkner and
William Spratling criticized Saxon's playing the role of aristocratic southern

The Vieux Carré in the 1920s, before renovation. Courtesy The Historic New Orleans Collection, Museum/Research Center, Acc. No. 1979.325.5221.

gentleman; in *Sherwood Anderson and Other Famous Creoles* (1926), they lampooned him (and all of the other major players in the Vieux Carré of the 1920s), his caricature showing him reclining on an elaborately embroidered pillow, reading a copy of *Eminent Victorians,* his caption reading, "The Mauve Decade in St. Peter Street."[5] At the same time, even though his reputation was secure as *literateur* and heir apparent to Grace King (he dedicated his *Fabulous New Orleans* to King), it was rankling to him that he was writing journalistic articles and romantic histories, not novels like his contemporaries, Sherwood Anderson and William Faulkner.[6]

In March 1923, at one of Grace King's "Thursday evenings" Saxon met Cammie Garret Henry, the owner of Melrose Plantation in Natchitoches Parish, and was invited to visit her home. On Lyle Saxon's first visit to Melrose on April 1, 1923, he conceived the idea of writing the novel *Children of Strangers.* He wrote the story "Cane River" in 1925 and quickly followed it with "The Long Fall" and then "Lizzie Balize," which became two chapters of the novel. Although these stories were followed by the four Louisiana "histories"—*Father Mississippi* (1927), *Fabulous New Orleans* (1928), *Old Louisiana* (1929), and *Lafitte the Pirate* (1930)—Saxon was obsessed by the story of his novel, which would be connected with the historical past of the Melrose Plantation, the original owner having been Marie Thérèse Coin-Coin, a Congoborn woman manumitted from slavery by the widow of her owner. Several descendants of the marriage between Marie Thérèse and Thomas Metoyer, member of a prominent white Natchitoches family, appear in Lyle Saxon's novel, which would not be published until 1937.[7]

Saxon became involved with the coterie of writers who met at the plantation, including his friends from *The Times-Picayune* and the French Quarter— Roark Bradford, Harnett Kane, Robert Tallant, Ada Jack Carver, Caroline Dormon, Gwen Bristow, and Rachel Fields.[8] "Aunt" Cammie Henry "provided the sympathetic milieu in which creative people could meet, exchange ideas, and work, and at a time no other place as this existed in this region outside New Orleans."[9] Melrose provided Saxon a respite from New Orleans, the drudgery of newspaper work, the boosting of the Quarter, and the bohemian literati, which he satirized in his novel.

By 1926, in fact, many of the writers of the French Quarter had left New Orleans. After writing *Dark Laughter* (1925) and feeling comfortable with the royalties from the novel, Sherwood Anderson left the city for Virginia. In 1927 when he was enjoying the hills and the bright, crisp fall days of Virginia, he wrote to Saxon, still a reporter for the *Times-Picayune* (though spending increasingly more time at Melrose), "God knows I don't envy your New Orleans now or your job."[10] In effect, the city had ceased being the antidote to America's standardization, a quality many of the writers had come there seeking. Lyle Saxon also realized that New Orleans could not offer him the time that he needed for contemplation and writing. Encouraging Saxon about his novel in progress, Anderson wrote (August 1927): "Anything good has to come slowly. Some women have a lot of children and none of them any good. Writing such tales is a good deal like having children. You have to become pregnant. Then carry the thing around inside you while it grows."[11] Some of Saxon's friends tried to encourage him by comparing him with Faulkner. For instance, Caroline Dormon wrote in December 1934 that she had just read *Light in August,* and she wondered why everybody was so excited about William Faulkner: "If these samples I have read represent him fairly . . . I should hate to think he is the American hope in literature! Why, Lyle, you can beat him writing so far. . . . One of these days, I will read a novel by Lyle Saxon which . . . will curl up the thin sheets of bright metal (probably tin) that glitter on Faulkner and these other *poseurs*."[12]

In *Children of Strangers,* Saxon himself speaks satirically about these superficial writers from the city through his character Guy Randolph, the white owner of Melrose: "Oh, writers! friends came here, and they talked me to death. Such a bunch of idiots you never saw. They were divided into two classes: one saw everything as symbolical . . . and found everything quaint: they saw the surface, and it was just as picturesque as hell. They talked about folklore and all that sort of bunk. The other group talked about the plight of the share-croppers. God! As though I wouldn't get rid of the share-croppers if I could."[13]

In his novel Saxon planned to deal with the problems of race and caste, themes treated earlier by Cable and King, but he would describe Louisiana characters, the place and its customs, realistically, not "symbolically," as Faulkner did in his short stories and novels. He would not portray Melrose and the Creoles of color as "quaint," or "picturesque." Ironically, to deal with race on a more realistic level, Saxon felt compelled to use a rural setting, where the Creole situation paralleled that of New Orleans, but allowed him a certain detachment from the familiar, stereotypical attitudes toward color and caste. The major character, Famie Vidal, is a Creole of color and a direct descendant of the original founders of the Melrose Plantation. In violation of the ethics of her caste, she falls in love with a white man and has a child by him. She neglects the Creole of color who marries her and puts her child above him. When her son leaves for the North, she sells her land and family heirlooms to the white owner of Melrose to send him money, and in return he decides to desert her completely by "passing" into the white world. To make matters worse, she begins to associate with "negroes," and finally decides to marry the black Henry Tyler. The family finally deserts her because "Famie had humbled them all. Her name had become a byword, and men laughed at her when they talked together. She was a traitor to her people, and she made her relatives ashamed that her name was the same as theirs."[14]

Saxon praised the traditional virtues of the rural community of Melrose Plantation and Ile Brevelle, but he criticized the cruelties imposed by the racial and caste structures on individuals living in the old-fashioned plantation economy. Wrestling with questions of black-white and black-Creole relationships, Saxon demonstrated the irrationality of a society based on such racial myths and exposed his ambivalence about playing the roles of southern aristocrat in New Orleans and romantic historian of the city and the state. Like Tinker in *Toucoutou* (1928), Saxon attempted to portray the world of the Louisiana Creole of color in realistic, rather than symbolic, terms, to portray more than a "quaint" Louisiana community; but the very selection of such a unique setting as the Ile Brevelle limited the reading public's readiness to apply the novel's situation to its own.

In October 1935 Lyle Saxon accepted the directorship of the Louisiana Writers' Project of the WPA. Even though he had not completely finished writing his novel, he was already known familiarly as "Mr. New Orleans" and "Dean of New Orleans Writers."[15] Assisted by Edward Dreyer, he edited voluminous materials sent in by field workers on the subjects of Louisiana's population, topography, customs, arts, and folklore. In his letters to the Melrose group, Saxon complained that his work was depressing and time-consuming, but in spite of the time spent on preparing *A Guide to the State: Louisiana* and the *New Orleans City Guide, Children of Strangers* was finally published on July 6, 1937.[16]

Marcus Christian

In 1936 Saxon asked Marcus Christian, a reporter for the black newspaper *The Louisiana Weekly,* to participate in a Negro unit of the Federal Writers' Project. The Negro unit would be housed at Dillard University and would "collect Negro material for a history of the Negro in Louisiana."[17] Christian, who was also a poet and owner of a small dry cleaning business, accepted the offer: "I told him that I thought it was great and showed him bits from the small collection of facts that I had already gathered together as well as some articles from the *Louisiana Weekly* that I had written four years back. The very fact so excited me that I blurted out that I'd even be glad to do that sort of work for nothing. He smiled one of his indulgent smiles and said: 'Oh, you'll get paid.'"[18] Christian remarked on their handshake that evening, describing Saxon's gesture as "that impulsive outward swing of his hand that nearly described an arc, but an arc that in its downward swing, hesitated just long enough to give your hand time to rise slightly and meet his in a gesture of genuine fellowship. . . . A clasping of hands in an expansive, mellow, hail-fellow mood."[19]

Marcus Christian, whose father and grandfather were both teachers in Mechanicsville (now Houma), Louisiana, had arrived in New Orleans in 1917 at seventeen years old, having been orphaned at thirteen. He was unable to continue his education there except in night school. He developed a cleaning business and a printing press, which were both housed in his shotgun home. By the time Lyle Saxon met him, Christian held the post of poetry and contributing editor for the *Louisiana Weekly,* and had published poems in the *Weekly,* the New Orleans *Daily States* and *Item-Tribune,* and such national forums as *Phylon,* the *Crisis, Opportunity,* the *New York Herald-Tribune,* the *Pittsburgh Courier,* and the *Baltimore Afro-American.* Mel Washburn, columnist of the *Item-Tribune,* had called him "the poet laureate of New Orleans Negroes."[20] During the WPA years and later, Christian edited a book of poetry, *From the Deep South* (1937), and was included in *The Negro Caravan* (1941), edited by Sterling Brown, and *The Poetry of the Negro* (1949), edited by Arna Bontemps; he wrote the long poems *In Memoriam—Franklin Delano Roosevelt* (1945) and *Common Peoples' Manifesto of World War II* (1948),

Marcus Christian, in his office at the University of New Orleans, 1973. Courtesy Archives and Manuscripts/Special Collections Department of the Earl K. Long Library, University of New Orleans.

the historical *Negro Soldiers in the Battle of New Orleans* (1955), the book of poetry *High Ground* (1958), the long Whitmanesque poem *I Am New Orleans* (1968), and the historical *Negro Ironworkers of Louisiana, 1718–1900*. When he died on March 21, 1976, he left numerous unpublished poems and pieces of fiction and nonfiction as well as voluminous notes and diaries.[21]

As researcher of Negro folklore and poet, Christian participated in the movement of black writers of the 1930s to recover the dialect and customs of the common people, whom Langston Hughes considered to be the salvation of black people. The interest of such leading writers as Hughes, Zora Neale Hurston, Sterling Brown, Arna Bontemps, and Margaret Walker was a movement toward a new black aesthetic, a continuation of the 1920s New Negro Movement, or Harlem Renaissance. In his essay "Why I Returned," Arna Bontemps answers the question, "Why should I not act colored?" by stating that "white people have been enjoying the privilege of acting like Negroes for more than a hundred years. The minstrel show, their most popular form of entertainment in America for a whole generation, simply epitomized, while it exaggerated, this privilege."[22] Christian's research into the life of blacks in Louisiana remained unpublished because of editors' continuing lack of interest in black views of black Louisiana life, which is particularly ironic when one considers the great volume of popular histories and novels about Negro folklore that saw print in the 1930s, 1940s, and 1950s—Roark Bradford's *All God's Chillun* (1928) and *John Henry* (1931), Robert Tallant's *Voodoo in New Orleans* (1946) and *The Voodoo Queen* (1956), and Allan Lomax's *Jelly Roll* (1950), to name a few.

The Negro Writers' Project was a Who's Who of Negro intellectuals during that same three-decade period. Lawrence D. Reddick, professor of History at Dillard University, became the first director of the project, but was soon succeeded by Christian. The original members of the group were Reddick, Christian, Clarence A. Laws, Octave Lilly, Jr., Eugene B. Willman, Alice Ward-Smith, and James La Fourche. Later under Christian's directorship the group's membership changed, still including Lilly and Reddick, but also Horace Mann Bond, Elizabeth Catlett, St. Clair Drake, Arna Bontemps, Rudolph Moses, Benjamin Quarles, and Margaret Walker.[23] Frank Yerby and Randolph Edmonds were also professors at Dillard during the years of the WPA. The group compiled "The History of Black Louisiana" between 1936 and 1943, but the manuscript was never completely edited and published in book form; today it is a part of the Marcus Christian Collection in the Archives of the University of New Orleans.

In fact, most of the original research Christian and his group collected remained unpublished except for other writers' use of it as source material, acknowledged and unacknowledged. In the prefaces of the state and city guides and in *Gumbo Ya-Ya* Lyle Saxon noted the assistance of Christian's group in compiling the material on black subjects. However, the credit given Christian is certainly not commensurate with his significant contribution in writing the book, as easily judged from studying his primary research notes and essays as filed in the Christian Collection. Saxon researched thoroughly the facts and legends surrounding Marie Laveau and other voodoo leaders. Christian's critical notes on the limitations of Tallant's *Voodoo in New Orleans* and *The Voodoo Queen: A Novel* and Tallant's repeated use of source material found in the Christian Collection strongly suggest Tallant's unacknowledged use of Christian's research in his books.[24] Christian also commented on current white productions of the John Henry legend, which he researched and planned a book on himself. Christian's papers include also clippings, notes, and manuscripts on numerous other Louisiana subjects, including Bras-Coupé, the *gens de couleur, Les Cenelles,* Alice Dunbar-Nelson, miscegenation, Creole dialect, litigation on matters of race, Melrose, and Negro culture in New Orleans from 1860 to 1880. His correspondence includes letters to Eleanor Roosevelt, Lyle Saxon, Langston Hughes, A. P. Tureaud, Arna Bontemps, Sterling Brown, W. E. B. DuBois, John Blassingame, and many others.[25]

Christian was aware of the major blind-spots of southern white writers and historians during that time, and in a handwritten note to himself, he pointed out the purposeful omission of contributions by blacks in most histories written by whites. As the researchers in the Dillard group began to unearth much new historical data, he observed:

> Very soon we began to take an attitude which was consistently critical of most histories—particularly those written from the typical viewpoint of a certain period, and very early concluded that most of them were a blending of regional prejudices and romance. We soon concluded that the omission of one-fourth, one-third, or one-half of the population from the true history of the state or region had been a deliberate, purposeful act on the part of most southern historians and was at variance with all documentary data, particularly so, since that region's whole "way of life" had been predicated largely upon the presence of this one-fourth, one-third, or one-half of the total population.
>
> Very soon we began to suspect that there was an important Negro or person of Negro descent in nearly every historical woodpile and worked accordingly.[26]

Clearly, black literature and other forms of art, as well as contributions of blacks to sociology, history, and science, did not exist for most white historians of New Orleans and Louisiana culture, for Charles Gayarré, Grace King, Saxon, Tallant. When Tallant cited *Les Cenelles* (1845), an anthology of poems by a group of New Orleans free men of color, in the section, "The Literary Heritage" of *The Romantic New Orleanians,* he called the book "one of the most curious productions of literary New Orleans." The literary magazine in which most of the poems had appeared, *L'Album Littéraire,* "was odd," he said, "only because of the race of the men who owned, edited and wrote it, and the fact that they could do so, not because of its contents, which were of high quality."[27]

In spite of the friendship between Christian and Saxon, Christian realized that because of the state of black-white relationships in the South of the time, the WPA would never actually publish his "History of Black Louisiana" and he would be only a contributor to the white-edited publications of the Federal Writers' Project. He disagreed with some of the material in the *Louisiana State Guide,* and was also concerned about Saxon's overall plan for the Dillard Project. The group had submitted items to the WPA which were not included in the Louisiana guide. Christian wrote in a typed note:

> Good material to refute on Marie Laveau in the *Louisiana State Guide,* a book on which Negroes were supposed to have collaborated. Yet they asked us for materials on free people of color and their culture, but nothing on Voudou or Laveau. . . . It is probably true as I always held, that Saxon never intended for the History of the Negro in Louisiana to be published under WPA auspices. On the other hand, because we had undeniably good material, he could not in his conscience let it go to waste or go to a white institution. Hence, the compromise of turning it over to me. He probably concluded that if Negroes had any sense they would work to get it out. He didn't know Negroes![28]

While continuing to collect scholarly material on black Louisiana and attempting publication, Christian maintained a critical vigilance on publications dealing with black subjects by white members of the WPA, especially Robert Tallant, Harnett Kane, and Roark Bradford. Christian considered Tallant's book *Voodoo in New Orleans* to be "a flamboyant bouquet" of Negro folklife and superstition; he thought that it made good reading but "the researcher interested in the history of authentic folk material free from author-coloration will be forced to travel farther still. . . . It contains little Voodoo history that is not known."[29] He criticized Tallant's portrayal of voodoo in New Orleans because, he said, Tallant sets the tone for the entire book in his introduction, where he discusses the white man's wonder at the almost completely black world of South Rampart Street. Tallant writes, for example, that "the white man walking on South Rampart Street is a foreigner. Unless he has some business errand here he is soon conscious of this fact. He may even begin to wonder if a Negro ever feels as strange when he walks on a white man's street, though he knows Negroes understand white men much better than white men understand Negroes. It seems to the white man that on South Rampart Street the Negro has in his mysterious way built a world for himself, and an amazing and colorful one at that."[30] According to Christian, Tallant's wonder "heightens the color of every prosaic thing, and gives a sometimes exaggerated focus to many parts of his story."[31]

Christian also found several errors in Tallant's book, and discusses these in

Robert Tallant, third from left, seated, at the Little Basement Bookstore, operated by Tess Crager, far right, a popular meeting place of writers from the 1920s to the 1950s. The Cragers ran their own press, publishing a number of the books of New Orleans's authors. Courtesy The Historic New Orleans Collection, Museum/Research Center, Acc. No. 1983.215.5.

his notes, for he himself had done a thorough job of studying voodoo in New Orleans, the sources and background of Marie Laveau, and the traditions associated with voodoo in the city. Christian notes that Tallant is in error when he says that slave raids on the African slave coast which brought voodoo worshippers to the West Indies began about 1724; Christian's studies showed that the slave raids began earlier, and by 1743 voodoo practices had already appeared in the Louisiana colony. The 1773 court trial, known as the "Gris-gris Plot," was evidence, Christian noted, that voodoo was already rooted in Louisiana culture by that time. Christian's research showed that voodoo was often used for insurrectionary purposes, both in Haiti and in the United States; as Tallant also notes, the dangers of insurrection led Governor Galvez to forbid the importation of slaves from the West Indies in 1782 because of their knowledge of voodoo.[32]

Christian felt that much of the "morbid interest manifested in the voodoos" during the early 1800s grew out of local white interest in what they considered "very strange happenings." Many newspaper descriptions of voodoo celebrations were also associated with Milneburg and with white underworld characters, and in the minds of many readers, voodoo rituals were often connected with prostitution, a tie that lasted even up to the time of Storyville. Fannie Sweet, one of the popular white Madames of the notorious area, was a believer in voodoo and her parties were said to have often been connected with voodoo ritual. In addition, as Tallant suggested, more than anything else, whites feared that there was a complicated network of blacks in revolt against their white owners and the people they worked for. Lyle Saxon wrote in *Fabulous New Orleans* that Marie Laveau and Doctor John had many Negro servants in their employ and that these servants continually brought information from the wealthy white homes to them. Therefore, the wealthy whites were often subject to blackmail or to the power of the voodooists.

A part of the interest of whites in voodoo, Christian suggested, was the fear and sensationalism caused by the integrated nature of the practices. What seems to have fascinated Tallant and many others who read about voodoo is that it held an attraction for whites as well as blacks. One of the first things Tallant mentions in discussing voodoo history is that whites joined the cult in New Orleans almost from the beginning, and at the largest gatherings of voodoos on the St. John's Eve celebrations there were always many whites who participated. Tallant writes that around 1850, voodoo—or "hoodoo," as blacks often called it—was at its height of popularity in the city. Newspapers defended the cultists. Voodoo queens became more open, and many New Orleanians "sought the services of *Voodooiennes,* sometimes for a lark, sometimes with great seriousness, and it was everyone's desire to witness a Voodoo rite."[33] Such rites on Lake Pontchartrain during the last part of the nineteenth century, Tallant wrote, brought thousands of observers, including reporters and politicians, and it was obvious that the practice was widely known and accepted. Tallant quoted blacks who had seen such ceremonies, among them Grandma Beauvois, "an old black woman with white hair and but one very belligerent eye," who described "the black-cat rite" as an important part of most ceremonies. A live black cat was thrown into boiling water and then skinned; "After that" she said, "they eat the flesh and divide the bones. Black-cat bones has lots of power and makes good gris-gris."[34]

Tallant remarks that voodoo practices in Louisiana also fascinated the national press of the 1880s and 1890s. In *Harper's Weekly* of November 7, 1885, for example, Lafcadio Hearn published "The Last of the Voudous," which described Doctor John, or John Montanet, a well-known voodoo priest in New Orleans before the most famous of the voodoo queens, Marie Laveau, came to the fore. Both Doctor John and Marie Laveau would later play important roles in Ishmael Reed's *The Last Days of Louisiana Red.*[35] Others writing for northern journals and magazines also wrote about the voodoo cults. Tallant quotes a description of a rite from C. D. Warner's *Studies in the South and West*: "While the wild chanting, the rhythmic movement of hands and feet, the barbarous dance, and the fiery incantations were at their height . . . it was so hard and bizarre that one might easily imagine he was in Africa or in hell."

Christian criticizes Tallant's descriptions of voodoo ceremonies at Congo Square on the grounds that basing them on material like the preceding passage by Warner rendered them derivative. Tallant's description of the dances at Congo Square was based on Henry C. Castellanos's book, *New Orleans As It Was* (1895) and the *Times-Picayune* article by William G. Nott, "Marie Leveau [*sic*], Long High Priestess of Voodooism in New Orleans" (1922). Castellanos's accounts, on the other hand, drew from Helene d'Aquin's *Souvenirs d'Amerique et de France Par Une Creole* (1882), but what contemporary writers like Tallant did not know was that d'Aquin's descriptions were based on ceremonies not in New Orleans, but in Santo Domingo.[36] Christian also notes that Lyle Saxon had drawn most of his material about voodoo in *Fabulous New Orleans* from the *Times-Picayune* article, and Tallant had simply restated his information.[37] Christian thought that the sensationalism of Tallant's book made it very popular reading, but sometimes truth had been sacrificed for effect.

The same might be said of Zora Neale Hurston's *Mules and Men,* which was published in 1935. In her study of hoodoo, carried out mainly between 1927 and 1928 in New Orleans and Algiers (on the West Bank of the Mississippi River), Hurston worked under several of the followers of Marie Laveau, whom she calls "the queen of conjure." Among these were Luke Turner, who was purportedly Laveau's nephew, Anatol Pierre, Eulalia, Father Joe Watson, or the "Frizzly Rooster," Dr. Duke, Dr. Samuel Jenkins, and Kitty Brown, and Hurston was initiated into the service of each. Hurston's book was generally ignored when it was published because of her colloquial, unscientific style of research and writing. But, as Arnold Rampersad notes in the foreword to the 1990 edition of *Mules and Men,* she promoted the idea of cultural relativism, which her mentor, Franz Boas, advocated, the idea that cultures should "be seen on their own terms and not according to a scale that held European civilization to be the supreme standard." Moreover, she viewed New Orleans as "the hoodoo capital of America. Great names in rites that vie with those of Hayti in deeds that keep alive the powers of Africa."[38]

The Marie Laveau story is an important part of the myth of New Orleans, and Tallant was instrumental in perpetuating her image as both saint and sinner. Christian was always interested in discovering the factual material and explaining how the legend evolved and grew. Christian notes that there was not just one organization of voodoo worshippers, as many writers have characterized the tradition, but there were many cults, and each was rivalling the other for dominance. There were a number of voodoo queens and kings (traditionally, the *mamaloi* and *papaloi*). Several of these predated Marie Laveau, whose name has almost become synonymous with the practice of voodoo in

New Orleans. In much of his research, Christian attempted to trace the geneal-
ogy of Marie Laveau and to identify which of the many Marie Laveaus who
lived in New Orleans at the time was the real voodoo queen, but that became
almost impossible. While Tallant and Christian seem to concur in most of the
biographical details of Laveau's life, they do differ in others. It was not clear,
for example, whether Marie Laveau actually had either a daughter or granddaughter who fit the description in Tallant's book. In this case, Christian wrote,
Tallant "not only conjures up a Marie II, but seems intent to supply a Marie
III."[39] More significantly, Christian pointed out how close Laveau's house at
1030 St. Ann Street was to the Parish Prison and Congo Square. Noting that
Marie Laveau was listed in the City's Directory as a *victualler,* Christian sur-
mised that as she got older, she confined her trade to the inmates and officials
of the Parish Prison, where she carried food to convicted persons, and thus
was associated with the strange deaths and other occurrences at the prison. But
it is probable that the mysteries were not as "darkly ritualistic" as some would
suggest, Christian wrote. "Then, here, as an old woman who had seen suffering among the poor of both races, she turned faith-healer and spiritual adviser,
backed by a traditional knowledge among free colored women of herbs and
simples."[40] Christian suggests, in other words, that Laveau's life was never as
flamboyant as writers like Robert Tallant would have us believe; in fact, she
was probably more of a spiritual advisor and healer than the Satanic figure that
many white writers and news people presented. He also notes that many
thought the services of Marie Laveau were similar to those of spiritualist
churches in his day. The occurrences in Congo Square, he thought, were not as
perverse as Tallant would have us believe; people would bring something to
the Square—a goat, a chicken, or money—to help those who were less fortu-
nate than they.[41] According to Hurston, the dances on Congo Square were primarily pleasure dances, not hoodoo, because "hoodoo is private." Laveau really did give dances on the first Friday night in each month and served crab
gumbo and rice and held a great feast once a year on the Eve of St. John's,
June 24.[42] Beyond that, we can't be certain.

Nevertheless, fantasy or not, Christian concedes that Marie Laveau, the historical figure, had become a legend "as indigenous to New Orleans's Franco-
American traditions as are the Mardi Gras, Gumbo, Jambalaya, and lagniappe."[43] She was associated with writers like Lafcadio Hearn, who many
people said was one of her lovers, George Washington Cable, who saw her
first as an old lady and wrote about her in his article, "Creole Slave Songs,"
and she continued to be an inspiration to other writers, including Zora Neale
Hurston, Edward Larocque Tinker, Lyle Saxon, Robert Tallant and, among our
contemporaries, Ishmael Reed and Tom Dent.[44] Although the truth about
Marie Laveau would probably never be known, Christian attempted to find
out some of the facts, at least to explain the black perspective on this pur-

ported voodoo priestess, who was very quickly becoming a white creation of black folklife in New Orleans.

After Tallant's fictional account, *The Voodoo Queen*, was published in 1956, Christian collected several articles from the *Times-Picayune* which dealt with Tallant's fear and timidity of retribution by voodoos. One of the articles was headed, "This Guest Will Make Himself Scarce"; it described an autograph party given for Tallant, but the guest-of-honor did not appear.[45] The hostess, Tess Crager, the owner of the Little Basement Bookstore, a meeting-place for literati of the *Double-Dealer* and WPA days, asked Tallant for an explanation. He said that after receiving a mysterious voodoo cloth, "wild horses couldn't drag me to the party. Whatever happens, you might call it psychosomatic, but I call it hoodoo." Much of the press apparently felt that Tallant had bitten off more than he could chew in writing about voodoo. A later article reported that Tallant had been cut off the air waves during a radio program when he was about to discuss his newly published novel. Tallant, the broadcaster suggested, might have caused the interruption because he was afraid to face an audience of voodoos, who probably knew that his real knowledge of the subject was limited, but a rational explanation was later published.[46]

Another writer during this period who used the subject of African-American folklore was Roark Bradford, who published *Ol' Man Adam an' His Chillun* (1928), which became in another version Marc Connelly's play *Green Pastures* and *John Henry* (1931).[47] John Henry was the subject of much of Marcus Christian's research over the years; he was particularly interested in finding out the facts surrounding this African-American legend, which was well known not only in the South and the rest of the United States but also in the Caribbean. Apparently Christian did not take issue with Bradford's presentation of the John Henry story, but his criticism of another writer's account, James Cloyd Bowman's *John Henry: The Rambling Black Ulysses* (1942), is also a valid criticism of Bradford's development of the legend. Christian wrote of Bowman's book that "despite these words and his excellent material—much of it similar to that in Bradford's story, however—his story is rather a caricature of a legendary figure rather than a monumental account of a monumental folk figure."[48]

Christian realized that John Henry had become a legend, as large as or larger than Marie Laveau in African-American folklore. In a short typescript, he wrote: "If ever you are in New Orleans, and you are a lover of the strange and mystifying twists and turns of the many odd threads woven into the fabric of American Negro folklore, you will do well to visit No. 376 Customhouse Street and look about you. For it was on this street and in this house that the Great John Henry—the original John Henry—lived out his last remaining days and it was from this house that he was taken to his final resting place on May 14, 1874."[49] Christian's research showed that a number of men by the name of

John Henry were in New Orleans during the time the legendary one was said
to live there. From 1870 to 1904, in fact, the New Orleans Directory listed a
large number of John Henrys, married and unmarried, with various occupa-
tions. There was also a long list of crimes charged to men who bore that name.
The similarities between the police accounts and the stories of the legendary
John Henry are striking, and, as Christian observes, somehow significant:

> Even though he was but a common brawler, petty thief, robber, and
> murderer, there was something about him, even though he was al-
> ways cast in the role of protagonist against the society in which he
> found himself. There was something about his very crimes which
> somehow seemed to be a silent indictment of society. His penchant
> for crime was so great that one begins to believe that surely here was
> a man which, in his own way, mirrored the wrongs of a white south
> against his own black race. His sure path to crime on all occasions
> seemed to prove beyond any doubt that the milieu in which he found
> himself, and not he, was the sinner.[50]

Christian compares John Henry to Till Eulenspiel, Robin Hood, and Jean
Valjean, of Victor Hugo's *Les Misérables,* for he was a person who fought out
against the society that he lived in and refused to limit himself within its narrow confines.[51]

Christian was more than simply curious about the John Henry myths; he
also planned a book, tentatively titled "John Henry: A Study in Facts and Folklore." In his introduction he remarks, "What is said here may either serve to
clarify many aspects of the career of this mythical and legendary figure, or
make even more vague and indistinct the outlines which proclaim him a
"nachal man."[52]

The objections Christian had with the treatment of John Henry by Bradford
could have been rooted in Bradford's minimalization of a bigger-than-life hero;
in Bradford's version, Henry becomes the champion cotton-picker, roustabout,
and railroad hand, a bad man with a big mouth, but he is also a caricature who
speaks an inaccurate and unpersuasive black dialect, in the minstrel tradition
of black humor. Such a portrait must have rankled Christian, with his penchant
for meticulous research and historical accuracy. Throughout his life, Christian
continued to collect details about the people of African-American folklore and
history and to critique publications about the subject by white authors; however, most of his research and analysis remains unpublished.

Aside from his role as prolific historical writer and folklorist, Marcus Christian was also a poet. In fact, some 1,175 poems, most of them unpublished, are
in the University of New Orleans Christian Collection. A friend and correspon-
dent of such poets as Arna Bontemps, Langston Hughes, and Sterling Brown,
then director of the Washington, D.C., Negro Writers' Project, Christian

looked toward folklore, language, and music for the themes and styles of his poetry and was interested in preserving Afro-New Orleanian speech, music, and traditions. In addition to writing about such serious subjects as race relations in the United States, black involvement in World War II, and the relationship between blacks and Jews, he also wrote with wit and humor about love and the problems of miscegenation, creating many blues songs about these situations. One such song is "Aint Nothing Else for a Zigaboo to Do." The first three stanzas begin with the same two lines, "O, there ain't nothin else for a Zigaboo to do / But to love and to laugh and be happy."[53] The persona, another Langston Hughes's Jesse B. Simple, bemoans the plight of blacks, or Zigaboos, laughing through the pain, but the final stanza ends with a melodramatic solution:

> *(In desperation rising.)*
> *O, I am going to take a deep wet fall*
> *And get away from it all*
> *From the police courts and the tenements*
> *From whites who go with their heads held high,*
> *And whites who say that we oughta die;*
> *Away from people who steal and rob*
> *From twenty-dollar rent and a ten-cents job;*
> *From prostitutes that cry of rape,*
> *And the unfair laws that we cant escape;*
> *O Lawd,*
> *There's no hope for such people as I*
> *So let this Zigaboo die!*

In addition to racial themes there are many poems about love and sex, which place Christian in the bohemian tradition of New Orleans writers and musicians of the 1920s and '30s, both black and white. Probably he realized his poems would remain largely unpublished, for it was almost inevitable, given the times, that he would be *silenced,* not only by the disinterest of white publishers in black writers but also by his departure from the black middle-class ethos, which despite Hughes and Sterling Brown, many black editors still expected. Hughes had declared the manifesto of the new black poet in his essay, "The Negro Artist and the Racial Mountain" (1926):

> Let the blare of Negro jazz bands and the bellowing voice of Bessie Smith singing Blues penetrate the closed ears of the colored near-intellectuals until they listen and perhaps understand. . . . We younger Negro artists who create intend to express our individual dark-skinned selves without fear or shame. If white people are pleased we are glad. If they are not, it doesn't matter. We know we are beautiful. And ugly

too. The tom-tom cries and the tom-tom laughs. If colored people are
pleased we are glad. If they are not, their displeasure doesn't matter
either. We build our temples for tomorrow, strong as we know how,
and we stand on top of the mountain, free within ourselves.[54]

One poem that exemplifies this creed, written in Negro dialect, is "Creole
Mammah Turn Your Damper Down." In the final stanza:

> *Creole Mammah, lissen heah,*
> *You know Ah am your monkey man;*
> *Ah swear Ah loves you honey chère*
> *Mo dan ennything in dis doggone land;*
> *Lissen, Baby, to your Lawd's comman—*
> *En doncha cheatcha lovin man—*
> *Ah said,*
> *Doncha cheatcha lovin man.*

Many of Christian's poems fall into the categories that he called "Fantastiks
and Grotesks" and "The Heroic Mold" (cf. the "grotesques" of Sherwood
Anderson's fiction and Faulkner's *New Orleans Sketches*). Included in the
"The Heroic Mold" are "Carnival Torch-bearer," interesting because the torchbearers, who are always black, play an important but demeaning role in the
Mardi Gras parades. Although the torchbearers proudly carry their beacons to
light the way for the floats and bands to follow, they still go on foot like the
horses, which carry the parade's knights and dukes.

> *In nondescript clothes and run-down, broken shoes,*
> *His small, dark face unnaturally lean,*
> *He walks the brightly lighted avenues*
> *With smoking, flaming torch of kerosene.*
> *He lights the way for one more King tonight,*
> *Just as his dark forbears have always done*
> *From Caesar to some lesser ones in might—*
> *Tomorrow night will be a different one.*
> *What are a thousand years but one tomorrow?*
> *What are five hundred years but one long night?*
> *None sees his face—pinched hard by want and sorrow—*
> *Although he carries in his hands a light.*
> *Lighting a dream, he dreams another dream*
> *Of dives on Poydras Street where bright lights gleam.*

The poem personifies the class stratification that was and is so much a part of
the Mardi Gras festivities, and while Christian sees the torchbearer as an individual, as very few others do, he nevertheless points out that in spite of the

man's apparent hunger and misery, he is not thinking about his next meal; he is thinking about the little money that he will get from this activity, and how he will use it in the dives on Poydras Street.

Like Hughes, Christian also wrote political poems, in which he shows his consciousness of race relations in America and the state of the world as it entered World War II. Among this group is "Aferica Salutes the flag"; he uses the term *Aferica,* he explains in a footnote, "because it symbolizes the exact position of the Negro in America. You have all of Africa in that word, and with only one letter substituted you have all of America." The Black American salutes the flag; his description of the flag, a "wind-whipped, tattered piece of bunting," shows the sympathy of blacks toward the chaotic world in which America was involved. The black American points to his respect for the flag whose command he also follows, but in spite of his participation in the war, having put his life on the line for America, he is still dying "by fagot and by rope" in this country. Still, he salutes the flag now because he still has hope that things will change. In the 1940s such a hope endured. By the 1960s blacks recognized that hope would not be enough to change America's ways. We see some of that hope in Marcus Christian, but also a great measure of realism and criticism of America's position vis-à-vis blacks.

In his long poem, "I Am New Orleans," printed "in commemoration of the 250th Anniversary Celebration of the Founding of the Crescent City— 1718–1968," Marcus Christian, like Walt Whitman ("Song of Myself") and Margaret Walker ("For My People") narrates in many voices the stories of his people, New Orleanians.[55] He celebrates the city's founding, its folklore— Bras-Coupé, Marie Laveau, Bloody O'Reilly—its epidemics and wars, the immigrants from many countries who have settled there:

> I am New Orleans—
> Queen City of the South;
> As fabulous—as fantastic and unreal as the
>   cities of the Arabian Nights.

> I am America epitomized:
> A blending of everything—
> Latin, Nordic, and Negro,
> Indian, European, and American.

The persona speaks in many voices—as narrator-observer, African vendor ("Belle des figues!" "Bon petit calas! Tout chauds, chère, tout chauds!" "Ah got duh nice yahlah bananas lady!"), the jazz aficionado ("Papa Bonnibee, beat dem hot licks out! / Ah sed, Poppa Stoppa, let dat jazz cum out! / En efyuh donh feel it / "Tain't no use tellin' yuh / Jess what it's all about!"), "plump little brown girls / with heavy-laden grocery pushcarts, / Follow[ing] their double-jointed dadies [*sic*] around," children singing their songs at play, a grandfather telling stories to his grandchildren, stories of Compair Lapin instead of ole Brer Rabbit.

> *Many voices—Many languages.*
> *I have been alternately cursed and praised in the hoarse gutterals of*
>   *the African and the German;*
> *I have been condemned and cajoled in the machine-gun polysyllables*
>   *of the Italian;*
> *I have been damned and glorified*
> *In the French of the Sorbonne, of Paris, and of the Communes.*
> *I have been alternately execrated and blessed by the Indian, the*
>   *Spaniard, and the Irishman.*

Marcus Christian, as writer and scholar, had New Orleans, the city and its multi-ethnic cultures as his subject. He maintained a publicly unexpressed dialogue with the major writers and scholars of New Orleans during the 1930s, 1940s, and 1950s—black and white—and many of the city's contemporary black writers as well, among them Tom Dent and Brenda Marie Osbey.[56]

SIX

ധ

Abstractions of Time and Place: Williams and Percy

Tennessee Williams's A Streetcar Named Desire *and* Suddenly, Last Summer

After leaving his home in St. Louis, Tennessee Williams came to New Orleans in 1938, hoping to find a job with the Federal Theatre of Lyle Saxon's Federal Writers' Project.[1] Unlucky in that, he continued in the French Quarter at a cheap boardinghouse, wrote about his experiences in several one-act plays, including "Lord Byron's Love Letters," "Auto-Da-Fé," and "The Lady of Larkspur Lotion" (collected in *27 Wagons Full of Cotton and Other One-Act Plays,* [1945]), and in short stories published later in the collection *One Arm* (1948).[2] He began a lifelong fascination with a city where writers still got together and talked about their books and living well could be very cheap. In the early plays, Williams dramatizes his continuing debate between realism and illusion, as romantic "degenerates" try to live within their dreams, while fighting off the reality of living on a shoestring in the French Quarter. In "The Lady of Larkspur Lotion," Mrs. Hardwicke-Moore fantasizes about being the owner of a Brazilian rubber plantation while in reality she lives in a cheap boardinghouse in the French Quarter, drinks larkspur lotion for alcohol, and earns money as a prostitute. The landlady, Mrs. Wire, constantly forces her way into the passive Mrs. Hardwicke-Moore's world, demanding the rent, and reminding her that "I'm done with dead-beats! . . . Completely fed-up with all you Quarter rats, half-breeds, drunkards, degenerates, who try to get by on promises, lies, and delusions!"[3] A writer who also lives in

Tennessee Williams, seated third from left, *with,* from left, *Frank Merlo, Elia Kazan, and Charles Feldman, during the film production of* A Streetcar Named Desire, *1950. Courtesy of the Photography Collection, Harry Ransom Humanities Research Center of the University of Texas at Austin.*

the boardinghouse, working on his 780-page masterpiece, argues that he and Mrs. Hardwicke-Moore have a right to live in their "world of pitiful fiction." He asks the landlady, "What satisfaction can it give you, good woman, to tear it to pieces, to crush it—call it a lie?"

According to Williams's mother, Edwina Williams, "Tom found New Orleans a complete contrast to St. Louis, a city he hated. . . . He became acquainted with a new kind of life in the French Quarter, one of wild drinking, sexual promiscuity and abnormality."[4] In biographer Thomas Richardson's words, New Orleans provided for Williams "the shock of freedom against the puritanism of his nature," a "city of night and release."[5] There Williams was surrounded by lost and lonely people, but like Faulkner he found in his "grotesques" some meaning which they had culled from experience. Oliver Winemiller of the title story "One Arm" is such a character. The one-time boxing champion, left with only one arm after a disastrous automobile accident, "looked like a broken statue of Apollo, and he had also had the coolness and impassivity of a stone figure."[6] When he faces the electric chair for killing one of the rich men that he hustled, he begins to reflect on his life after receiving hundreds of letters from men for whom he had prostituted himself, and he looks at the letters as "bills from people" to whom he owed feelings. He dies in the electric chair holding the unpaid bills, "but death has never been much in the way of completion."[7] Such characters as Alma Tutwiler of "The Yellow Bird" and the tubercular artist of "The Angel in the Alcove" populate the Vieux Carré of this early period of his writing. It is an exotic city, but also a desperate one for the many artists and dreamers who inhabit it hoping for a break or at least a chance for expression. In his characterization of New Orleans and its characters, Williams shows the influence of Poe and Baudelaire, to whom he refers in "The Angel in the Alcove"; there the loss of Mrs. Wayne, the woman who would tell the landlady horrific stories to poach food from her as she cooked, was probably "the greatest pathological genius since Baudelaire or Poe."[8] Williams describes the "unreal city" of New Orleans in that short story as having an understanding with the moon, "an intimacy of sisters grown old together, no longer needing more than a speechless look to communicate their feelings to each other. This lunar atmosphere of the city draws me back whenever the waves of energy which removed me to more vital towns have spent themselves and a time of recession is called for. Each time I have felt some rather profound psychic wound, a loss or a failure, I have returned to this city. At such periods I would seem to belong there and no place else in the country."[9] Richardson observes that Williams, "unlike other American artists, was influenced significantly by the exotic unreality of New Orleans, so much, in fact, that the city became an informing image for his art."[10]

After success with *The Glass Menagerie* (1944), Williams spent his visits in New Orleans in more fashionable quarters, but he always favored the French Quarter. In 1947, while staying in a second-floor apartment on the corner of St. Peter and Royal with a beautiful skylight over the desk where he wrote in the mornings, he created one of the best-known images of New Orleans in *A Streetcar Named Desire*.[11] In this masterpiece Williams takes the city's courtesan image, its bohemian culture, and its position somewhere between the Old South (as symbolized by the Garden District) and the New South of immigrants and blacks (as symbolized by the "declining" Vieux Carré and Elysian fields—the Faubourg Marigny) and contributes the tensions of love/desire/beauty and death to the myth of New Orleans.

The setting of *Streetcar* is 632 Elysian fields, where one can "almost feel the warm breath of the brown river beyond the river warehouses with their faint redolences of bananas and coffee" and hear "the music of Negro entertainers at a barroom around the corner"; European immigrants, blacks, and whites live together in a kind of "warm and easy" way.[12] Grace King had used

The Desire Streetcar. Courtesy The Historic New Orleans Collection, Museum/Research Center, Acc. No. 1974.25.37.103.

the term "fluid society" to describe this area of the city in "Bonne Maman." Into this unassuming immigrant neighborhood, where men and women go bowling for entertainment and men drink beer and play poker, walks Blanche DuBois, broken voice from the past, Belle Reve—the Old South. In her white suit, pearl earrings and necklace, white gloves and hat, she is obviously out of place.

Hoping that she has wandered into the wrong neighborhood, Blanche explains to her sister's neighbor, "They told me to take a street-car named Desire, and then transfer to one called Cemeteries and ride six blocks and get off at—Elysian Fields." Robert Tallant's bus driver gave similar directions to Mrs. Candy in the novel *Mrs. Candy and Saturday Night,* published in the same year as *Streetcar.* In fact, during 1946-48 New Orleans was a choice subject for popular fiction, histories, and films. *Streetcar* and Williams's early short stories and one-act plays should also be seen in dialogic relation to such popular novels as Frances Parkinson Keyes's *Dinner at Antoine's* (1948), Truman Capote's *Other Voices, Other Rooms* (1948), W. Adolphe Robert's *Brave Mardi Gras* and *Lake Pontchartrain* (1946), Robert Tallant's *Voodoo in New Orleans* (1946), and Frank Yerby's *The Foxes of Harrow* (1946), which sold widely at the time of their publication. When Mrs. Candy of Tallant's novel goes to the cemetery to put flowers on her husband's grave, she boards "a streetcar marked 'Cemeteries' to reach the business district of New Orleans." To go "downtown," north of Canal Street, she has to transfer to the Desire car. When she arrives at the cemetery, she has a perceptive conversation with her dead husband about the virtues of remarrying.[13] In Tallant's comedy, the Desire streetcar takes Mrs. Candy to the cemetery to gain wisdom from the dead. Mr. Candy's advice to his wife is to have a party and remarry, to enjoy life.

But the directions in *Streetcar,* as well as its characterization and theme all operate on a much deeper level. John M. Roderick writes that Blanche's travel through the city on the streetcar lines can be interpreted as "a symbolic prophecy of her movement that will echo throughout the play. . . . Before she can truly arrive at Elysian Fields—resting place of the blessed dead in Greek mythology—Blanche must travel the sacrificial path from desire to death and be purged for this epiphany."[14]

Throughout most of the play, Blanche continues to play the role of the southern belle who has recently lost her family estate. She tries to maintain the facade even after her sister's husband, Stanley Kowalski, has found out the truth of why she has come to New Orleans after being fired from her teaching position in Laurel, Mississippi. As Blanche explains to Mitch, the man whom she had hoped to marry until Stanley told him about her past, her promiscuity is tied to her fear of death: "Death—I used to sit here and she [her mother] used to sit over there and death was as close as you are. . . . The opposite is desire. So do you wonder? How could you possibly wonder!" (120). New Orleans, or Stanley and Stella Kowalski's home on Elysian Fields, is Blanche's last refuge after she has failed in her previous escapes from death through courting desire. But New Orleans holds no answer for Blanche because, despite its seductive, Old World charm, it is also, paradoxically, "an environment created by and for the modern urban survivor—the Stanley and Stella Kowalskis of this world."[15]

The epigraph of *Streetcar* comes from the fifth stanza of Hart Crane's "The Broken Tower," which the poet completed just a month before his suicide in the Caribbean near Florida.[16]

> *And so it was I entered the broken world*
> *To trace the visionary company of love, its voice*
> *An instant in the wind (I know not whither hurled)*
> *But not for long to hold each desperate choice.*

The persona of Crane's poem contemplates his "desperate choices"—love or death. The signs that he hears are unclear because the bells have broken the tower and are swinging wildly. His own words reflect the Word, which promised hope, but seems bent only on delivering despair. He will attempt to build a new tower "that is not stone (Not stone can jacket heaven)—but slip / Of pebbles—visible wings of silence sown / In azure circles." This tower, his poetry, though apparently fragile, will be able to encompass heaven and love. Williams is not so affirmative in portraying Blanche's choices in *Streetcar*. She had come to New Orleans, "the broken world," in search of her illusions of love, but she is forced to face reality and the death of her dreams.

When Mitch takes off the lantern that Blanche used to subdue the light and so disguise her age, she asks him why. He replies that he just wants to be realistic, to see her in the light. But Blanche responds, "I don't want realism. I want magic!" In the New Orleans of *Streetcar*, however, magic is only temporary. Just before Stanley enters Blanche's room and rapes her, while Stella is at the hospital having their baby, Blanche attempts to call Western Union and send off a telegram to her old college sweetheart Shep Huntleigh, a wealthy businessman now in Dallas: "Take down this message! 'In desperate, desperate circumstances! Help me! Caught in a trap. Caught in—' Oh!" (128). Blanche had entered New Orleans to trace desire, perhaps love, but she can not hold on to her illusion of love. Life's choices are desperate: in New Orleans the dream of the Old South is dead; in the brutal world of Stanley Kowalski, she can not even play the role of southern belle.

For Faulkner New Orleans was a courtesan, no longer young, but full of mystery and enchantment; to Tennessee Williams, the city was a prostitute, taking what it needed and demanding payment, but giving no love in return. "Yes, we all use each other," says Catharine Holly in *Suddenly, Last Summer* (1958), "and that's what we think of as love, and not being able to use each other is what's—*hate*. . . ."[17] In this play Williams transmuted many of his anguished personal experiences into drama: the guilt he felt over his sister Rose's lobotomy, what he considered his mother's complicity in approving the procedure, and his own homosexuality. In *Suddenly, Last Summer* Violet Venable

demands that the young Catharine Holly "cut . . . out of her brain" the hor-
rible story of Violet's son's death at the hands of Spanish boys he had used
sexually (423); Williams based Violet's character largely on his own mother
and her son, Sebastian, on himself.[18]

Williams had previously explored the idea of being eaten alive as a kind of
atonement for one's sins in the short story "Desire and the Black Masseur."
There, the black masseur, "the giant," devours the body of the masochistic
Anthony Burns; at the same time church services next door to the masseur's
home end; the rites are over, and "quiet had returned and there was an air of
completion."[19] The connection of being devoured with the idea of sacrifice to
a god continues in *Suddenly, Last Summer,* where, Catharine explains,
Sebastian always envisioned himself as a "sacrifice to a cruel God," and Violet agrees that he was always searching for God. As Sebastian watched the
carnivorous birds attack the sea turtles where they hatched on the Terrible
Encantadas, he thought he had seen God. The insectivorous plants grow ever
more monstrous in his garden, every year demanding their sacrifice. Sebastian
and his mother had become "a famous couple" and had constructed an art form
out of their lives, but Violet refuses to see that Sebastian's sacrificial death
was the completion of the image he had composed.

Williams's New Orleans, like Faulkner's, represents that part of Williams's
psyche which was in rebellion against the Puritan influences of his youth. The
"exotic unreality" of this city would seem to allow its denizens to follow their
illusions, but there was always a demanding landlady, or a "realistic" Mitch,
or the demands of unlimited desire to prevent them from escaping reality. New
Orleans was the city of illusion and desire, which could be satisfied fully only
in death. The ritually slain Sebastian shares with Blanche DuBois the fascination with illusions and Dionysian realities the city represents, but their death
and insanity are all that the city can really give. [20]

Walker Percy's The Moviegoer *and* Love in the Ruins

Unlike Blanche DuBois of *A Streetcar Named Desire* or Quentin Compson of
Absalom, Absalom! Binx Bolling of Walker Percy's *The Moviegoer* cannot retreat from the world through either insanity or suicide; in a 1984 interview
Percy said that in his fiction he was "starting where Faulkner left off, starting
with Quentin Compson who didn't commit suicide. . . . Suicide is easy. Keeping
Quentin Compson alive is something else."[21] Binx Bolling is alive in New Orleans conducting his search for life's meaning. In order to escape the cultural
complexity of the city and particularly the tradition of southern stoicism which
his Aunt Emily represents, he has moved to Gentilly, an undistinguished area

Walker Percy, leaving bookstore in Covington, Louisiana, ca. 1982. Courtesy of Rhoda K. Faust, Maple Street Book Shop, New Orleans.

("Except for the banana plants in the patios and the curlicues of iron on the Walgreen drugstore one would never guess it was part of New Orleans").[22] In this, his first novel, Percy is already moving away from the allure of the romantic myth of New Orleans. In his own life, Percy moved away as well, living in the fashionable Garden District in 1947 when he and his wife, Bunt, first came to New Orleans, but soon moving to the quiet, then relatively undiscovered suburb of Covington, north of Lake Pontchartrain. In Covington, the

Percys "would not be too caught up in the social swirl of Uptown New Orleans."[23]

When *The Moviegoer* appeared in 1961, Judge J. Skelly Wright had just issued a Federal decree to end segregation of the public schools in New Orleans and other schools of the Fifth Circuit, in line with the 1954 United States Supreme Court decision, *Brown v. Board of Education of Topeka, Kansas,* which, in effect, reversed *Plessy v. Ferguson* (1896).[24] Robert Coles, whose biography of Walker Percy places the author in perspective sociologically, philosophically, and literarily, has compared the "search" that he himself discovered in reading *The Moviegoer* with the "search" of the schoolchildren that Coles met in New Orleans during its desegregation crisis.[25] The black children Coles worked with raised many of the same questions that Percy's Binx Bolling raised in the novel. As they initiated school desegregation against persistent violent reactions of white parents, the boycott of the schools by most white students, the rioting, cursing, stoning, and other harassment by white parents, they contemplated the meaning of the tumult; an eight-year-old black girl mused, "I will ask myself if it's worth it. I will ask myself why God made people like He did those white people who shout all those bad words at me. I will ask myself if it makes any sense, to keep walking by them, and trying to smile at them, and trying to be polite, when I'd like to see them all dead . . . to thank those white folks. They're testing me!"[26] The black child tried to use Christian teachings to reverse her feelings of alienation. As he wrote about the children's questioning and read *The Moviegoer* about Binx Bolling's "search," Coles himself experienced what Percy calls "an aesthetic reversal of alienation": "There is a great deal of difference between an alienated commuter riding a train and this same commuter reading a book about an alienated commuter riding a train. . . . The nonreading commuter exists in true alienation, which is unspeakable; the reading commuter rejoices in the speakability of his alienation and in the new triple alliance of himself, the alienated character, and the author. His mood is affirmatory and glad: Yes! that is how it is!—which is an aesthetic reversal of alienation."[27]

Binx Bolling in *The Moviegoer* is, as Percy has written, "a man who finds himself in a world, a very concrete man who is located in a very concrete place and time."[28] While on the surface he is a stock and bond broker living an ordinary life in a duplex on Elysian fields in Gentilly in the 1950s, he knows also that he is an alienated human being, who is "coming to himself" again as he begins his search, "in somewhat the same sense as Robinson Crusoe came to himself on his island after his shipwreck, with the same wonder and curiosity."[29] In pleasant exile, like Robinson Crusoe on his island, Binx pursues his search for meaning; at the same time he manages a small branch office of his uncle's brokerage firm and lives in a tiny basement apartment of a raised bungalow on Elysian Fields. He is, in other words, living according to "the Little

Way," which Percy described in his 1968 essay, "New Orleans, Mon Amour": "The peculiar virtue of New Orleans, like St. Theresa, may be that of the Little Way, a talent for everyday life rather than the heroic deed."[30]

Movies and movie stars offer Binx a sense of "heightened reality" in his decidedly detached existence (16). When he sees William Holden in the French Quarter walking towards Galatoire's Restaurant, place and time seem more significant than they do in everyday reality. Movies also enable Binx to isolate time, as when he sees a western with his cousin Kate and remembers his sophomore year at Tulane when he saw a western in the same theater at the same time of year. The result was a repetition, "the re-enactment of past experience toward the end of isolating the time segment which has lapsed in order that it, the lapsed time, can be savored of itself and without the usual adulteration of events that clog time like peanuts in brittle" (79-80). Seeing the movie *Fort Dobbs* with his girlfriend and secretary, Sharon, and his dying half-brother, Lonnie, is similarly rewarding; Binx calls it "a good rotation" because it's "the experience of the new beyond the expectation of the experiencing of the new" (144). Movies, like train rides and disasters, give one a jolt out of the malaise of the everyday; each creates a situation during which "the world is lost to you, the world and the people in it, and there remains only you and the world and you no more able to be in the world than Banquo's ghost" (120).

It is significant that the novel takes place during Mardi Gras week, a period of "heightened reality" for many New Orleanians. Uncle Jules, for example, "could not conceive being anywhere on earth Mardi Gras morning but the Boston Club" (98).[31] Jules, who has everything a New Orleanian could possibly desire, including money, friends, and status, had been Rex of Mardi Gras and was "an exemplary Catholic" whose role as King of the Krewe of Rex meant being accepted totally by the social elite of the city.[32] For Binx, however, Mardi Gras is just one more chance to be caught in the malaise, yet when his Uncle Jules asks him to go on a business trip to Chicago on Mardi Gras Day, he is traumatized by the thought of losing what sense of identification he still maintains: "It is nothing to him [Uncle Jules] to close his eyes in New Orleans and wake up in San Francisco and think the same thoughts on Telegraph Hill that he thought on Carondelet Street. Me, it is my fortune and misfortune to know how the spirit-presence of a strange place can enrich a man or rob a man but never leave him alone, how, if a man travels lightly to a hundred strange cities and cares nothing for the risk he takes, he may find himself No one and Nowhere" (98-99).

Kate Cutrer, daughter of Jules Cutrer and stepdaughter of Binx's Aunt Emily, did not inherit her father's "Catholic unseriousness" nor her stepmother's southern stoicism. The only character in Percy's novel who is more abstract and alienated than Binx, she loves arriving in Chicago with Binx on his business trip because she can at last be "an anyone who is anywhere"

(190). In his conversations with Kate, Binx finds that he must first identify the tone she has adopted and then subtract that from her words to discover what she is actually trying to say. When she says on the train that "suicide is the only thing that keeps her alive," Binx notes that she is speaking in her "bold" tone and he is concerned about her (194-95). Sometimes her gestures remind him of the college girls before the Korean War (another Lucy Lipscomb of *The Thanatos Syndrome*), who smoked cigarettes, rode in convertibles, and acted independent, like one of Faulkner's epicene women, Helen Baird, or Pat Robyn, or Charlotte Rittenmeyer. At other times her voice takes on its "objective tone," from her social work experience. The accident that killed her fiancé, Lyell, has also left her without an anchor, with nothing more than gestures or rebellion to sustain her. She has made two suicide attempts and finally realizes that she cannot survive without believing in something. "I am a religious person. . . . What I want is to believe in someone completely and then do what he wants me to do" (197). She decides that she will marry Binx if he will play God, be someone she can believe in and tell her what to do in each instance, letting her move one step at a time toward an acceptance of reality and her place in it. Kate, Percy's fragile southern woman broken by her recognition of society's spiritual malaise, is a comment on Faulkner's Pat or Charlotte and Tennessee Williams's Blanche. Kate pretends to be one of the liberated modern women that Faulkner imagines, but Percy emphasizes her vulnerability, as Faulkner and Williams eventually demonstrate Charlotte's and Blanche's as well.[33] Kate needs Binx, and he marries her, accepting the challenge. "In the absence of an absent or silent God," Max Webb writes, "Binx accepts responsibility for Kate's life. In effect, he is an Abraham who is forced to become an imitator of God, not merely a faithful follower."[34]

In *The Moviegoer,* Walker Percy is already moving away from the use of New Orleans topography and culture as significant elements in his fiction. His subject even with his first novel is basically the diagnosis of the human mind in the latter part of the twentieth century. In choosing to live in Gentilly instead of the Garden District, Binx turns away from the aristocratic elite and the mythical tradition of the Old South, which he could have inherited. By turning away from the Mardi Gras spirit of Jules and the Boston Club, he has also separated himself from another important aspect of New Orleans culture: its myth of gaiety and festival. He begins to listen to his own voice at the end of the novel, which counsels commitment, but only after isolating himself from the allure of the myth of New Orleans. In subsequent novels he moves more clearly toward satire, using "allegorical fable" to reveal the culture's disease and to suggest a prescription for its cure.[35]

The increased satire and abstraction of Percy's later novels make less geographically defined settings more suitable vehicles for the development of theme and character. In Percy's third novel, *Love in the Ruins* (1971), he makes clear that the failure of modern society which he described in *The Moviegoer* is not limited to New Orleans, or even to the South; he is writing "reverse satire," not about the end of New Orleans or of the South, but of the world, "in order to warn about present ills and so avert the end."[36] Studying his later novels helps us to understand the polarities of the fictional New Orleans which he creates in *The Moviegoer.* Since nothing that the writer could say about the coming apocalypse in the traditional novel (i.e., *The Moviegoer* and *The Last Gentleman*) would wake up spiritless twentieth-century American readers to the dangers of the world, in subsequent novels Percy would use shock, insult, and violence. The "postmodern consciousness," it seems, is too anesthetized to receive the writer's news, whether bad or good.

Neither time nor place are reliable in *Love in the Ruins,* for most of the events of the novel are parts of a dream that occur when Dr. Thomas More, Percy's "middle-aged, alcoholic rake of a hero," falls in a ditch on his way to town from a Howard Johnson's motel in a deserted shopping plaza.[37] There he has stowed away three women that he "loved" during a period that he predicts will be the end of the world. For 350 pages the reader follows More's dream-vision, during which time he carefully plans three days, starting at 9 a.m. on July 1, when he is sure that black guerrillas from the swamp have taken three shots at him through the window of his enclosed patio, while he drinks his usual breakfast of Tang, two duck eggs, two ounces of vodka, and a dash of Tabasco sauce. Dr. More also gives us an overview of his life and even his family, who had settled in Louisiana many years after the life of their oldest known ancestor, the British Sir Thomas More, Renaissance author of *Utopia.* In brief, Tom, a fairly conscientious middle-aged doctor, dreamer, and inventor, has grieved over the disfiguring death of his daughter Samantha from neuroblastoma, or brain cancer. He has also been deserted by his wife, Doris, because of his inability to communicate with her, except physically. His grief has led to an attempted suicide, after which he committed himself to a mental institution. Since leaving the institution (without full permission), he has invented the Ontological Qualitative-Quantitative Lapsometer, which works by adding the correct amount of heavy sodium or chloride to a person's brain to stabilize the individual by making his/her body and spirit coincide with each other. Hardy speaks of the 350-page dream vision as "myth time."[38]

The setting of *Love in the Ruins* is an abstract crossroads, where More, like Binx in Chicago, may very well find himself to be a "No one and Nowhere." Beyond the interchange where the novel begins and ends can be seen Fedville—a federal complex which includes the hospital; medical school, with its infamous Pit, a place of intellectual exchange among faculty and students; a NASA facility; the Behavioral Institute; the Geriatrics Center, where many senior citizens suffer mysterious deaths when the "transformation switch" is chosen as the best alternative to their continued death-in-life; and the Love

Clinic, a Brave New World re-creation, where sexual problems are handled inventively by behavioral scientists and doctors. Beyond the cypresses lies the Honey Island swamp, where "the dropouts from and cast-offs of and rebels against society" live. These include the young flower people in their "hummocks," who tempt More to give up his life of drudgery and become their *shaman,* and the "ferocious black Bantus," guerrillas who plan attacks on outlying white suburbs and perhaps ultimately the Federal complex itself. One of the suburbs under attack, Paradise Estates, lies between the town and the swamp. While the town is a place where conservatives are clearly predominant, Paradise is Percy's satiric picture of the American dream place where everyone gets along—northerners and southerners, Jews and Gentiles, liberals and conservatives, scientists and businessmen. Paradise Estates is "a pleasant place where Knothead and Left—but not black—dwell side by side in peace" (18).

As in *The Moviegoer,* Percy is fascinated by the strange interplay of voices in his black characters' speech and intentions. There, Binx never knows just how he should react to Mercer, his Aunt Emily's black butler: "My main emotion around Mercer is unease that in threading his way between servility and presumption, his foot might slip. . . . Behind his mustache, his face, I notice, is not at all devoted but is as sulky as a Pullman porter's" (22). In *Love in the Ruins,* the racial theme is more pervasive, for Percy wants his readers to understand, as Michael Pearson has argued, "that the racial issue and the spiritual dilemma are very much linked."[39] The "egregious moral failure of Christendom" in America, Percy has written, is evidenced in the attitudes of whites toward blacks: "In the one place, the place which hurts the most and where charity was most needed, they have not done right. White Americans have sinned against the Negro from the beginning and continue to do so, initially with cruelty and presently with an indifference which may be even more destructive. And it is the churches which, far from fighting the good fight against man's native inhumanity to man, have sanctified and perpetuated this indifference."[40] As Tom begins to fall off to sleep in the ditch, he thinks again that the United States has failed. "Moon Mullins [the cartoon character]," he says, "blames it on the niggers." Then More ponders the question: "Was it the nigger business from the beginning?" (57). In a sardonic voice, More conceives a new creation myth: God had given "the lordly Westerners, the fierce Caucasian-Gentile-Visigoths," the new Eden and allowed them to keep it when they passed the first big test (believing in Jesus, "the outlandish Jewish Event"); but when he gave them the second test, a little one (not to violate "a helpless man in Africa"), they failed. Now all Africans have to do is wait, for "sooner or later the lordly Visigoth-Western-Gentile-Christian-Americans would have to falter, fall out, turn upon themselves like scorpions in a bottle," and the Africans would take over (57). Tom's fear of a black takeover is typical of the whites of Feliciana Parish, and Percy's characterization of blacks as "a help-less man in Africa" shows that he cannot divorce himself from his community's discourse to think independently about the historical role of Africans.

The targets of Percy's satire are both black and white, for while he thinks that Caucasians have been despicable leaders, More is certain that African-Americans would be worse. In Tom's nightmare, along with the Heavy Sodium fallout which will kill thousands in Feliciana Parish due to the misuse of his lapsometer, the blacks take over Paradise Estates and have plans to attack the president and vice-president as they visit the NASA plant. "There are riots in New Orleans, and riots over here. The students are fighting the National Guard, the Lefts are fighting the Knotheads, the blacks are fighting the whites. The Jews are being persecuted" (342). But with a sweeping caricature of black militants of the late 1960s and 1970s equal to that of Ishmael Reed in *The Last Days of Louisiana Red*,[41] Percy belittles the would-be Bantu leaders, such as Uru, who attempts the attack on Paradise Estates, but fails and ends up returning north to head the Black Studies Department at the University of Michigan. For a while, Uru attempts to dominate such loyal southern blacks as Victor Charles, who will feel forever obliged to Dr. More for attending his aunt during her illness. Of course, Tom notes that even Victor Charles, as helpful as he is, "good-natured, reserved," like Mercer, still has "the faintest risibility agleam in his muddy eyes" (146). Even though southern blacks in Percy's fiction continue to work with whites, often in menial roles, they always maintain a "double discourse," knowing more than they appear to, understanding the bitterness of southern racism, and the white characters continue to distrust them for doing so.

Finally, after his long nightmare vision, Tom More remembers his daughter Samantha's advice to him before her death: "Don't commit the one sin for which there is no forgiveness. . . . The sin against grace. If God gives you the grace to believe in him and love him, and you refuse, the sin will not be forgiven you" (374). In the epilogue to the novel, which takes place five years after the events of the narration, Tom is, ironically, living in the Slave Quarters apartments in town with his new wife, Ellen Oglethorpe, his former nurse, and their children. He apparently has forgiven himself for Samantha's death. And although he has taken on a poorer practice, he seems self-confident about his state of affairs: "I feel like God's spoiled child. I am Robinson Crusoe set down in the best possible island with a library, a laboratory, a lusty Presbyterian wife, a cozy tree house, an idea, and all the time in the world" (383). Like Binx Bolling, he has recognized "that he must become more involved, that he must create the meaning of his life existentially by his own actions"[42], and he has decided to accept the Little Way, living one day at a time. He still drinks too much, gives way to desire instead of love, and has not given up the urge to know the scientific truth of mind-body relations, or, in other words, still values gnosis over faith.[43] More has decided to live out the best compromise that he can imagine in "the dread latter days of the old violent beloved U.S.A. and of the Christ-forgetting Christ-haunted death-dealing Western World" (3).

Percy portrays New Orleans satirically in the postmodern world; Tennessee Williams portrays it symbolically in the modernist tradition of William Faulkner and his contemporaries. Built upon abstractions, both Williams's and Percy's fictional cities were more overtly metaphorical than those of earlier writers. Williams, like Faulkner, was not as interested in re-creating a historical myth of New Orleans as in developing a metaphor for the Dionysian aspect of the self. In Williams's theater, New Orleans became the city as prostitute and illusion, or the city of night. His modern city's diversity marked the death of the Old South myth. In *The Moviegoer* Percy is not interested in developing beautiful metaphors of the modernists' "broken world"; his interest is in developing consciousness, and his world is largely interior. New Orleans is the scene of his first protagonist's search for meaning, but only because he thought that he must begin with a concrete place and time. The later novels are more surely about the "sovereign wayfarer" on a crossroads anywhere in the latter part of the twentieth century.[44] Yet Percy adds to the myth of New Orleans by diminishing its exoticism and placing it solidly within the apocalyptic temper of this century.[45]

SEVEN

ய

African-American Dialogues and Revisionist Strategies: Dent, Reed, Kein, and Osbey

The Free Southern Theater (FST) was founded by Gilbert Moses and John O'Neal in 1963 as a touring theater based in the Mississippi Delta. It began as a workshop at Tougaloo University and planned to present performances during the "Freedom Summer" of 1964. Moses and O'Neal's objectives were to bring theater to people who were struggling for racial change, to bring it without an admission charge, and to use it to promote the cause of the civil rights movement. The FST dealt with both art and politics, provided images to counter prevailing black stereotypes, opened up communication, and provided a cultural and historical dimension for the civil rights movement. Free Southern Theater tours took the group, which soon included Denise Nichols, Roscoe Ormon, and seven to nine others, to churches, schools, and community festivals. After the plays, group members organized discussions for people to voice their reactions. A community workshop program attempted to get local people involved in all levels of theater production. The company was racially integrated; their audiences were primarily black people in small towns.[1]

In November 1964 the theater moved to New Orleans. As black community theaters began to develop in other parts of the country (e.g., the Black Arts Repertory Theatre founded by LeRoi Jones in 1965 in Harlem), Gilbert Moses proposed that the FST become a black theater. In the early days of the theater, FST had performed plays by Samuel Becket, Sean O'Casey, Berthold

Brecht, Martin Duberman, and Ossie Davis. Speaking of the urgent need of
the Free Southern Theater to perform plays by black writers, co-founder
O'Neal argued: "There is no truth that speaks so clearly to me as the truth of
my own experience. If I cut to the essence of my own truth there will lie a
truth for all men. One can only achieve that kind of statement, however, in the
context of specific historical cultural, political, economic circumstances."[2] The
argument by O'Neal, Gilbert Moses, and others that the FST should be a theater "for black people established by black people—and not a liberal idea established for the good of the black people" led to the theater's move in 1966 to
the Desire area of the Ninth Ward.[3]

During the late 1950s and the 1960s, New Orleans civil rights leaders
played significant roles in the strategic organization of the Movement. According to Dr. Henry Mitchell, the Southern Christian Leadership Conference
(SCLC), which Dr. Martin Luther King, Jr., was later to head, was organized
in uptown New Orleans at Reverend A. L. Davis's Baptist church on Third
Street in 1957. The Consumer's League, which was founded by Reverend
Davis, Avery Alexander, Raymond Floyd, and Dr. Henry Mitchell soon after-
wards, worked in conjunction with "non-direct action" groups, such as the National Association for the Advancement of Colored People (NAACP), the Urban League, and the Ministerial Alliance, to integrate and demand fair
employment practices by businesses, first on Dryades Street, then on
Claiborne, St. Claude, and Desire—all neighborhoods with large shopping areas used primarily by blacks. While attorneys A. P. Tureaud, Ernest N. Morial,
and others represented the NAACP in testing many of the Jim Crow practices
and laws in the courts, attorneys Earl Amedee, Lolis Elie, Lawrence Wheeler,
and Alvin Jones fought in the courts for the Consumer's League. The Congress of Racial Equality (CORE), based in New Orleans with Oretha Haley as
regional director, led campaigns to integrate the lunch counters of businesses
on Canal Street through pickets and sit-ins by many young people. Through
most of the 1960s New Orleans was also the terminus for CORE's "freedom
rides" through the South.[4]

Tom Dent and BLKARTSOUTH

In 1965 Tom Dent—poet, playwright, journalist, and civil rights activist—returned to New Orleans from New York, where he had been a member of the
Umbra literary workshop and co-editor of its journal, *Umbra*. The Umbra poets included David Henderson, Calvin Hernton, Ishmael Reed, and Lorenzo
Thomas.[5] In New York, Dent also met with older black writers, including
Langston Hughes, John Killens, and Ralph Ellison, and worked with the civil
rights movement as a press attaché of the NAACP Legal Defense Fund. In

Tom Dent. Photo by Ellis Lucia.

"Ten Years After Umbra," Dent recounts the youthful intellectual and sensuous expansion that the young Umbra poets felt on beginning their careers:

> *We had seen*
> *our minds reach out*
> *touch fingertips*
> *music crawl in like lazy smoke on Friday nights*
> *taste the wind and*
> *leave us a whiff of real road.*

In spite of some hesitation and distrust, those were days of moral optimism, as the Umbra writers left the intellectual and artistic life of New York's lower east side, some to go south to Mississippi and the freedom rallies and struggles of the civil rights movement.

as for me
the dirt roads of Mississippi
are a long way from anywhere.

but then the sun will rise
just as easy tomorrow over this black earth

join me there. [6]

In the last lines of the poem, Dent (the persona) issues a call to David [Henderson] and Calvin [Hernton], to whom the poem is dedicated, to meet him again after the civil rights experience and the Free Southern Theater, when "the jammed years are over," the years of dedication to the tumultuous social change and the working out of the ideals of the civil rights movement.

Dent hoped to continue the intellectual and literary dialogue of the African diaspora in New Orleans when he began to work with the Free Southern Theater there in 1965. He had grown up in New Orleans, son of Albert W. Dent, who was president of Dillard University from 1941 to 1969. Having known Marcus Christian as a boy growing up on the Dillard University campus, he had learned the value of recovering and preserving Afro-Louisiana culture and printing one's own work if publishers were not interested.[7] Through literary and dramatic workshops, such as the Free Southern Theater, BLKARTSOUTH, the Southern Black Cultural Alliance, and the Congo Square Writers' Union, Dent was attempting to execute a kind of "cultural nationalism" in the South, and especially New Orleans. In an interview he compared what he and other young writers in New Orleans were doing with the development of jazz at the turn of the century:

> If jazz, as we think of it, began to take off from New Orleans, it was because between 1890 and 1920 all of the influences of black music coalesced in New Orleans during that period. . . . Now, in terms of literature . . . it can't really happen for us except in places where there are enough people of talent who are familiar with all traditions germane to them. . . . And what you need to do is expose them [young people] to the Brathwaites, the Killens's, the Baldwins. . . . this is really the key to artistic production.[8]

In December 1968 the first of a series of publications from the Free Southern Theater writing-acting workshop, which came to be known as BLKART-SOUTH, appeared. The publication was called *Echoes from the Gumbo* and was later renamed *Nkombo*. Tom Dent, (sometimes Kush, in these publications), and Val Ferdinand, now known as Kalamu ya Salaam, were co-editors. BLKARTSOUTH was created originally to encourage the writing of new dramatic material for the FST and to develop writers and actors from the New Orleans community. As Dent wrote in the first issue: "This workshop was created as part of our program because we know that for a black theater to have viability in our communities we must have a working tie to those communities—something more than mere performances of plays every now and then (no matter how relevant the material). The community must have a stake in the life of the theater. This is the real meaning of community theatre."[9]

BLKARTSOUTH, along with Umbra, the Free Southern Theater, and the Southern Black Cultural Alliance, was in the mode of these "communities of people who are trying to build cultural forms."[10] It was not only a writing and publishing organ but also served as a vehicle for communicating and critiquing the work of its members. From the beginning of the workshop it was clear that poetry, rather than fiction or drama, was the dominant mode of expression among these young black writers of the 1960s. They wrote poetry that reflected the speech of black folks on the streets, at church, on barstools, on basketball courts, and shared the objectives of LeRoi Jones/Amiri Baraka, Maulana Ron Karenga, and other leaders of the Black Aesthetic Movement of the 1960s, who believed that "literature conditions the mind and the battle for the mind is the first half of the struggle."[11] Kalamu ya Salaam characterized the new black poetry as having to do mostly with rhythm, images, and sound. In terms of rhythm, the poetry had to dance, "to ride/be/hear/feel"; the images "can/should connect one consciousness with another's" and would often come from blues ("Blues singers were our first heavy poets"); a poet's unique sound is "the ultimate expression of creativity." Referring to jazz musician Charlie "Bird" Parker, Kalamu spoke of Baraka as "the bird of black poetics."[12]

The poems published in *Nkombo* centered on basic concerns of the 1960s Black Aesthetic Movement—the meaning of blackness, the battle of the sexes, frustrations about the effectiveness of the Black Revolution, questions of identity, responses to the assassination of Martin Luther King. In an attempt to discover the "ethnic roots" of "blackness," the writers emphasized the vernacular, which, they felt, expressed the culture more fundamentally than bourgeois traditions. The first issue listed the directors as "chefs de cuisine," the writers as "cooks," and the clerical assistants as "Kitchen Help"; the leaders of the workshop consistently projected a "folksy," communal image. The editors considered the journal to be a communal effort: entries appeared without names of the authors, just numbers; the names of authors appeared only in the table of contents. Alluding to NASA's recent successful space flight to the moon, Tom Dent queried his elder: "Well Langston / nothing much has changed. / White folks gone to the moon but we still down in the ghetto lookin for a nickle / to shoot pool."[13] In 1969, however, a slightly more individualistic approach seemed to prevail: several volumes of poetry by individual members of the group were published, among them, poems by Quo Vadis Gex, Nayo (Barbara

Malcolm), Raymond Washington, and Ronald Fernandez. The August 1972
Nkombo was devoted to plays written by Kalamu ya Salaam, Norbert
Davidson, and Tom Dent during and following the active years of the FST.

The last issue of *Nkombo*, published in June 1974, pays tribute to black
jazz and blues as theme and form, celebrates songs of "the people," and remembers earlier generations and black traditions. In support of the nationally growing Black Arts Movement, whose spokesmen saw an extant "African-American cultural tradition" as well as a broader black aesthetic which
encompassed Third World culture, the last issue of *Nkombo* included a wider
variety of black poets—of the past and present. Besides the members of
BLKARTSOUTH, it included poems and prose of Marcus Christian and Octave Lilly (members of the Colored Project of the Louisiana Federal Writers' Project of the WPA), Richard Haley, David Henderson, John O'Neal,
and Alice Walker.[14] The 1930s black aesthetic espoused by Hughes, Sterling
Brown, Hurston, Christian, and Margaret Walker is also reflected in the
choice of poetry, which often adopted a blues tenor, as in Marcus Christian's
"Segregation Blues":[15]

> *Aincha heard the news*
> *That gave me Segregation Blues?*
> *O they beat my brother*
> *And they slapped my mother*
> *And they roughhoused my sister*
> *And jailed my pa—*
> *I'm gonnah walk-walk-walk—*
> *Cuz I got thuh Segregation Blues*
> *Got corns and bunions,*
> *But I'm gonnah wear out all my shoes.*
>
> ....
>
> *O I can't go here,*
> *I live there I'm dead,*
> *And Uncle Sam himself*
> *Can't tell me where to lay my head—*
> *Like Mister Hitler's Jews,*
> *I got thuh Segregation Blues—*
> *Got thuh Housing Project Street-car,*
> *Jim Crow, Segregation Blues.*

In the tradition of dialect poetry, and also bearing the ironic tone of Langston
Hughes's blues poems, Christian's poem reflects the protest spirit of the 1960s
in the wake of the post-World War II disillusionment by blacks who had returned to America to find things very much the same. The editors of *Nkombo*
felt themselves at the intersection of civil rights and cultural nationalism. The

later "hip" jazz poetry of writers like David Henderson, a member of the Umbra Workshop in New York reflects the growing northern cynicism, which envisioned a conspiracy of whites against blacks and imminent revolution by blacks. Henderson visited the FST in New Orleans in the summer of 1967 and participated in its writing workshop there; he used the New Orleans experience as source material for several of his earlier poems. In one of his poems, published in *Nkombo* and in *De Mayor of Harlem,* he uses the form of a radio discussion (duet). Two whites discuss how to handle a race riot; Henderson refers on the surface to the actual events that surrounded the flood caused by Hurricane Betsy in September 1965. The devastation of that hurricane caused severe damage to the largely black community in the Ninth Ward of New Orleans, which includes the Desire Housing Project.

> *a phone duet over the radio*
> *the night*
> *we got our leading lady out of jail*
> *they were talkin' about handling niggers*
> *the white folks was*
> *one suggestion:*
> > *in event of a riot*
> > *to flood the canals in the negro section*

> *they probably got the idea*
> *from the last flood/*
> *when the big department stores were threatened*
> *when they had to blow the industrial canal*
> > *to siphon some water off*

> *happened to be right near black town the bombs fell*
> *many blacks drowned*
> *others were ferried by private boats*
> > *for a fee*
> *many blacks drowned*
> > *the city*
> > *never did get*
> > *all the names.*

The poet, reflecting a popular sentiment of the time, strongly suggests that Hurricane Betsy's destruction of the lower Ninth Ward occurred not from the storm itself but was instead perpetrated by a white establishment that, determined to prevent flooding of the central business district, opened the Industrial Canal to overflow into the ward. The repetition of the line, "many blacks were

drowned," resounds with the persona's continuing shock, or feeling of disbe-
lief, that something so diabolical could possibly have been public policy.

The poetry of *Nkombo* referred to actual black experiences: poetry should
be more than beautiful words; it should call for action. As LeRoi Jones had
written in "Black Dada Nihilismus," "Poems are bullshit unless they are / teeth
or trees or lemons piled / on a step. . . . / We want live / words of the hip
world, live flesh & / coursing blood."[16] Black experience takes the form of a
careful interplay of song, rhythm, and theme in a poem by Lloyd Medley.
There the persona asks a black woman to contribute a song to the movement.

> *Say sister,*
> > *We wan you to sing*
> > *us a song.*
> > *A song that will make us*
>
> > *dance into your body*
> > *and move and groove to the*
> > *tempo of our destinies*
> > ....
> > *We want to hear battle chants*
> > *that ring in our ears and wipe*
> > *out armies, leaving the streets*
> > *red with blood.*
> *Say sister,*
> > *We want to be free*
> > *and we want you and your powerful sounds*
> > *of rebirth to help do it.*
> *Say sister sing us a song.*

Note the familiar address, "Say sister," and the communal point of view, "Sing
us a song," both of which serve to include others within the fold of the movement. For the poem is a love song and yet a revolutionary statement. Using
bold, sensual language, the male persona uses more than moral persuasion to
win the "sister's" support. He attempts to convince her that poetry, music, song
were all to be used to support blacks and the Revolution.

A new organization of writers, the Congo Square Writers' Workshop,
founded in 1972 by Tom Dent and Lloyd Medley, followed BLKARTSOUTH;
directed by Tom Dent, the group published the journal *Bamboula* in 1976 and
several issues of a newspaper, *The Black River Journal.* Its purpose was similar to that of *Nkombo*: "to give the 'Southern writer' a vehicle for publication
and . . . to document emphatically the 'Southern Experience,' particularly the
New Orleans experience."[17]

In the same year, Dent published his own first book of poetry, *Magnolia*

Street. In 1978 his play *Ritual Murder* was published in *Callaloo* and was performed at the Ethiopian Theater, directed by Chakula cha Jua. *Ritual Murder* was followed by the collection of poetry, *Blue Lights,* in 1982. Dent's poetry focuses on portraying the culture of black New Orleans, which Dent sees as "a particularly strong outpost of the African diaspora through its cultural continuum of music, dance, cooking, dress, speech, drumming . . . more crucially related culturally to the Caribbean diaspora and the mother continent than to mainstream America."[18] Black New Orleans culture, Dent observes, "has been so brilliantly rendered through music, but almost totally ignored in literature." His poetry evokes characters and feelings of the New Orleans black traditions, like Miss Lucas and Lawrence Sly, a typical young black New Orleanian; included also are the musician-entertainers, like Louis Armstrong and Danny Barker, and the violent hero-criminals, like Bras-Coupé (see chapter 2) and Mark Essex, a young unemployed black who staged a shoot-out from the roof of a Howard Johnson's motel across from the City Hall on January 7, 1973, killing several policemen. About five hundred policemen surrounded the area, thinking that a riot was in progress. As Michael Pearson has noted, Walker Percy seems to have predicted the incident in the near-riot described in *Love in the Ruins.*[19]

In "Secret Messages" Dent describes the ironic voices of, and the masks worn by, so many of the black New Orleans regulars:

> *rain*
> *rain drenches the city*
> *as we move past*
> *stuffed black mammies*
> *chained to Royal St. praline shops*
> *check it out*
>
> *past Bourbon St. Beer cans*
> *shadowed moorish cottages*
> *ships slipping down the riversnake past*
> *images of the bullet-riddled bodies of*
> *Mark Essex & Bras-Coupé*
> *buried in the beckoning of the blk*
> *shoeshine boy*
> *when it rains it pours*
> *check it out*
>
> *past blk tap-dancers of the shit-eating grin*
> *the nickle & dime shake-a-leg*
> *shades of weaving flambeau carriers*

of the dripping oil & the grease-head
"we are mardi gras" one said
check it out

....

& maybe someday when nobody is
checking it out the drummers will come to life in
St. Louis No. 1 at midnight
beating out the secret messages
& all the masks will drop.
jest like we said they would.
secret messages
secret messages of the gods.

rain
rain drenches the city
as we move past grinning stuffed black mammies
the god of fallen masks offstage
waiting, waiting . . .

The speaker in the poem suggests that what Tallant, Saxon, and Percy feared was in fact true: the blacks were wearing masks, they had a network, and there were "secret messages" between them. "The shit-eating grin" was a bitter mask, as Binx Bolling knew Mercer, his Aunt Emily's black servant, wore, imperfectly at times. One day all the masks would fall, as the masks of Bras-Coupé, Robert Charles (who caused the New Orleans riot of 1900), and Mark Essex fell.[20]

In Dent's second book of poetry, *Blue Lights and River Songs,* there are many songs written on the occasion of listening to, or dedicated to, African-American jazz musicians—Thelonius Monk, Ray Charles, Louis Armstrong, Danny Barker, Jelly Roll Morton, Walter Washington, Cool Papa Bell—and to poets of the diaspora—Langston Hughes, Keorapetse Kgositsile, Kalamu ya Salaam, and other Umbra and Congo Square writers. "The longer poems," as Jerry Ward notes, are modelled "on the rhythmic movement and the sight-sound of rivers"; just as rivers "determine the shape of land masses (and to a lesser degree the configurations of history), Dent's poetic practice gives palpable shape to history, musical response, heroic lives."[21] Dent is particularly conscious in these poems of the history of the civil rights movement in the in Alabama, Mississippi, and Louisiana, and of how woefully its struggles were forgotten in the New Orleans of the seventies, "the dying city," "the elegantly crumbling city," "the museum city of indifference."[22]

Dent's play *Ritual Murder* grew out of the Free Southern Theater's demand for viable black theater.[23] Dent portrays the cultural experience of a young black man, Joe Brown, Jr., from the Desire Housing Project. The style of the play is a television documentary in which "the narrator," who "hosts" the documentary, confronts all of the major characters in Joe Brown, Jr.'s life and asks why the young man killed his best friend at a Ninth Ward street bar on Saturday night. Like the movies in *The Moviegoer* and *A Confederacy of Dunces,* by John Kennedy Toole (1980), television is of crucial importance to the play's structure and theme.[24] Joe Brown's wife and teacher love the life they see on their televisions; Joe, however, is frustrated by a screen on which he can't find his own image. He dreams about surfing and about being willed $66 million by a rich uncle. At his job, where he shucks oysters, he continues his imaginative escape by reading a book in the bathroom when he should have been working. "I say, boy," his boss says when he catches Joe, "I pay you to read or shell oysters?" (72).

Joe can't settle down to his "real" world; he can't help thinking there's something better. When his friend says offhandedly there is no hope, the frustrated and disillusioned Joe "for no apparent reason" stabs him three times in the chest. James, the victim, doesn't blame Joe because he knows that Joe really didn't have any control over his actions or his situation. It was his passion, the desire for hope, and his frustration, that overtook him.

One of the flashpoints of Joe's frustration is his inability to express it, and, indeed, throughout the play articulation plagues the characters. The most articulate-sounding people—the social worker and the psychiatrist—may seem glib enough but in fact are only mouthing the jargon of their discipline; phrases like "culturally deprived area," "cultural and economic gap," and "level of competency" do little to communicate real ideas or emotions. And the mother, the wife, and the teacher cannot, or refuse to, understand Joe's full humanity, in part because he cannot express it and in part because they, too, are limited in their ability to articulate their perceptions of their world. For them the way to explain a complex act, Joe's murder of his friend, is to reduce it to simplistic terms: they categorize him as a dreamer, or a boy with a temper who hangs out with a bad crowd. All these characters lack the empowerment of language, and they are reduced to powerless beings who acknowledge their impotence to change the way things happen. Even Joe Brown and James Roberts cannot express what the act signifies.

> Narrator: [To James Roberts] Do you feel you died for anything? Is there any meaning in it?
> James Roberts: Yes, I died for something. But I don't know what it means.
> Narrator: [To Joe Brown, Jr.] And did your act mean anything?
> Joe Brown, Jr. (Softly) I suppose so. But I can't imagine what. (79)

The audience is left with the task of piecing things together and coming up with its own answer.

The fact that Joe Brown is a product of "Desire" is, of course, significant. The name itself is ironic for a housing project that has become known as the most dangerous in New Orleans. When Dent wrote the play, its theme reflected the violence of the place. Built perhaps idealistically in the late 1950s to house the poor, the federally subsidized projects were by the 1970s increasingly dense concentrations of frustration and crime. While Blanche DuBois of *A Streetcar Named Desire* also "must travel the sacrificial path from desire to death" which, in her case, means insanity,[25] there is no corollary compassion or personal epiphany for Joe Brown or James Roberts. They are nothing more than statistics; even their names are undistinguished, and their lives and deaths fit only for the "crime-of-the-day section of the white *Times-Picayune*" (68). Dent implies the only distinction between them in his stage directions for the end of the play: "Play *Summertime* for Joe Brown Jr., and play a very funky *Summertime* for his friend James Roberts who he knifed to death" (81). Perhaps the "funkier" *Summertime* is a tribute to the sacrificial victim.

In portraying the culture of black New Orleans in his poetry and plays, Tom Dent has re-created the generally unrecognized characters of black New Orleans culture—the Lawrence Slys, the Joe Brown, Jr.'s, and has revealed their hidden beauty and the intensity of their oppression. He constantly reminds his readers of the masks that New Orleans African-Americans wear, at the time suggesting that they will not wear them forever. His poetry is also a dialogue with the past, as he engages his heroes of literature, music, and sports in discussions of their achievements and of race and racism.

Hoodoo as Ishmael Reed's Multicultural Aesthetic

Ishmael Reed, also a member of the Umbra Workshop in the 1960s and a friend of Tom Dent, has appropriated voodoo, also known as vodoun or the African-American version, hoodoo, as the model for his writing. In some ways Reed sees himself as a cultural outsider in New Orleans in general and, to some extent, among his contemporary literati. He blames feuding between him and Dent on such cultural differences: "Tom Dent eats lobster; I eat Kentucky Fried Chicken. He's a bourbon black as he once said to me, and his father runs a university [Dillard University]. He's very 'fair' looking, as they say, I'm brownish red."[26] Despite such differences, Reed considers hoodoo to be "the true Afro-American aesthetic," and indeed, it shapes his fiction.[27] The syncretism of hoodoo with its amazing ability to blend with other religions (Catholicism in New Orleans, Protestantism in many other parts of the South) becomes a model for Reed's literary methods, which he calls a "multicultural aes-

Ishmael Reed. Photographer: Jay Blakesberg.

thetic."[28] His characters *signify,* or use "double-voicedness," by talking in codes and using the vernacular as well as formal language, receiving various levels of understanding by other characters and the reading public. As *loas* (gods), the characters live on various levels, while spirits speak through them and allow them to prophesy.[29] Reed uses the voodoo idea of *synchronicity,* which "views time as a circle of revolving and re-evolving events," to work out the double discourses involved in the plots of his novels.[30]

Reed views New Orleans mainly as the entry point into the United States of the ancient voodoo culture on its journey from its origins in Nigeria, Dahomey, and Togo, then through Cuba and Haiti. In "Shrovetide" Reed defines *voodoo,* or *vodoun* (from the Dahomean and Togo words, meaning "the unknown") as "the fusion of dance, drums, embroidery, herbal medicine, and cuisine of many African nations whose people were brought to Haiti during the slave trade."[31] He elaborates on Tallant's flamboyant myths of Marie Laveau and Doctor John (whom Reed considers to have been her greatest rival) in his fiction, particularly in *The Last Days of Louisiana Red*.[32] Reed also recognizes in his essays and fiction what he considers to be New Orleans expressions of hoodoo, which have had what he sees as "outbreaks" from its founding. In the novel *Mumbo Jumbo,* "the Jes Grew epidemic" is the result of such overt expressions of pluralistic spirit and the love of dance and song. In the novel the Jes Grew contingent, led by the Voodooists, are an anti-Western spirit. Descendants of the Egyptian god Osiris, they have already taken over New Orleans, but are in a struggle in the rest of the country with the Atonists (the *a-tonal*) who, hating nature and spirit, fight to maintain dominance in the Western world.

In *Shrovetide in Old New Orleans,* Reed discusses expressions of hoodoo in New Orleans, including Mardi Gras, gumbo and other Creole cuisine, and jazz. In Mardi Gras, the satiric juxtaposition of remnants of the Confederacy and the romantic longing for "a southern monarchy," on the one hand, and on the other hand, "the oppressors' parody of themselves," is African in spirit, Reed points out. The Mardi Gras Indians and the emphasis on the occult are also retentions of African traditions. "Mardi Gras," Reed concludes, "is a bright moment on America's death calendar."[33]

Gumbo, which Reed describes in an epigraph to *The Last Days of Louisiana Red* as "a most distinctive type of evolution of good cookery under the hands of the famous Creole cuisinières of old New Orleans . . . an original conception, peculiar to this ancient Creole city alone, and the manner born," is also another name for Reed's form of satire.[34] Gumbo is an improvisation, syncretic—African, Spanish, Native American, French—a symbol for the kind of parody and intertextuality that forms the substance of Reed's fiction.

Jazz, created in New Orleans, along with dance, is probably the most influential expression of hoodoo culture in America, according to Reed. The spirit of jazz is in direct opposition to the Atonist/establishment of *Mumbo-Jumbo*. The be-boppers signified upon jazz tunes, sometimes by speeding up the rhythm, providing a new melody, or embellishing the existing chords by extending them vertically, or altering the given pitches, or making chord substitutions.[35] Reed uses the improvisational form of jazz, particularly be-bop, in the many subplots and intertexts of his novels. "Charlie 'Yardbird [Thoth]' Parker is an example of the Neo-Hoo-Doo artist as innovator," says Reed.[36]

Another aspect of Reed's fiction which seems to derive from the hoodoo aesthetic is his tendency to be both a historian and a mythmaker. Mason calls him "an historical fabulist" whose emphasis is on the fantastic and the surreal.[37] Reed may use real names and places, as is the case with New Orleans, Berkeley, President Harding, for example, but he emphasizes "figurative multiplicity, not the singular referential correspondence" which Tom Dent and many other members of the Black Aesthetic Movement emphasize.[38] Reed sees history as process and our vision of historical situations as really the work of many fabulists, such as the mass media, the romantic "historians" (cf. Saxon's *Fabulous New Orleans*), the published folklorists. In all of his works he attempts both to create new myths and to reveal the conspiracy that accounts for our "fabulous" idea of history.

Reed uses surrealism, the fantastic, and many of the innovations of metafiction; his prose suggests a pastiche of parody, jazz rhythms, quickspliced cinema projection, photos, headlines, drawings, and symbols.[39] As Joe Weixlmann has noted, Reed writes revisionist detective stories, but his fiction is ultimately reflexive, in the tradition of late twentieth-century metafiction.[40] His use of New Orleans folklore and traditions—voodoo, jazz, gumbo—does not, in effect, create new myth so much as it satirizes the ways of thinking that do not allow for the multiethnicity of the true New Orleans spirit.

In *The Last Days of Louisiana Red* the central conflict is between Ed Yellings's hoodoo workers, known in Berkeley as Gumbo Workers, who follow the teachings of Doctor John, *and* the "Louisiana Red" contingent, led by the black New Orleanian Lisa (Minnie Yelling's nanny) and the white English graduate student, Kasavutu, who follow the teachings of Marie Laveau. The followers of Marie Laveau have an interest in continuing the contemporary American hate-ethic and apathy among America's workers, a syndrome that Reed calls "Louisiana Red." The Louisiana Red workers kill Ed Yellings because his faction has come up with a cure for cocaine addiction and is working on a cure for cancer, both of which would be deadly for the Louisiana Red epidemic. Reed chooses to emphasize the rumored rivalry between the historical Marie Laveau and Doctor John, and comes down on the side of the man, with the woman playing the role of villain.

Also central to Reed's plot is his satire of black leadership during the 1960s and 1970s. Reed's description of the Moochers is a devastating attack on black revolutionaries. Minnie, daughter of Ed Yellings and leader of the Moochers, is heavily influenced by Nanny Lisa, who indoctrinates her with stories of Marie Laveau's superiority over Doctor John. Parallels between the fictional character Minnie and the mythical character Antigone recur; "Louisiana Red," for example, can also be seen as a plague on Berkeley (America), a modern version of the Oedipus myth. Further, in Reed's reconstruction of the Greek myth, Minnie strongly parallels Antigone in her desire to destroy the existing patriarchy. As a woman Moocher, Minnie worships only herself and, in fact, actually wants to be a Sphinx or a high-priestess. LaBas, chief detective in the novel and a major voice through which the *loas* speak (based on Legba of voodoo tradition), serves as the modern Creon, who is left at the end of the novel to manage the remaining Gumbo Workers and other earthly workers of Hoodoo when the conspiracy of Nanny Lisa and Kasavubu is revealed. As we might expect, Minnie's two brothers, Street and Wolf, two would-be black leaders, kill each other, Wolf being the true heir-apparent (Eteocles), and Street (Polyneices), the new kind of street leader, more militant than any of the others, an escaped criminal whose only strategy is violence. In *Love in the Ruins* Walker Percy sketches a sweeping caricature of black militants of the late sixties and seventies equal to that of Ishmael Reed's. There Percy belittles the would-be Bantu leaders, like Uru, who attempts to lead an attack on Paradise Estates but fails and ends up returning north to head the Black Studies Department at the University of Michigan.

Although Antigone is fated to die in the old myth, in Reed's new myth, LaBas does not kill her counterpart; in effect, LaBas steps out of the mortal sphere into the sphere of the supernatural to plead for Minnie's return, even though she has been killed. Blue Coal, Chairman of the Board of Directors (Zeus), has become so disgusted with Minnie's continuing desire to put men down that he throws her into LaBas's hands. In the end, LaBas reunites Minnie and Sister (Antigone and Ismene).

By the end of the novel, Reed has satirized virtually every sphere of American society—black leadership, supporters of the status quo in American society (the Atonists of *Mumbo-Jumbo*), and black women. He has continued the tradition of the myth of New Orleans as a center of mystery and the occult but has gone further to create his own "historical fable" in which the conjectured rivalry between Marie Laveau and Doctor John has escalated into war between the contingents that have been corrupted by the American apathetic spirit and the "true" hoodoo followers. The abstraction and reflexiveness of Reed's style place him squarely in the age of postmodernism or "metafiction." Like Walker Percy, he is using New Orleans culture as a metaphor for a way of seeing, for a double-voicedness.

Voices of Community:
Sybil Kein and Brenda Marie Osbey

The woman of color is clearly a part of the myth of New Orleans. Lafcadio Hearn's tragic mulattoes, the "tropical lilies" of the quadroon balls, created by man for man; Faulkner's courtesan; Grace King's whores; Cable's and Tallant's dangerous *voodooiennes,* with Marie Laveau as the archetype; Marcus Christian's healers: each contributes a different shading to the colorful mystique of the city. But these women have certainly been "more sinned against than sinning." Until recently the voices of black New Orleans women writers were seldom heard, the rare exception being an Alice Dunbar-Nelson or a Zora Neale Hurston, the latter often considered an outsider looking in at the world of voodoo; a few other women writers were hidden in newspapers, church magazines, sorority publications. But a new community of African-American women writers has come to the fore, as Brenda Marie Osbey, Sybil Kein, Quo Vadis Gex-Breaux, Fatima Shaik, Debra Hils-Clifton, Adèle Gautier, and Mona Lisa Saloy have made themselves heard. Along with them has been a group of more nationally known white New Orleans women writers, among them Shirley Ann Grau, Ellen Gilchrist, Anne Rice, Valerie Martin, and Sheila Bosworth.

In the poetic works of Sybil Kein and Brenda Marie Osbey we hear new personal voices, concerned with recovering the lost truths of New Orleanian women and their folklore. Their poetry introduces a personal perspective on the experiences of African-American women of Louisiana in contrast to the poetry of social protest in the tradition of the Black Arts Movement. Kein uses revisionist strategies to recover the lost "truths" of history. Osbey re-creates "communities of narrative" which articulate the consciousnesses of those too often silenced by their community.

Sybil Kein: Revision of History

Sybil Kein is a New Orleans-born poet, dramatist, and scholar whose major interest is to preserve and re-create the history, folklore, and language of the Louisiana Creole culture and language in her creative and critical work. Her first book of poetry, *Gombo People* (1981), includes poems written both in Louisiana Creole and English.[41] In her study and use of Louisiana Creole language, she refers to the Afro-French language, which includes an African syntax and a French-based vocabulary. This language, says Kein, was probably developed in the sixteenth century "as a quick way of communication between the French and the African."[42] In an introduction to *Gombo People,* the editor and printer of the book, Ulysse S. Ricard, describes the volume as "un livre sur les creoles de la Nouvelle-Orleans, *ecrit dans la langue creole, et par un auteur creole qui parle la langue do so moune*" (a book on Creoles of New Orleans by a Creole author who speaks the language herself), in the tradition of Armand Lanusse's *Les Cenelles,* the collection of poems by Louisiana *gens de couleur* published in 1845. In her poetry, Kein hopes to preserve the language and culture of Creoles, not because the Creole culture is in danger of dying, but because it is evolving. "There are so many groups coming into New Orleans as they did two hundred years ago," she writes, "bringing their cultures, e.g., the Haitians and the Spanish-speaking people. They are making a new impact on the city and will increase the ingredients of the *gombo,* which I see as New Orleans."[43]

Kein is a poet-historian. Many of the characters of her poems in *Delta Dancer,* which followed *Gombo People* in 1984, are historical figures whom

Sybil Kein. Photographer: Joan Martin.

the author has carefully researched.[44] One of Kein's purposes in *Delta Dancer* is to present historically "truthful" portraits of antebellum black and Creole characters; her portraits, of course, reflect her point of view as a New Orleans woman of color. In "Fragment from the Diary of Amelie Patine Quadroon Mistress of Monsieur Jacques R——" she describes, for example, the quadroon

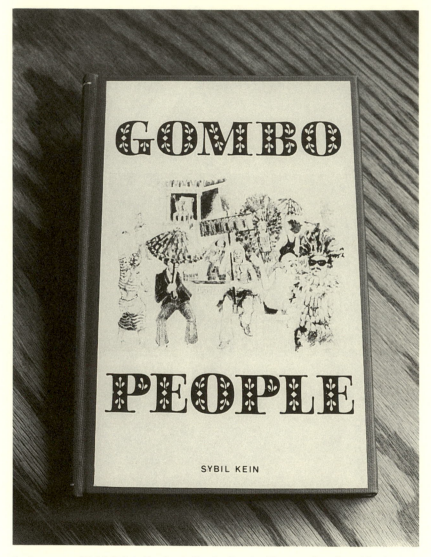

Jacket cover of Sybil Kein's first book, Gombo People. *Photographer: Joan Martin.*

mistress, whom she says "is often painted as a whore and sometimes as a figure that is distorted historically."[45] In her revisionist approach, Kein is intent on showing that "there was a human side to her."[46] In her poem she describes the complex position of the quadroon mistress as "bought, adored, despised paramour, / blight made flesh; hidden, held in / dire esteem, yet sought for bare beauty, fate begging." The mistress contrasts her beautiful passion to the new wife's "frivolous morality and peasant crudeness." However, the unabashed sentimentality of the speaker threatens to defeat her purpose; the quadroon mistress seems hopelessly romantic: "Should I wrap my hair around the bed posts to cover those Cupids and their forever taut bows?. . . Who will feel the vapors / rising under my skin. . . . Who will muff my little cries, unruff these violet sheets that stare coldly at my spine?" The quadroon woman accepts the stereotype that she is the passionate creature who incites the man to passion, even if the wife is cold.

Kein's poem "Toucoutou" is based on the court case of the early 1900s in which a woman found to have an ounce of black blood brought suit to retain her status as white but lost the case (see chapter 2). In Kein's work, the focus is on the woman herself—the anger, shame, shock, the evidence of French, Indian, and African ancestry behind "taut blue veins," "faint skin." In Edward Larocque Tinker's novel and Joseph Beaumont's song about Toucoutou, the emphasis is on the African-American community, which criticized Toucoutou pitilessly for her defection. Similarly, in Alice Dunbar-Nelson's "The Stones of the Village," the community of the protagonist Auguste Picou criticizes him so much for his defection that he decides to leave the South (see chapter 3).[47] In Kein's poem Toucoutou's self-image vanishes before this loss of the "infinite untouchable / privilege of being / white," which is the society's standard of beauty and acceptance.[48] Kein describes Toucoutou as having the accepted white face, "rose-bud mouth, small French nose, Indian-brown hair curved to frame the portrait"; but showing behind the white appearance is the "ghost-grey" of the slave ancestors, and when the court declares Toucoutou black, her apparently white image vanishes, as her face is consumed by anger and self-hatred.

Despite this rather serious subject, in other of Kein's poetry her sense of humor, sometimes light-hearted, often wry, is pervasive. Nevertheless, the humor barely covers the unforgivable, unresolved tensions of the color-line and the dilemma of the person of color. The "Letter to Madame Linde from Justine, Her Creole Servant" ironically portrays the loyal servant as a free woman of color, not a slave, who, to save her daughter's honor and her own position as free servant from the white Madame Linde's vindictiveness, threatens to make known the employer's lesbian affair:

> Madame, I am not condemning your particular capacity For such love, nor am I judging the sincerity of your lover Madame Celeste. I am, however, writing this to demand that You see to it that my place as your free servant is secured For as long as I live, and that the honor of my daughter is Preserved as fitting a young woman of her beauty and station. I am sure that you will therefore reconsider the foolish

Threats to my daughter and myself that you made on yestereve, And
consequently take whatever action necessary to rectify this affaire.[49]

In *Gombo People* and *Delta Dancer* Kein also deals with the question of Creole and Cajun identity, classifications that Brenda Marie Osbey seems to ig-
nore.[50] *Creoles of color,* whom Kein calls "Creoles" for brevity, are people of
mixed Spanish or French and West Indian or African origin. This differs from
Cajuns, originally called "Acadians," who were descendants of Nova Scotians
expelled from their country by the British; they immigrated to Louisiana in the
1800s and settled for the most part in rural Southwest Louisiana. Kein alludes
to the popular conception that Cajuns are white, while Creoles of color are
black, even if they are often *cousines*. In spite of the racial hierarchy, Cajuns tend
to be considered of a lower socioeconomic class than their cousins, the Creoles.
In "La Chaudriere Pele La Gregue . . . " ("The Pot Calls the Coffee Pot . . . "),
the speaker argues that Cajuns and Creoles are brothers and the white-black
distinctions should be discarded:

> *But my friend, do not throw away the spice*
> *Because it is too light or too dark.*
> *If you do that you will not have Gombo*
> *Ever again, but a foul melted stew made up of*
> *The denied flesh of your ancestors.*

Another humorous, light-hearted poem in *Delta Dancer* that simulates the Creole dialect is "Cofaire?" ("How Come?").

> *My cousine Tee-Ta, she say she Cajun;*
> *et me, I'm Creole, name Tee-Teen,*
> *She still live up on de Bayou, you know,*
> *but me, I move to New Orleen.[51]*

Both cousins have the same last name—Boudreaux; they cook the same food
and like to dance and sing, but when the Cajun cousin comes to New Orleans
she says she is white and does not speak to the New Orleans Creole cousin.

> *Well,* dit pas rien, *she do what she please,*
> *and me, I just laugh all de time.*
> *"Cajun" and "creole," we cousine, that's for true;*
> *cause her "French" folks is "French"—same as mine!*

The persona is interested in their common ancestry; the cousins are united by
the French connection, even if not the African, just as Honoré and Honoré,
f.m.c., were brothers even if they lived on different sides of the culture. That
culture was interracial.

Brenda Marie Osbey. Photographer: Chandra McCormick.

Brenda Marie Osbey:
"Communities of Narrative"

Like Kein, Brenda Marie Osbey re-creates the experiences, attitudes, ways of seeing, and consciousness of the people she knows best, Afro-Louisiana women. Her poetic community in her first three collections of poetry, *Ceremony for Minneconjoux* (1983), *In These Houses* (1988), and *Desperate Circumstance, Dangerous Woman* (1991), is based largely on the Tremé cultural district of New Orleans, which includes the old Congo Square of the eighteenth and nineteenth centuries, now Louis Armstrong Park,[52] and surrounding parishes and bayous during the period from the turn of the century to around 1949. The Tremé area may be the literal landscape of many of the poems, but Osbey also creates a figurative landscape of cultural and personal history which, in turn, forms a context within which one "can see that Black New Orleans women devise ways to be in control of their lives, to channel their abilities and need for expression."[53]

Osbey has chosen to use narrative form because she relates stories from the New Orleans black experience, many that she has been told or has read about or knows personally, and "embroiders" or "reinvents" them. Her interpretation of narrative, she says, "does not require that I report to the reader an entire story: beginning, middle, and resolution. The poems are snapshots, frames. . . . In a way, perhaps I'm doing a quilt work. I don't feel compelled to reveal too much of my characters' lives. It's one of the obligations of the reader to work that out."[54] In her narratives, or dramatizations, she uses multiple voices—various levels of spoken English as well as jazz, blues, and nursery rhymes. As I have pointed out elsewhere, Osbey consciously uses the peculiar language of her characters in the poems; in fact, an individual character may use different voices herself.[55] For instance, the same character may use standard American English, her own spoken voice, and an ancient African communal voice. In a work like "Ceremony for Minneconjoux" several voices appear. The poem begins in a communal (third-person) voice:

> *it was years back you know*
> *down bayou la fourche*
> *she named her daughter*
> *minneconjoux*
> *so that people would not mistake*
> *her indian blood.*

Yet the sense of the spoken language of the various characters comes through in the narration. As the narrative progresses, the third-person point of view becomes more obviously that of Mama Lou's daughter Lenazette: "she come

Mardi Gras Indian. Photographer: Joan Martin.

through the run-down page fence gate / and looked up at him on the ladder / what the hell was he doing she meant to know?" Then the voice shifts into the first-person narration of Lenazette (about one-third through the poem): "i wore my braids down now / connected together at the ends. i have always liked things / connected together at the ends." Finally, in the last two pages of the poem, the speaker becomes Minneconjoux, Lenazette's daughter: "when i was ten i left mammazette / to go live in the city with mama lou." The shifts in perspective in "Ceremony" and in other poems of Osbey's first volume emphasize, through the connections among the various characters, the interrelatedness of generations.

The spirit of hoodoo hovers over, and emanates through, Osbey's poetry. The emphasis is not so much on the rites and rituals associated with the religious practice, but on the spiritual life that the belief system encourages. Osbey herself has said that she sees hoodoo "as a series of life principles . . . in the way that it shapes one's attitudes about life, birth, and death."[56]

One aspect of the religious value system shared by Osbey's characters is a reverence for the dead and for the communion of spirits, dead and alive. The mission of the poet as historian/geographer is to trace the cultural terrain of a place and people.

> *the geography i am learning*
> *has me place myself*
> *at simultaneous points*
> *of celebration*
> *and all you see and hear in me*
> *is these women*
> *walking in the middle of the road*
> *with their hoodoo in their hands.*
>
> ....
>
> *this place no one chooses*
> *is the land i tarry in.*
> *this ritual i go through*
> *is as old as its name*
> *and the prophet-women who dance it.*
>
> first you place one foot
> and then the other.

The poet/persona has "actively remembered" the past and re-created it for others one step at a time. She has built her "house of bones," her familial, ancestral, community past, and in "reading" her poems, we may conjure up our own past and enrich our lives.

The poems of *In These Houses* are divided into three sections: "Houses of the Swift Easy Women," "House of Mercies," and "House of Bones"; the three sections can be seen as entering into deeper levels of spirit and communion, or community. On the first level, Osbey creates portraits of her typical New Orleans women—strong, rebellious (even within the restrictions of their society), often insane or violent. "These women," Osbey writes in the title poem of this section, "know subtlety / sleight of hand / cane liquor / island songs / the poetry of soundlessness." Characters like Thelma V. Picou, Ophelia (who loved beauty and violence), Clarissa/Reva (a case of mistaken or multiple identities), and the wastrel woman all carry their *blues* around with them, almost always camouflaging them with their swagger. The blues were personal expressions, each woman with her lone voice singing of her pain, but transcending the pain through her song and then realizing that she is a part of the group, the community.

In the second level the women visit and exit from the "House of Mercies," which is, by its description, a hoodoo house, a defiantly white wooden structure. Coming out they are different, having shared their secrets and listened to the wise women, or "prophets": "so careful when they leave / to close the rusted page-fence gate / looking about / some cherished article / almost covered in the folds of their skirts. . . no woman swaggers or smiles / making her exit / from this house of mercies." The house of mercies is like a way station where these women can reveal their secrets. Only "the bone-step women," like the Féfé and Bahalia women of *Ceremony,* dare to come out openly and be witnesses of these women's blues; in "Elvena" no one will come forward and call her name but the hoodoo women, who can "read" her sorrow and give her grace. *Féfé,* a creolization of the Haitian term *vévé,* is a sign, or pattern, in voodoo, which represents the *loas,* or gods, and is used to identify anything conjure-related. The Bahalia women were associated with a religious sect in New Orleans, which has died out today as public worship and has become primarily private. The "Bone-Step Women," like the other hoodoo women, understand a woman's sorrows; by reading bones, as some people read dice, candle flames, or Tarot cards, they see into a person's innermost being.[57] The "Bone-Step Women" say to women like Elvena, one of Osbey's lost female souls who needs to find the truth and return to wholeness and health and the community:

> *only the bone-step women*
> *would ever come for her in broad daylight*
> *carrying their satchels of longing*
> *like easy parcels on turbaned heads.*
> *carrying that woman along*
> *between the folds of their red cotton skirts*
> *calling aloud, to no one in particular*
> tell the truth
> tell the truth and do right
> *carrying that woman along like one more burden*
> *one more parcel*

that amounts to nothing much
moving along the broken road
that leads to bayou st. john.

The third level of *In These Houses* includes more explicit pictures of the writer/ artist and her task of building a house for her memories. This section reminds the reader that there are many more steps to be taken in this re-creation of the past.[58] In "Consuela," healers break the circle of the ring game, and Consuela is warned that to give up one's song means to pass on one's soul. The poet must hold on to her stories in order to hold on to herself, but this poet is building a house that no one can tear down, a circle that cannot be broken. In "Portrait," the photographer takes a picture of the "young writer woman," who has been raised by the vegetable man/photographer, August Anthony Peter Le Jamn, and the photographer's aunt, Sue Lee, who took in white people's wash, but also taught little colored girls French. The female photographer is taking a shot in front of her ancestral home, so full of this contradictory history of the New Orleans African American. Others must follow in her footsteps:

and as you work
without proper materials
or light of day
these are the words you must recite
repeat them daily
until you hear how true they are:
this is the house
i have carried inside me
this is the house
made of artifact and gut
this is the house
all my bones have come from
this is the house
nothing
nothing
nothing can tear down.

In her third collection of poetry, *Desperate Circumstance, Dangerous Woman,* Osbey continues to evoke the haunting prophetic voice that has made all of her poetry a unique history of Louisiana community and culture. The Bahalia women, the Féfé women, the Bone-step women enter our lives and carry out the same healing process that they perform in the lives of Osbey's characters. In re-creating stories from her ancestral past, Osbey is giving written form to oral narrative by unselfconsciously using the voices of various generations of characters and traditions. In effect, she is creating a new form of poetic narrative "which will bear witness to the fact that the narrative function can still be metamorphosed, but not so as to die. For we have no idea of what a culture would be where no one any longer knew what it meant to narrate things."[59]

Osbey's poetry, the dialogue of Tom Dent, the poets of BLKARTSOUTH and the Congo Square Writers, Ishmael Reed, and Sybil Kein all add significantly to the myth of New Orleans. In their poetry, plays, and fiction, they create, evoke, and revise the folklore, mythology, and language of African traditions in New Orleans culture. Dent re-creates portraits of the ordinary black New Orleanians, in the housing projects, the bars, the parades. His characters speak in the vernacular; like Joe Brown, Jr., in *Ritual Murder,* they are often inarticulate, but their culture is strong: the music, the parades, the organizations, the attitudes toward life dominate the landscape. The poet sees them as wearing masks, which are so commonplace that nobody usually notices. Ishmael Reed diverges from the realistic stance of Dent and others of the BLKARTSOUTH workshop and creates a new myth of African-American history, using hoodoo, which he considers to be "the primary African American folklore" as theme and structure of his fiction. He emphasizes the strong cultural link between New Orleans, home of hoodoo in the United States, and Africa, especially Dahomey, where he says that *Voudoun* originates, and the Caribbean, particularly Haiti, where hoodoo's expression has been particularly dominant.

The black women poets, Sybil Kein and Brenda Marie Osbey, add to the myth of New Orleans in significant, but dramatically different ways. Sybil Kein consciously revises the old myths of New Orleans Creole culture. In her poetry she uses Creole language, transcribing oral into written language, and she has recorded Creole ballads in five languages—Haitian Creole, Louisiana Creole, French, Spanish, and English—demonstrating the Caribbean and Spanish influence on Creole culture.[60] Through irony, she comments on the innuendos and misinterpretations which have maligned the Creole women of color in so much of the literature about the city; she attempts to set the record straight by creating characters who contrast with the stereotype: the Creole servant who blackmails her white mistress, the Cajun (white) girl who comes from the country and will not recognize her Creole (black) cousin because racial classifications are more rigid in the city than in the country.

Brenda Marie Osbey's characters are also, for the most part, Creole, but she does not self-consciously transcribe Creole dialect, nor does she use the signification *Creole* in her works. She uses blues, call-response rhythms, ring games, and hoodoo characters, traditions, and ceremonies in the development of her narrative poems—all retentions of African traditions in the diaspora, all reflective of the African, French, Spanish, and Native American culture of New Orleans. She writes "communities of narrative," so that her characters and the events of their lives are developed in more detail than in the poems of any of the other authors that we have discussed; they recur in subsequent poems as well and work out their problems together. Calvin C. Hernton has observed of Osbey's work that "in addition to influences from the American Indian and French and Spanish cultures, the styles of speech and the general aura of the women reflect a certain Africa mystique . . . carried over into the New World and blended with the indigenously developed folkness of southern black women."[61] As opposed to the poetry of Tom Dent and the other poets of BLKARTSOUTH, Osbey is primarily interested in the inner lives of her women, not the public debate about race and ethnicity; her characters, while reflecting the fusion of the various cultures that influence their lives and their possibilities of self-expression, are primarily engaged in expressing their personal blues and finding grace or healing through the community. Throughout her poems there is a respect for ancestors and the community. She is searching for the epiphanies that the culture can evoke.

Conclusion

ய

"**M**yth is speech stolen and restored. Only, speech which is restored is no longer quite that which was stolen: when it was brought back, it was not put exactly in its place."[1] Or, in other words, myth in the Barthean sense is the appropriation of the culture for authorial purposes. The writer appropriates the rituals, behavior, attitudes, language, ceremonies of New Orleanians and puts them in a form that demands interpretation and reinterpretation. "I plant words / and bring up myself / even if no one sees me / i can be the history of migrations coming up through city pavements / reminding them of where home really is," writes Brenda Marie Osbey.[2] The Bras-Coupé episode lives in the writings of George Washington Cable, in the "Bibi" that was never published and *The Grandissimes,* which was; in the Creole song, "The Dirge of St. Malo" (published in Cable's "Creole Slave Songs"); Merimée's "Tamango," which came before; the Marcus Christian research that remains unpublished and largely unread; the poems of our contemporary Tom Dent.[3] The history becomes legend and folklore and enters the literature, music, art, and the imagination.

We have seen how myths in literature work to portray and contribute to the continuing development of a culture. Humanistic geographers are interested in defining the influence of place images on our acceptance and recognition of a place. Several studies have been done on the impact of literature on our understanding of cities and places.[4] But my perspective here has been that of the culturalist and the literary critic, that is, the intersection of literature and culture and how each informs and influences the other. If we view culture as the "webs of significance" that Geertz describes, or, in other words, a system of symbols which we must interpret rather than study scientifically, then the analysis of culture and literature must share a common method; in both we are interpreting the meaning of symbols, or forms.[5] Culture, the template upon which we base our attitudes and behavior and create our music, art, architecture, patterns of play and work, can be *read* in the texts that we have studied; the interplay between literature and culture reveals meanings about the tensions embedded in the literary work's theme and in the culture itself.

Within the webs of significance that surround the city of New Orleans are many myths. Two of them are the myth of race, color, and racial identification, based on the ideology of racial superiority and inferiority, and the myth of the city as woman.

The Myth of Race, Color, and Racial Identification

"The Negro Problem" was a unique one in Louisiana because the colony was nearly one hundred years old before it became a part of the United States, and by that time, the particular situation of *les gens de couleur libres* as a separate race and caste and their legal status as *quasi-citizens* had been legally defined by the French *Code Noir* in 1724 and the Spanish equivalent, *Las Siete Partidas* of 1789; attitudes toward race were anything but American.[6] Free persons of color could own slaves and, on the other hand, often bought freedom for slaves—family members, spouses, and friends; they owned real estate and were recognized in the courts, but they were restricted from voting and from marrying white persons. However, the free men of color are virtually absent from literature. "The tragic mulatto" theme, which became so popular in literature during the late nineteenth and early twentieth centuries did not include the free man of color. He was not a pathetic figure, but more of a threat to the white reader because of the violence with which he was usually associated. The idea of the Grandissimes *frères,* the black and white Honorés, condemned Cable much more readily than the character pairing of Aurora Nancanou, the white mistress, and her slave and friend, Palmyre. Faulkner's Charles Bon was so abstractly drawn that it is difficult to compare him to the violent presence of a Joe Christmas or the realistic treatment of a Lucas Beauchamp, both from Yoknapatawpha County. The Creole men of color were shadows, too ethereal and undefined to interest writers or readers of the period.

The free women of color, who were required by the *Code Noir* to wear *tignons* (head scarves) to establish their identity, were prominent subjects of fiction, however. In Cable's early stories they were the innocent victims of an unforgivable caste system; they were neither black nor white and had no place except as the mistress of some white man who would care for them. Such white women writers of Cable's time as Grace King and Kate Chopin looked at these women askant, portraying them in the most positive sense as neat landladies and conscientious nurses and hairdressers, but more negatively as prostitutes or madames of houses of prostitution. Contemporary black women writers, if they have not dismissed the symbolic import of the Creole woman of color in the past, have attempted to speak from her point of view, as does Sybil Kein in several of her poems. The idea of the octoroon and quadroon women as the creation of the white man in Lafcadio Hearn and William Faulkner, and to some extent Cable, is a myth which betrays the white male writers' disregard for the black woman as a person and congratulates him for his "sophistication" and worldliness, unacceptable in most of the American landscape and by most of his own psyche.

The problem of racial identification and *passing* is a theme handled by many authors at the turn of the nineteenth and into the early twentieth century, among them Charles Chesnutt, Alice Dunbar-Nelson, Edward Larocque Tinker, Lyle Saxon. During that period, several cases that attempted to establish a person's racial identity as white took place. As with the fictional cases of Toucoutou and Paul Marchand, F.M.C., people of possible mixed ancestry sued for their rights as full citizens of Louisiana. In one such case, *State v. Treadaway,* which was brought before the Louisiana Supreme Court in 1910, a woman and her husband were prosecuted for miscegenation because the woman was a Caucasian and the husband was a "mulatto," a term used at the time to classify any person of mixed racial ancestry. The couple had been acquitted in the lower court and the acquittal was affirmed by the State Supreme Court because it was decided that the husband was an octoroon, not a Negro. To be a Negro was to have more than just an admixture of Negro blood. The statute that the couple was accused of violating, it was decided, was not intended to include octoroons as Negroes.[7] The idea of class distinctions due to shades of color is not unique; however, in the United States, New Orleans's minute attention to racial differences within a group of blacks, and the difficulty in distinguishing those differences because white and black were often little more than legal terms unsubstantiated very often by physical appearance, was unique.

In much of the fiction and poetry, authors portray black characters as wearing a mask. Walker Percy's Mercer of *The Moviegoer* wears a mask; he plays the game, but actually sees much more. He exhibits DuBois's idea of the "double-consciousness," a "sense of always looking at one's self through the eyes of others, of measuring one's soul by the tape of a world that looks on in amused contempt and pity. One ever feels his twoness,—an American, a Negro; two souls, two thoughts, two unreconciled strivings; two warring ideals in one dark body, whose dogged strength alone keeps it from being torn asunder."[8] New Orleans poems, plays, and fiction often include this theme of the mask covering the double-consciousness, and the fearful implication is that one day, blacks will remove the mask, "jes like we said they would," as Tom Dent suggests.

Dent describes the removal of that mask in "Secret Messages": "& maybe someday when nobody is / checking it out the drummers will come to life in / St. Louis No. 1 at midnight / beating out the secret messages / all the masks will drop. / jest like we said they would. / secret messages / secret messages of the gods." In taking off the mask, a black may become another Bras-Coupé or John Henry, two of the great criminal-heroes of African-American folklore. They, and their historical counterparts—the Maroon leaders of the Pointe Coupée Slave Revolt of 1895; Toussaint l'Ouverture and Dessalines, who led the Santo Domingan Revolution, also 1895; Robert Charles, who started the famous New Orleans race riot of 1900—were all heroes because they revolted against, and transcended, the unfair system of race.[9]

Voodoo, or hoodoo in writings as diverse as Grace King's "Madrilène," Alice Dunbar-Nelson's "The Goodness of Saint Rocque," Edward Larocque Tinker's *Toucoutou,* Ishmael Reed's *The Last Days of Louisiana Red* and *Mumbo Jumbo,* and Brenda Marie Osbey's *In These Houses,* is always associated with the supersensory power of blacks, a power which extends back in space and time to Africa, and reflects the fear of that power by whites. Certainly, the literature of New Orleans emphasizes how integral voodoo practices are to the city's culture, from the spiritualist healing of hoodoo women to the All Saint's Day ceremonies practiced in respect for the dead. Palmyre of *The Grandissimes* is dreaded because of her power; Clemence is killed in response to her act of laying a gris-gris in the Grandissimes home for Agricola Fusilier. But Aurora diligently performed the rites of the worship to protect her home and to win the favor of the voodoo gods. This religion of African and Caribbean origin practiced by both whites and blacks of all classes becomes a symbol of the interdependence of the various strains of the New Orleans pluralistic culture.

Another facet of the myth of race and racial identification in New Orleans literature is the possibility that occurs to the author, the reader, and sometimes self-consciously to the white characters, that the black race is the other self, the doppelganger. Anne Goodwyn Jones points out that the southern women writers that she discusses in *Tomorrow Is Another Day,* among them Grace King and Kate Chopin, "reconstruct racial relationships such that black and white women, especially, find themselves in both literally and symbolically significant relationships, often as one another's hidden self."[10] The identification of most readers with Grace King's "Little Convent Girl," who discovers in shock that she is "black" when her mother appears on the ship to take her home, makes this story one of Grace King's most popular. The same identification between black and white characters and the confusion of racial identity makes "Desirée's Baby" and "La Belle Zoraïde" two of Kate Chopin's best-loved works.

The vision of the black character as the other self is not limited to the work of white women authors. Cable and Faulkner deal with the complexity of the symbolic interrelationships between black and white half-brothers and half-sisters in *The Grandissimes* and in *Absalom, Absalom!* As discussed in chapter 2, the careful pairing of the two Honorés in Cable's novel, even their identical name, makes an ironic comment on the irrationality of racial divisions and the depth of their destructiveness. As the white Honoré watches his brother contemplate suicide by drowning in the canal, he is filled with horror at the magnitude of his brother's problem and in that moment sees racism as a "morhal, political, commercial, social mistake" that "drhags us a centurhy behind the rhes' of the world!" In *Absalom, Absalom!* Faulkner is more explicit in showing the desire of Henry Sutpen and Charles Bon for a common identity. "Because Henry loved Bon. He repudiated blood birthright and material security for his sake."[11] Elizabeth S. Muhlenfeld argues that each of the characters in *Absalom* must have his or her imaginative construct of the Negro to serve as a buffer to "absorb the shock of self-confrontation."[12] However, the imaginative construct of the black person is more likely the confrontation itself—the confrontation with the other self. For Henry it was Bon and vice versa: "It was not Judith who was the object of Bon's love or of Henry's solicitude. She was just the blank shape, the empty vessel in which each of them strove to preserve, not the illusion of himself nor his illusion of the other but what each conceived the other to believe him to be.—the man and the youth, seducer and seduced, who had known one another, seduced and been seduced, victimised in turn each by the other."[13]

The City as Woman

Perhaps the most popular myth of the city in recent years is that of New Orleans as courtesan. As discussed in chapter 4, Faulkner developed this concept to encapsulate his ideas of this city as exotic, old, sophisticated, and tolerant. His myth was both attractive and pejorative, for the courtesan, while beautiful and free, was also without morals. Her gods, symbolized in the city's religions, Catholic and voodoo, were "voluptuous" and "ornamental." They allowed miscegenation without guilt or shame demanded of the oppressor or the victim. Faulkner's ambiguous portrait of the courtesan was later reconfigured by Tennessee Williams, whose most famous courtesan image was Blanche DuBois, the fallen southern belle who came to New Orleans because she thought she could avoid reality there. "I don't tell truth, I tell what *ought* to be truth. And if that is sinful, then let me be damned for it!" When Mitch tears the paper lantern off the light bulb, Blanche yells, *"Don't turn the light on!"*[14] The light would reveal too much, would force a confrontation with the reality that Blanche fends off through her fantasies of magic and romance. But, like Blanche, the female image of the city in Williams's plays promises desire and magic, not realism, but never really lives up to it.

"Nuns and naked ladies," said Walker Percy says of New Orleans.[15] The city is contradictory; it is both sensual and pious—another image of decadence.

New Orleans is Grace King's "La femme en grande tenue," a "Parisian woman." The city is portrayed as strong and yet feminine, like the *filles à la casette* who came to the Louisiana colony to marry the founders, like the rebellious women who fought against the Union occupation during the time of "Beast" Butler, like the Era Club women who led reform movements to institute hospitals, asylums, prisons, and a juvenile court system at the turn of the last century.

The idea of the city as woman traverses the literary landscape. Brenda Marie Osbey adds the féfé women, the "bone-step women," and other hoodoo women to the field of literary symbols of women associated with the city. She emphasizes the richness of community and the possibility of healing. Her "community of narrative" is created by stories handed down by women from generation to generation: "Experiences, reminiscences, episodes, picked up as only women know how to pick them up from other women's lives," writes Grace King, "and told as only women know how to relate them."[16]

The myth of the city as woman, and other aspects of the myth of New Orleans as it has been worked out in the dialogue between writers across boundaries of race and gender, demand further exploration. Future studies should include the influence of music, the visual arts, and film on the continuing dialogue.

W

Notes

1. Literary Dialogues and the Development of an Urban Myth

1. During the years of the Federal Writers' Project of the Works Progress Administration in Louisiana and in the following decade several books were published about the history and folklore of New Orleans and writings inspired by the city. Besides the WPA's *New Orleans City Guide* (Boston: Houghton Mifflin, 1938), there was Lyle Saxon, *Fabulous New Orleans* (New York: Century, 1928); Robert Tallant, *The Romantic New Orleanians* (New York: Dutton, 1950); *Gumbo Ya-Ya: A Collection of Louisiana Folk Tales* (New York: Bonanza Books, 1945); and Harnett Kane, *Queen New Orleans: City by the River* (New York: Morrow, 1949). See also Etolia S. Basso, ed., *The World from Jackson Square* (New Orleans: Tulane UP, 1968), and Violet H. Bryan, "Land of Dreams: Image and Reality in New Orleans," *Urban Resources* 1 (Spring 1984): 29–35. See Blaine A. Brownell and David R. Goldfield, eds., *History: The Growth of Urban Civilization in the South* (Port Washington, NY: National University Publications, 1977) for a description of the special position of southern cities and their close relationship with their rural hinterlands.

2. For further discussions of ethnicity and cultural groups in New Orleans, see Hodding Carter, ed., Th*e Past as Prelude: New Orleans 1718–1968* (New Orleans: Tulane UP, 1968); Sarah Searight, *New Orleans* (New York: Stein and Day, 1973); George Reinecke, "The National and Cultural Groups of New Orleans, 1718–1918," in *New Orleans Ethnic Cultures,* ed. John Cooke (New Orleans: Committee on Ethnicity in New Orleans, 1978), 6–25.

3. Roland Barthes, "Myth Today," in Myth*ologies,* trans. Annette Lavers (New York: Hill and Wang, 1972), 99. See also Donald Fanger, *Dostoevsky and Romantic Realism* (Chicago: U of Chicago P, 1965), for a discussion of the urban myths of Petersburg, London, and Paris created by Dostoevsky, Gogol, Dickens, and Balzac. The writers who have developed the most significant

literary portraits of New Orleans have also looked beyond the surface details
and contributed to the "myth" of the city. As Fanger writes about the romantic
realists: "The very moral sensitivities that let them see the sickness of their
cities ... led them to depict their cities ultimately in moral terms—taking
moral here to mean a concern with the quality and possibilities of life. It is
these terms which shape the myth of each, and each writer's investigation
must be seen as a quest for myth" (259).

4.   See Clifford Geertz, "Ideology as a Cultural System," *The Interpretation of
       Cultures* (New York: Basic Books, 1973), 216. Geertz compares the opera-
       tion of cultural practices in the human mind to the operation of genetic
       systems in organic processes:"Culture patterns—religious, philosophical,
       aesthetic, scientific, ideological—are 'programs'; they provide a template or
       blueprint for the organization of social and psychological processes, much as
       genetic systems provide such a template for the organization of organic
       processes."

5.   Barthes 112.

6.   W. Lawrence Hogue, *Discourse and the Other: The Production of the Afro-
       American Text* (Durham, N.C.: Duke UP, 1986), discusses how the dominant
       literary establishment has controlled the production or non-production of
       African-American texts and images from the nineteenth century to the
       present. Also see such studies of women's literary traditions as Elaine
       Showalter, *A Literature of Their Own* (Princeton, NJ: Princeton UP, 1977),
       Barbara Christian, B*lack Women Novelists: The Development of a Tradition*
       (Westport, Conn.: Greenwood, 1980), Tillie Olsen, *Silences* (New York:
       Delacorte, 1978), and Nelly Furman, "The Study of Women and Language:
       Comment on Vol.3, no. 3," *Signs* 4 (Fall 1978): 182–85, for discussions of
       women's exclusion in the language and social practices in a patriarchal
       society.

7.   M. M. Bakhtin, *The Dialogic Imagination,* ed. Michael Holquist, trans.
       Holquist and Caryl Emerson (Austin: U of Texas P, 1981), 276–77.

8.   Cheryl A. Wall, ed., introd., *Changing Our Own Words: Essays on Criticism,
       Theory, and Writing by Black Women* (New Brunswick: Rutgers UP, 1989),
       8–10.

9.   Alexis de Tocqueville, *Democracy in America,* ed. Phillips Bradley, trans.
       Henry Reeve, rev. Francis Bowen (New York: Vintage, 1945), vol. 1: 388–
       89. The original text was *De la democratie en Amerique,* 4th ed. (Paris:
       Charles Gosselin, 1836–40).

10.   Rodolphe Desdunes, *Nos Hommes et Notre Histoire* (Montreal, 1911), rpt.
       Our People and Our History, trans. Sister Dorothea Olga McCants (Baton
       Rouge: Louisiana State UP, 1973); Alice Dunbar-Nelson, "People of Color in
       Louisiana, Part I," *Journal of Negro History* (Jan. 1917): 51–78 (rpt. in *An
       Alice Dunbar-Nelson Reader,* ed. R. Ora Williams (Washington, DC: UP of
       America, 1976); Charles B. Roussève, Th*e Negro in Louisiana: Aspects of
       His History and His Literature* (New Orleans: Xavier UP, 1937); John W.
       Blassingame, *Black New Orleans: 1860–1880* (Chicago: U of Chicago P,
       1973).

11. Sally Kittredge Evans, "Free Persons of Color," *New Orleans Architecture,*
     vol. 4: *The Creole Faubourgs* (Gretna, LA: Pelican, 1974). Also see H. E.
     Sterkx, T*he Free Negro in Ante-Bellum Louisiana* (Rutherford, NJ: Fairleigh
     Dickinson UP, 1972), and Thomas Marc Fiehrer, "The African Presence in
     Colonial Louisiana: An Essay on the Continuity of Caribbean Culture,"
     Lo*uisiana's Black Heritage,* ed. Robert R. MacDonald, John R. Kemp, and
     Edward F. Haas (New Orleans: Louisiana State Museum, 1979).

12. H. E. Sterkx, *The Free Negro in Ante-Bellum Louisiana* (Rutherford, NJ:
     Fairleigh Dickinson UP, 1972), 247–48.

13. Blassingame 12. The population figures are from Evans 25.

14. See Roussève 25–26; Laura Foner, "The Free People of Color in Louisiana
     and St. Domingue: A Comparative Portrait of Two Three-Caste Slave
     Societies," Jo*urnal of Social History,* 3 (1970): 406–30; Helene d'Aquin
     Allain, *Souvenirs d'Amerique et de France, par un creole* (Paris, 1883), 14–
     18; Donald Everett, "Emigres and Militiamen: Free Persons of Color in New
     Orleans 1803–1815, *Journal of Negro History* 38 (Oct. 1953): 387–402;
     Fiehrer 3–31.

15. Sister Audrey Marie Detiege, *Henriette Delille, Free Woman of Color:
     Foundress of the Sisters of the Holy Family* (New Orleans: Sisters of the Holy
     Family, 1976).

16. Armand Lanusse, "Epigramme" (1845), in *Les Cenelles,* ed. Lanusse, trans.
     and ed. Regine Latortue and Gleason R. W. Adams (Boston: G. K. Hall,
     1979), 95.

17. Grace King, *New Orleans: The Place and the People* (New York: Macmillan,
     1895); William Faulkner, *New Orleans Sketches,* ed. Carvel Collins (New
     York: Random House, 1958); Harnett Kane, *Queen New Orleans: City by the
     River*; Walker Percy, "New Orleans, Mon Amour," *Harper's* Sept. 1968: 80.

18. Probably the most widely known accounts of Marie Laveau (1794–1881) are
     those of Robert Tallant's *Voodoo in New Orleans* (1946; Gretna, LA: Pelican,
     1974) and T*he Voodoo Queen: A Novel* (1956; Gretna, LA: Pelican, 1974).
     Also see Marcus Christian's manuscripts on the subject in the Marcus
     Christian Collection, the Archives and Manuscripts Department of the Earl K.
     Long Library of the University of New Orleans.

19. Arnold K. Rampersad, foreword, M*ules and Men* by Zora Neale Hurston
     (1935; New York: Harper & Row, 1990), xxii–xxiii.

20. See particularly Ishmael Reed, *The Last Days of Louisiana Red, Mumbo
     Jumbo, Shrovetide in Old New Orleans,* and Brenda Marie Osbey, *Ceremony
     for Minneconjoux* and *In These Houses.*

21. Per Seyersted and Emily Toth, eds., *A Kate Chopin Miscellany* (Natchitoches,
     LA: Northwestern State UP, 1979), 116; Robert Bush, *Grace King: A
     Southern Destiny* (Baton Rouge: Louisiana State UP, 1983), 34–35.

22. Rodolphe Desdunes discusses the role of the Comité des Citoyens (free
     persons of color) in bringing *Plessy v. Ferguson* to court in 1896, pp. 143–45;
     Edward Larocque Tinker, *Toucoutou* (New York: Dodd, Mead, 1928); "Paul
     Marchand, F.M.C." (ca. 1928), unpublished, is found in typescript in the
     Charles Chesnutt Collection of Fisk University Library.

23.   See Larzer Ziff, *The American 1890s: Life and Times of a Lost Generation* (New York: Viking, 1966), 275–305.

24.   Helen Taylor, "The Case of Grace King," *Southern Review* 18 (Fall 1982): 685–702; W. Kenneth Holditch, "The Singing Heart: A Study of the Life and Work of Pearl Rivers," *Southern Quarterly* 20 (Winter 1982): 87–117.

25.   Susan Merrill Squier, ed., introd., *Women Writers and the City: Essays in Feminist Literary Criticism* (Knoxville: U of Tennessee P, 1984), 8.

26.   Ziff, chap. 13.

27.   Bakhtin 262–63.

28.   Robert Tallant, "My Fabulous Friend—Lyle Saxon," *Times-Picayune,* Magazine Section, Nov. 21, 1948.

29.   Joseph Logsdon, "Marcus Bruce Christian," *A Dictionary of Louisiana Biography,* ed. Glenn R. Conrad (Louisiana Historical Association, 1988), vol. 1: 1788–89.

30.   Sterling Brown, "Folk Life of the Negro," and Langston Hughes, "The Negro Artist and the Racial Mountain," in *Black Expression,* ed. Addison Gayle (New York: Weybright and Talley, 1970).

31.   Larry McCaffrey, *The Metafictional Muse: The Works of Robert Coover, Donald Barthelme, and William H. Gass* (Pittsburgh: U of Pittsburgh P, 1982); Joseph Dewey, *In a Dark Time: The Apocalyptic Temper in the American Novel of the Nuclear Age* (West Lafayette, Ind.: Purdue UP, 1990).

32.   Thomas J. Richardson, "The City of Day and the City of Night: New Orleans and the Exotic Unreality of Tennessee Williams," in *Tennessee Williams: A Tribute,* ed. Jac Tharpe (Jackson: UP of Mississippi, 1977), 631–42; Milly S. Barranger, "New Orleans as Theatrical Image in Plays by Tennessee Williams," *Southern Quarterly* 23.2 (Winter 1985): 38–54; Camille Paglia, *Sexual Personae: Art and Decadence from Nefertiti to Emily Dickinson* (New Haven: Yale UP, 1990), 434–35.

33.   Walker Percy, "Symbol, Consciousness, and Intersubjectivity," *The Message in the Bottle* (New York: Farrar, Straus and Giroux, 1954), 265–76; Michael Kobre, "The Consolations of Fiction: Walker Percy's Dialogic Art," *New Orleans Review* 16.4 (Winter 1989): 45–53.

34.   Walker Percy, "The Diagnostic Novel: On the Uses of Modern Fiction," *Harper's* June 1986: 39–45.

35.   Michael Pearson, "The Double Bondage of Racism in Walker Percy's Fiction," *Mississippi Quarterly* 41.4 (Fall 1988): 479–95.

36.   Larry Neal, "The Black Arts Movement," in *The Black Aesthetic,* ed. Addison Gayle (New York: Doubleday, 1971), 257–74.

2. Cable, Chesnutt, and the Dialectic of Race

1.   Donald Ringe, "'The Double Center': Character and Meaning in Cable's Early Novels," *Studies in the Novel* 5 (Spring 1973): 53. Ringe refers to the term "double center," used in the line from "Café des Exilés": "But, besides these, and many who need no mention, there were two in particular, around whom all the story of the Café des Exilés, of old M. D'Hemecourt and of

Pauline, turns as on a double center. First, Manuel Mazaro ... second ...
'Major' Galahad Shaughnessy." George Washington Cable, "Café des
Exilés," *Old Creole Days,* 1879; rpt. *Creoles and Cajuns: Stories of Old
Louisiana,* ed. Arlin Turner (Garden City, NY: Doubleday, 1959), 150.

2.   Edmund Wilson, P*atriotic Gore: Studies in the Literature of the American
Civil War* (New York: Oxford UP, 1966), 580.

3.   "'Sieur George," Cable's first published short story, appeared in *Scribner's
Monthly* in October 1873; *Doctor Sevier* was published by J. R. Osgood in
1884. Edward King, journalist for *Scribner's,* visited New Orleans in early
1873 to search for materials and writers for the magazine's "The Great South"
series. Articles about the mythical Old South by southern "local color"
writers, including George Washington Cable, Thomas Nelson Page, Joel
Chandler Harris, Grace King, Ruth McEnery Stuart, and Rebecca Harding
Davis, continued to be featured in *Scribner's/Century,* the *Atlantic Monthly,*
and *Lippincott's* for the next twenty years. "The Great South" series and
associated publications marked the interest of the Northeastern publishing
establishment in an era of reconciliation with the South following the
wrenching years of the Civil War. See Arlin Turner, *George W. Cable* (Baton
Rouge, Louisiana State UP, 1966), 52–53, and Thomas Richardson, "Local
Color in Louisiana," in *The History of Southern Literature,* ed. Louis D.
Rubin (Baton Rouge: Louisiana State UP, 1985), 199–208.

4.   Samuel Clemens, *Life on the Mississippi* (1883; New York: Lancer, 1968),
368. The *Picayune* newspaper began publication in New Orleans in 1837 and
continues to the present with slight changes in name over the years. The first
newspaper sold for less than a dime and was named for the Spanish silver
coin, the *picayune,* which was a half real or 6 1/4 cents. The paper was
renamed the *Daily Picayune* in 1937 and joined with *The Times-Democrat* to
become the *Times-Picayune* in 1914. See Thomas Ewing Dabney, *One
Hundred Great Years: The Story of the Times-Picayune from Its Founding to
1940* (Baton Rouge: Louisiana State UP, 1944).

5.   Cable, "My Politics," in *The Negro Question,* ed. Arlin Turner (Garden City,
NY: Doubleday, 1958), 14.

6.   Herbert Spencer, Th*e Study of Sociology* (New York: Appleton, 1882). See
Richard Hofstadter, *Social Darwinism in American Thought,* rev. ed. (Boston:
Beacon, 1955). Hofstadter writes that Spencer's book was first discussed in
the United States in 1872–73. In Hofstadter's words, Spencer argued that "a
science of sociology, by teaching men to think of social causation scientifically, would awaken them to the enormous complexity of the social organism,
and put an end to hasty legislative panaceas" (43).

7.   Hofstadter 95.

8.   Hofstadter 167–68.

9.   Edward Larocque Tinker, "Cable and the Creoles," *American Literature* 5
(1933–34), 316, 325.

10.   "My Politics": 12. A "quadroon" was a racial label which signified that the
person was one-fourth black; an "octoroon" was one-eighth black. See Grace
King, *New Orleans: The Place and the People,* chap. 14.

11. Cable argued for the continuation of integration in the public schools, which
     had begun during Reconstruction, in letters to the editor of the New Orleans
     Bulletin in 1875, the second of which he signed "A Southern White Man." He
     wrote the letters in response to the forcible expulsion of Negro students by a
     mob of white men in December 1874. The school was located in the same
     house where Madame Lalaurie tortured her slaves, which Cable wrote about
     in "The 'Haunted House' in Royal Street" in *Strange True Stories of
     Louisiana,* 1889. See Turner, *The Negro Question* 26–33.
12. Turner, *George W. Cable* 54. The *Code Noir,* or Black Code, was a compila-
     tion of laws which regulated the relations of blacks by whites first in Santo
     Domingo, beginning in 1695, and in Louisiana in 1724, under Governor
     Bienville. See Alice Dunbar-Nelson, "People of Color in Louisiana, Part I,"
     for a general discussion of its major tenets. In relation to "Bibi" and the later
     Bras-Coupé episode of *The Grandissimes,* it is important to know that the
     Code Noir required the execution of a slave who struck his master or one of
     the family "so as to produce a bruise or shedding blood in the face" (142),
     that a runaway slave suffered the penalty of having his ears cut off and being
     branded on his shoulder with a fleur-de-lis; for a second offense, he would be
     hamstrung and branded on the other shoulder, and for a third offense, put to
     death. In "'Tite Poulette" and the later *Madame Delphine,* Cable dealt with
     the *Code Noir*'s forbidding of intermarriage between blacks and whites, or
     "miscegenation."
13. Cable, *Madame Delphine,* 1881; rpt. *Creoles and Cajuns* 193.
14. Lafcadio Hearn, *Fantastics and Other Fancies,* ed. Charles Woodward
     Hutson (Boston and New York: Houghton Mifflin, 1914): 146–47.
15. Cable, "'Tite Poulette," *Old Creole Days,* rpt. *Creoles and Cajuns* 87. All
     subsequent references to "'Tite Poulette" will be from this edition; page
     references will be noted parenthetically in the text.
16. Tinker 321; Dion Boucicault, *The Octoroon, or Life in Louisiana,* in *Plays by
     Dion Boucicault,* ed. Peter Thomson (Cambridge: Cambridge UP, 1984).
17. William Faulkner, *Absalom, Absalom!* (1936; New York: Vintage, 1986),
     138.
18. Alice Hall Petry, *A Genius in His Way: The Art of Cable's Old Creole Days*
     (Rutherford: Fairleigh Dickinson UP, 1988), 111.
19. See Turner, *George W. Cable* 105.
20. Cable, *Madame Delphine* (New York: Scribner's, 1881; rpt *Creoles and
     Cajuns*). All subsequent references to *Madame Delphine* will be from the
     latter edition; page references will be noted parenthetically in the text.
21. Jean Lafitte and his brother Pierre were agents and bankers for the smugglers.
     Barataria is a concourse of islands stretching along the Gulf coast of Louisi-
     ana between the mouth of the Mississippi River and Bayou Lafourche. On
     these islands the privateers deposited their treasures before smuggling them to
     New Orleans. In 1813 Governor Claiborne declared the business piracy and
     offered a $500 reward for the arrest of Jean Lafitte, but Lafitte was pardoned
     for his participation in behalf of the United States at the Battle of New

Orleans in 1815. See Grace King, *New Orleans: The Place and the People* 191–207, and Works Progress Administration, *New Orleans City Guide* 392, 396.

22. Louis D. Rubin, *George Washington Cable: The Life and Times of a Southern Heretic* (New York: Pegasus Western, 1969): 101.

23. Cable, "My Politics" 14.

24. C. Vann Woodward, *The Strange Career of Jim Crow* (1955; New York: Oxford UP, 1964).

25. "Herbert Spencer in America," *Century Magazine* 24 (Sept. 1882): 789.

26. Cable wrote a historical sketch of New Orleans for the census in the spring of 1882, which was later included in the complete *Tenth Census*. Articles, later included in his *The Creoles of Louisiana* (New York: Scribner's, 1884), were published in the *Century Magazine,* Jan.–July 1883. See Turner, *George W. Cable* 109–11.

27. George E. Waring, "George W. Cable," *Century Magazine* 23 (Feb. 1882): 603.

28. Letter of Hjalmar H. Boyesen to George W. Cable, 17 Mar. 1877, in Arlin Turner, "A Novelist Discovers a Novelist: The Correspondence of H. H. Boyesen and George W. Cable," *Western Humanities Review* 5 (Autumn 1951): 346.

29. See Hofstadter's discussion of Herbert Spencer, pp. 30–50, and on William Graham Sumner, pp. 51–65. Also, see William Graham Sumner, *Social Darwinism: Selected Essays* (Englewood Cliffs, NJ: Prentice-Hall, 1963); Richard D. Alexander, Da*rwinism and Human Affairs* (Seattle: U of Washington P, 1979); Alexander Alland, Jr., *Human Nature: Darwin's View* (New York: Columbia UP, 1985); and Robert C. Bannister, *Social Darwinism: Science and Myth in Anglo-American Social Thought* (Philadelphia: Temple UP, 1979).

30. George W. Cable, *The Grandissimes* (1880; New York: Scribner's, 1907), 197. All future references to *The Grandissimes* will be from this edition.

31. See the description of the transfer in Grace King, *New Orleans: The Place and the People* 160–70.

32. King 170.

33. Lafcadio Hearn, *Fantastics and Other Fancies,* ed. Charles Woodward Hutson (Boston: Houghton Mifflin, 1914), 3.

34. John Cleman, "The Art of Local Color in George W. Cable's *The Grandissimes,*" *American Literature* 47 (1975): 396–410.

35. William W. Evans, "Naming Day in Old New Orleans: Charactonyms and Colloquialisms in George Washington Cable's *The Grandissimes* and *Old Creole Days,*" *Names: Journal of the American Name Society* 30 (1982): 186.

36. See Joseph Egan, "Lions Rampant: Agricola Fusilier and Bras-Coupé as Antithetical Doubles in *The Grandissimes,*" *Southern Quarterly* 18 (1980): 74–80, and Violet H. Bryan, "The Image of New Orleans in the Fiction of George Washington Cable and William Faulkner: A Study of Place in Fiction," diss., Harvard U, 1981.

37. Robert O. Stephens, "Cable's Bras-Coupé and Merimée's Tamango: The Case of the Missing Arm," *Mississippi Quarterly* 35 (Fall 1982): 387–405. See also the Marcus Christian Collection, Box 11 of Historical Source Materials, Archives and Manuscripts Department, Earl K. Long Library, University of New Orleans, for a discussion of the sources of the Bras-Coupé legend.

38. Between 1791 and 1794 the Revolution in Santo Domingo led to the immigration of many Santo Domingans to Cuba, and then to New Orleans. According to Alice Dunbar-Nelson, 5,800 people arrived from Cuba in 1809, 4,000 of them *les gens de couleur,* or free people of color; this number later mounted to 10,000, adding substantially to the free Creole of color population in New Orleans. Toussaint l'Ouverture and Jacques Dessalines were leaders of the Revolution. See Alice Dunbar-Nelson, "People of Color in Louisiana, Part I," 152, and Donald Everett, "Free Persons of Color in New Orleans, 1803–1865," diss., Tulane U, 1952. The St. Malô Conspiracy was a part of the abortive slave insurrection of 1795 at Pointe Coupée, near New Orleans, on the plantation of Julian Poydras. See Stephens, "Cable's Bras Coupé" 394.

39. Ringe 54–56.

40. William Bedford Clark, "Cable and the Theme of Miscegenation in *Old Creole Days* and *The Grandissimes,*" *Mississippi Quarterly* 30 (1977): 605.

41. See Blake Touchstone, "Voodoo in New Orleans," *Louisiana History* 13 (Fall 1972): 371–86; Works Progress Administration, *New Orleans City Guide* 56–65; and Robert Tallant, *Voodoo in New Orleans.*

42. John Hope Franklin, *From Slavery to Freedom: A History of the Negro in America,* 3d ed. (New York: Random, 1969), and C. Vann Woodward, *Origins of the New South: 1877–1913* (Baton Rouge: Louisiana State UP, 1951), 159–63.

43. See "Darwinism in Literature," *Galaxy* 15 (1873): 5.

44. Tinker 318–19.

45. Sarah Searight, *New Orleans* (New York: Stein and Day, 1973), 90.

46. George W. Cable, *The Creoles of Louisiana* 220; Searight 83.

47. Joy J. Jackson, *New Orleans in the Gilded Age: Politics and Urban Progress, 1880–96* (Baton Rouge: Louisiana State UP, 1969), 171.

48. See Jackson, *passim.*

49. See Cable, "My Politics" 17–18. Andrew Carnegie, "The Gospel of Wealth," *The Gospel of Wealth and Other Timely Essays* (1889; Cambridge, Mass.: Harvard UP, 1965), 16, 25. Cable had met Carnegie at Richard Gilder's home in October 1883 and later visited him in Scotland in 1898. Carnegie continued their friendship later when Cable moved to Northampton. See Rubin 260, 268, 271.

50. In 1888 Cable started the Open Letter Club in cooperation with Professor William M. Baskervill of Vanderbilt University to provide for the Silent South's written expression and distribution of ideas on matters of race. In distributing his essay "The Negro Question in the United States," he had devised a list of interested southerners, including Charles W. Chesnutt. The

Club was successful in exchanging ideas through correspondence and symposia, but, as attacks on Cable mounted, he felt impelled to end the club early in 1890. See Turner, *George W. Cable* 263–72.

51. George Washington Cable Collection, Special Collections, Howard-Tilton Library, Tulane University; hereafter cited as "GWC."

52. "The Future American," part 2, p. 1, typescript, the Charles Chesnutt Collection, Special Collections, Fisk University Library. All references to manuscripts from this collection, which include Chesnutt's unpublished novels (including "Paul Marchand, F.M.C."), his journals, letters, and manuscripts, both published and unpublished, will be cited hereafter as "CC." "The Future American" was published in *The Boston Transcript* in three installments: "The Future American: What the Race Is Likely to Become in the Process of Time," Aug. 18, 1900; "The Future American: A Stream of Dark Blood in the Veins of the Southern Whites," Aug. 25, 1900; "The Future American: A Complete Race-Amalgamation Likely to Occur," Sept. 1, 1900.

53. Albion Tourgée, *A Fool's Errand* (New York: Fords, Howard and Hulbert, 1879); *Bricks Without Straw* (New York: Fords, Howard and Hulbert, 1886). Tourgée, like Cable, was condemned by southerners for his attitudes on racial equality. An Ohioan, he settled in North Carolina after serving in the Union Army during the Civil War and spending several months in Confederate prisons. See Daniel Aaron, *The Unwritten War* (Madison: U of Wisconsin P, 1987): 193–95.

54. "Paul Marchand, F.M.C.," typescript, 156 pp., CC.

55. Sylvia Lyons Render, *Charles W. Chesnutt* (Boston: Twayne-Hall, 1980).

56. Letter from Chesnutt to Harry C. Block, c/o Alfred Knopf, Inc., June 8, 1928, CC.

57. Helen Chesnutt, *Charles Waddell Chesnutt* (Chapel Hill: U of North Carolina P, 1952): 43–44. Caryn Ann Bell, "Critics of the Color Line: George W. Cable and Charles W. Chesnutt," M.A. thesis, U of New Orleans, 1979: 39.

58. See Turner, *George W. Cable* 265.

59. Correspondence between Cable and Chesnutt, CC. In the letter of Feb. 20, 1897 Chesnutt wrote to Cable to inform him that *The Atlantic Monthly* had accepted two of the stories that he had sent them for early publication. "One is 'The Wife of His Youth,' which I read to you last winter; it has an additional character, however, in connection with which I found the life-giving touch which I suspect made the story go. The other I did not mention to you, but I am sure you will like it."

60. "The Freedman's Case in Equity," in Arlin Turner, ed., *The Negro Question* 71. The essay was first published in *Century*, Jan. 1885, and later in *The Silent South.*

61. "The Silent South" in Turner, ed., *The Negro Question* 23. Also quoted in Bell 14.

62. Editorial, *Nashville Daily American,* Dec. 31, 1889. Also see Bell 58.

63. See Rubin 206–11.

64. de Tocqueville, *Democracy in America* 1: 72.

65.   "The Future American: A Stream of Dark Blood in the Veins of the Southern Whites" 1, CC.

66.   Cable, "The Negro Question in the United States," London *Contemporary Review* 53 (Mar. 1888): 443–68; New York *Tribune* and Chicago *Inter-Ocean*, Mar. 4, 1888. See incomplete typescript of "An Inside View of the Negro Question," CC. Correspondence between Cable and Chesnutt, CC and GWC. Letter from Gilder to Cable also quoted in Bell 45.

67.   Chesnutt, "What Is a White Man?" *The Independent* 30 (May 1889).

68.   "The Future American: A Stream of Dark Blood in the Veins of the Southern Whites" 4, CC.

69.   W. E. B. DuBois, "The Conservation of Races," a paper delivered to the American Negro Academy in the year it was founded, 1897, as quoted by Anthony Appiah, "The Uncompleted Argument: DuBois and the Illusion of Race," *Critical Inquiry* 12 (Autumn 1985): 21–36; rpt. *"Race," Writing and Difference* (Chicago: U of Chicago P, 1986).

70.   "The Future American: A Stream of Dark Blood" 8, CC.

71.   See Brenda Marie Osbey, "Faubourg Tremé: Community in Transition, Part 2: Solidifying the Community," The New Orleans *Tribune,* 7.1 (Jan. 1991): 12–14 concerning the damaging influence of the *Plessy v. Ferguson* decision on the spirit of the black New Orleans community.

72.   "Paul Marchand, F.M.C.," typescript, CC, 23. All future references will be from this manuscript, with page notations in text.

73.   Sylvia Lyons Render, *The Short Fiction of Charles W. Chesnutt* (Washington, DC: Howard UP, 1974), 3–4.

74.   Edward Larocque Tinker, To*ucoutou* (New York: Dodd, Mead, 1928). For a discussion of the historical court case, see Rodolphe Lucien Desdunes, *Nos Hommes et Notre Histoire* (1911), rpt. *Our People and Our History* 61–64.

75.   Render, *Short Fiction of Charles W. Chesnutt* 15.

76.   Cable, *The Grandissimes* 219.

77.   Chesnutt, "An Insider's View of the Negro Question," typescript, 14, CC.

78.   "Address to the Bethel Literary and Historical Association," n.d., CC.

79.   Chesnutt, "Post-Bellum, Pre-Harlem," *The Crisis* 40 (June 1931): 194.

3. Defining Race, Gender, and the Myth: King, Chopin, and Dunbar-Nelson

1.   Larzer Ziff, *The American 1890s: Life and Times of a Lost Generation* (New York: Viking, 1966), 277–304; Henry James, *The Bostonians* (1886; New York: Random House, 1956).

2.   Augusta Jane Evans, *Macaria* (1863; New York: Dillingham, 1887).

3.   Violet Harrington Bryan, "Frances Joseph-Gaudet, Black Philanthropist," *Sage: A Scholarly Journal on Black Women* 3.1 (Spring 1986): 46–49; Paula Giddings, *When and Where I Enter: The Impact of Black Women on Race and Sex in America* (New York: Bantam, 1984), 95–134; Gerda Lerner, *Black Women in White America: A Documentary History* (New York: Vintage,

1973), 437–575; Jill Conway, "Women Reformers and American Culture, 1870–1900," *Journal of Social History*, 5 (Winter 1971–72): 164–77.

4.   Blassingame 133, 146.

5.   Bettina Aptheker, *Woman's Legacy: Essays on Race, Sex, and Class in American History* (Amherst: U of Massachusetts P, 1982), 55–57.

6.   Aptheker 63.

7.   Grace King, "Monsieur Motte," *New Princeton Review*, Apr. 1886; *Monsieur Motte* (New York, 1888). Grace King recounts the conversation about Cable with Gilder in Grace King, *Memories of a Southern Woman of Letters* (New York: Macmillan, 1932), 60.

8.   Grace King to Fred Lewis Pattee, Jan. 19, 1915; quoted in Robert Bush, ed., *Grace King of New Orleans* (Baton Rouge: Louisiana State UP, 1973), 398, and Robert Bush, *Grace King: A Southern Destiny* (Baton Rouge: Louisiana State UP, 1983), 51.

9.   On King's early life and education, see Bush, *Grace King: A Southern Destiny*, chaps. 1–2.

10. King, *New Orleans: The Place and the People* xxi.

11. King, *New Orleans: The Place and the People* 68; see also Herbert Asbury, *French Quarter* (New York: Knopf, 1936), 7–8. Asbury refers to the Mississippi Company's immigration of *correction girls*, inmates from a Parisian house of correction, as well as the *filles à la cassette*, or *casket girls*, but, he notes sarcastically, no Louisiana family ever traced its ancestry back to the correction girls.

12. Grace King, *New Orleans: The Place and the People* 310.

13. Helen Taylor, *Gender, Race, and Region in the Writings of Grace King, Ruth McEnery Stuart, and Kate Chopin* (Baton Rouge: Louisiana State UP, 1989), 79–80.

14. Clara Juncker, "The Mother's Balcony: Grace King's Discourse of Femininity," *New Orleans Review* 15 (Spring 1988): 39–46.

15. Anne Goodwyn Jones, *Tomorrow Is Another Day: The Woman Writer in the South, 1859–1936* (Baton Rouge: Louisiana State UP, 1981), 127.

16. Grace King, *Balcony Stories* (1892; rpt. Ridgewood, NJ: Gregg, 1968), 2. Quotations from B*alcony Stories* are all taken from this edition; page notations will be given parenthetically in the text.

17. Clifford Geertz, "Ideology as a Cultural System," *The Interpretation of Cultures* (New York: Basic Books, 1973), 204.

18. King, "Bonne Maman," *Harper's New Monthly Magazine*, July 1886. Also appears in *Tales of a Time and Place* (New York: Macmillan, 1892). Quotations from stories of *Tales of a Time and Place* will be taken from this edition; page notations will be given parenthetically in the text.

19. Louis Armstrong was born in "Back-o'-town," which he described as "one of the four great sections into which the city is divided. The others are Uptown, Downtown and Front-o'-town, and each of these quarters has its own little traits." Armstrong, *Satchmo: My Life in New Orleans* (1954; Dacapo, 1986). Also, see Robert Tallant, *Mrs. Candy and Saturday Night* (Garden City, NY:

Doubleday, 1947); Mrs. Candy's house was on Cairo Street in "Back of
town," in general, the area around Lake Pontchartrain; "Front of town" was
the area near the Mississippi River.

20.   M. M. Bakhtin, "Discourse and the Novel," The *Dialogic Imagination,* trans.
Caryl Emerson and Michael Holquist (Austin: U of Texas P, 1981), 262. The
dialogically interrelated "double discourse" that characterizes the novel works
as a conversation between the various voices in the work (*heteroglossia*)
(324). See also Robert Bush, *Grace King: A Southern Destiny* 95–96. Bush
discusses the structure of *Monsieur Motte* as a musical composition, as "four
parts of a sonata." Clara Juncker discusses the "Cixousian chaosmos" of
King's writing: "the groping, rhythmic, repetitive, musical, and excessive
writing establishes an affective economy of femininity," 45.

21.   Bush, *A Southern Destiny* 105.

22.   See Bush, *A Southern Destiny* 61.

23.   King, "Bonne Maman," *Harper's New Monthly Magazine,* July 1886: 305.

24.   Deborah E. McDowell, introd., *Passing* and *Quicksand* by Nella Larsen (New
Brunswick: Rutgers UP, 1987), xii. McDowell states: "It is well known that
during slavery the white slave master constructed an image of black female
sexuality which shifted responsibility for his own sexual passions onto his
female slaves. They, not he, had wanton, insatiable desires that he was
powerless to resist. The image did not end with emancipation. So persistent
was it that black club women devoted part of their first national conference in
July 1895 to addressing it."

25.   For a detailed discussion of All Saints' Day, see Federal Writers' Project of
the Works Progress Administration, *New Orleans City Guide* (Boston:
Houghton Mifflin, 1938), 186–89.

26.   King, "Bayou l'Ombre," *Monsieur Motte* 25.

27.   Palmyre in both Cable's novel and King's story are passionate, violent
women of color. Cable was probably familiar with Palmyra, the ancient
Syrian city, which, under Septimus Odenathus and his widow, Zenobia,
became a powerful center of Roman military strength, but was defeated and
destroyed in A.D. 274 when Zenobia tried to seize land from the Roman
emperors and extend her power.

28.   King, "The Little Convent Girl," *Century* (1893); rpt. *Balcony Stories.*

29.   Bush, *A Southern Destiny* 152.

30.   Jones, *Tomorrow* 123.

31.   Emily Toth, *Kate Chopin* (New York: William Morrow, 1990), 124.

32.   Toth 134–36.

33.   "A Lady of Bayou St. John" was written Aug. 24–25 and published in *Vogue*
of Sept. 21, 1893, and "La Belle Zoraïde" was written on Sept. 21, 1893 and
published in *Vogue* of Jan. 4, 1894. Both were published in *Bayou Folk,* 1894.

34.   Kate Chopin, *The Complete Works,* ed. Per Seyersted (Baton Rouge:
Louisiana State UP, 1969). All future references to the works of Kate Chopin
will be to this edition.

35.   Joyce Coyne Dyer, "Techniques of Distancing in the Fiction of Kate Chopin,"
Southern Studies 24 (Spring 1985): 69–81.

36.   See Dale M. Bauer, *Feminist Dialogics: A Theory of Failed Community* (Albany: State U of New York at Albany P, 1988), 130.

37.   Bauer 143.

38.   Patricia Hopkins Lattin, "Childbirth and Motherhood in *The Awakening* and in 'Athénaise,'" *Approaches to Teaching Chopin's The Awakening,* ed. Bernard Koloski (New York: MLA, 1988), 41.

39.   Geertz 204.

40.   Suzanne W. Jones, "Place, Perception and Identity in *The Awakening,*" *The Southern Quarterly* 25 (Winter 1987): 118.

41.   Chopin commented on Cable's racial themes in her diary on May 12, 1894: "I read Mrs Hull's story through this morning. It is upon the theme which Cable has used effectively. A girl with negro blood who is loved by a white man. . . . I have no objection to a commonplace theme if it be handled artistically or with originality"; Per Seyersted, ed., *A Kate Chopin Miscellany* 90.

42.   Alice Dunbar-Nelson, *Violets and Other Tales* (Boston: Monthly Review P, 1895), and The Good*ness of St. Rocque and Other Stories* (New York: Dodd, Mead, 1899).

43.   Vernon Loggins, *The Negro Author: His Development in America to 1900* (Port Washington, NY: Kennikat, 1964), 364.

44.   Alice Dunbar-Nelson, "People of Color in Louisiana, Part I," J*ournal of Negro History* (Jan. 1916): 361–76; "People of Color in Louisiana, Part II," *Journal of Negro History* (Jan. 1917): 51–78. The essay is reprinted in R. Ora Williams, *An Alice Dunbar-Nelson Reader* (Washington, DC: UP of America, 1978); all references to the essay hereafter will be from this edition.

45.   Alice Dunbar-Nelson, "People of Color in Louisiana, Part I" 143–44.

46.   Charles Étienne Arthur Gayarré, Hi*story of Louisiana.* 4 vols. (New Orleans: Hansel and Brothers, 1903); Grace King, *New Orleans: The Place and the People.*

47.   Rodolphe Lucien Desdunes, *Nos Hommes et Notre Histoire,* rpt. *Our People and Our History,* trans. Sister Dorothea McCants.

48.   Gloria T. Hull, "Shaping Contradictions: Alice Dunbar-Nelson and the Black Creole Experience," *New Orleans Review* 5 (Spring 1988): 34–35; Hull, ed., *Give Us Each Day: The Diary of Alice Dunbar-Nelson* (New York: W. W. Norton, 1984), 297.

49.   Dunbar-Nelson's address while a student at Straight College (now Dillard University) is listed in her university records in the archives, Dillard University.

50.   *Give Us Each Day* 122–23.

51.   Alice Dunbar-Nelson, "Brass Ankles," in *The Works of Alice Dunbar-Nelson,* ed. Gloria T. Hull, Schomburg Library of Nineteenth-Century Black Women Writers (New York: Oxford UP, 1988), vol. 2: 311; "The Stones of the Village," 3: 3–33. All future references to the works of Dunbar-Nelson, except for "The People of Color in Louisiana, Parts I and II," will be from the three-volume Oxford edition; page notations will be given in the text. The term "Brass Ankles" was taken from the poem by that name by Edward Clarkson Adams in his book Nig*ger to Nigger* (New York: Scribners, 1928).

See the Marcus Christian Collection, Archives and Manuscripts Department, Earl K. Long Library of the University of New Orleans.

52. Virginia Cunningham, *Paul Laurence Dunbar and His Song* (New York: Biblo and Tanner, 1969), 123.

53. June 25, 1895. All correspondence mentioned in the text is from *The Paul L. Dunbar Papers,* ed. Sara S. Fuller, Ohio Historical Society, Columbus, microfilm ed., 1972.

54. Paul Laurence Dunbar, *Clorindy, or the Origin of the Cakewalk.* Music by Will Cook (New York: Witmark Music Publisher, 1898).

55. Kate Chopin, *The Complete Works* 952.

56. For a detailed history of Henriette Delille and the founding of the Sisters of the Holy Family, see Sister Audrey Marie Detiege, *Henriette Delille, Free Woman of Color: Foundress of the Sisters of the Holy Family* (New Orleans: Sisters of the Holy Family, 1976).

57. Evans, *Macaria.* Excerpt reprinted in "'Married Belles'—What a Woman Says," New Orleans *Tribune,* Mar. 29, 1865.

58. Eleanor Whiting, "Women's Work and Wages," *Lippincott's Magazine,* May 22, 1898: 676.

59. "The Decision," typescript, written between 1902 and 1909, published in *The Works of Alice Dunbar-Nelson,* ed. Gloria T. Hull, 196. "No Sacrifice" was written some time between 1928 and 1931; it is also published in *The Works of Alice Dunbar-Nelson,* 203–31. The Paul L. Dunbar figure in this story was named Gerald Kennedy.

60. For a detailed discussion of the Black Women's Club Movement, see Paula Giddings, *When and Where I Enter: The Impact of Black Women on Race and Sex in America* (Toronto: Bantam, 1984), particularly her description of the search for identity by three writers of this period: Jessie Fauset, Nella Larsen, and Zora Neale Hurston, 189–93.

61. See *Give Us Each Day* for biographical details.

62. *Give Us Each Day* 382. Lynching of African Americans continued to abound in 1930 when Dunbar-Nelson wrote about Russ in her diary (Aug. 22, 1923).

63. "The Stones of the Village," published for the first time in *The Works of Alice Dunbar-Nelson* 3: 3–32. "The Pearl in the Oyster," *The Southern Workman,* 1900; rpt. *The Works of Alice Dunbar-Nelson* 3: 51–64. Hull discusses the two stories in "Shaping Contradictions."

64. Gloria T. Hull, *Color, Sex, and Poetry: Three Women Writers of the Harlem Renaissance* (Bloomington: Indiana UP, 1987), 19.

65. Charles Dudley Warner, "New Orleans," *Harper's New Monthly Magazine,* 74 (Dec. 1886): 90.

66. Dunbar-Nelson, "April Is On the Way," *Ebony and Topaz* (1927): 52; rpt. *The Works of Alice Dunbar-Nelson,* vol. 2.

67. Allie Miller Hubert, member of the Delta Sigma Theta Sorority, wrote in a letter to Marcus Christian on March 24, 1971: "May I project my opinion that she did not have so much of the French Culture background nor Paul Laurence Dunbar so much of the plantation . . . traditions as expressed in his

writings." Marcus Christian Collection, Archives and Manuscripts Collection, Earl K. Long Library of the University of New Orleans.

68. Gloria T. Hull, introd., *The Works of Alice Dunbar-Nelson* xxix. The subject of black women's writing during the Harlem Renaissance is discussed in Gloria T. Hull, "Afro-American Women Poets: A Bio-Critical Survey," *Shakespeare's Sisters: Feminist Essays on Women Poets,* ed. Sandra M. Gilbert and Susan Gubar (Bloomington: Indiana UP, 1979); Hull, *Color, Sex, and Poetry*; and Deborah E. McDowell, introd., *Quicksand* and *Passing* by Nella Larsen. Deborah E. McDowell points out that "even in [Nella] Larsen's day, the Freudian 1920s, the Jazz Age of sexual abandon and 'free love'—when female sexuality, in general, was acknowledged and commercialized in the advertising, beauty, and fashion industries—black women's novels preserve their reticence about sexuality. . . . Jessie Fauset and Nella Larsen could only hint at the idea of black women as sexual subjects behind the safe and protective covers of traditional narrative subjects and conventions" (xiii).

69. Hélène Cixous, "The Laugh of the Medusa," *Signs: Journal of Women in Culture and Society* 1.4 (1976): 875–93.

4. The Double-Dealer *Movement and New Orleans as Courtesan in Faulkner's* Mosquitoes *and* Absalom, Absalom!

1. James K. Feibleman, "Literary New Orleans Between World Wars," *The Southern Review* 1 NS (July 1965): 702.

2. Feibleman 702.

3. See Malcolm Bradbury, "The Cities of Modernism," in *Modernism, 1890–1930,* ed. Malcolm Bradbury and James McFarlane (New Jersey: Humanities P, 1978), 96–104, for a discussion of the relationship between the literature of experimental modernism and the life of modern cities. As "culture capitals" of modernism, he cites Berlin, Vienna, Moscow, St. Petersburg, London, Zurich, New York, and Chicago.

4. H. L. Mencken, "The Sahara of the Bozart," Prej*udices: Second Series,* 1917, rpt. in *Prejudices: A Selection,* ed. James T. Farrell (New York: Vintage, 1958), 70, 79.

5. Thomas Daniel Young, "The Fugitives: Ransom, Davidson, Tate," in *The History of Southern Literature,* ed. Louis D. Rubin, Jr. (Baton Rouge: Louisiana State UP, 1985), 319–32.

6. Editorial, *The Double Dealer* 1 (Jan. 1921).

7. James G. Watson, "New Orleans, *The Double Dealer,* and 'New Orleans,'" *American Literature* 56 (May 1984): 214–26.

8. Sherwood Anderson, "New Orleans, *The Double Dealer,* and the Modern Movement in America" 3 (Mar. 1922): 126.

9.   David Cohn, review of *Darkwater* by W. E. B. DuBois, *The Double Dealer* 1 (June 1921): 254.

10.   John McClure, review of *Cane* by Jean Toomer, *The Double Dealer* 6 (Jan. 1924): 26–27.

11.   Joseph Hilton Smyth, review of *The Weary Blues* by Langston Hughes, *The Double Dealer* 8 (May 1926): 358.

12.   Hart Crane, "Black Tambourine," *The Double Dealer* 1 (June 1921): 232; William Faulkner, "Carcassonne," in *Collected Stories* (New York: Random House, 1934).

13.   Warner Berthoff, *Hart Crane: A Re-Introduction* (Minneapolis: U of Minnesota P, 1989): 114. Hart Crane, *White Buildings: Poems by Hart Crane* (New York: Boni and Liveright, 1926).

14.   See Sterling Brown, *The Negro in American Fiction and Negro Poetry and Drama,* 1937; rpt. *Negro Poetry and Drama and the Negro in American Fiction* (New York: Atheneum, 1978). Brown remarks on an increase in sociological realism among southern writers about Negro subjects, beginning with T. S. Stribling's *Birthright* (1922); however, he laments the continued use of Negro stereotypes by many of them. For example, he notes Roark Bradford's limited view of blacks. "His Negroes are nothing but easy-come, easy-go children, creatures of laughter and of song."

15.   Robert Bush, *Grace King: A Southern Destiny* (Baton Rouge: Louisiana State UP, 1983); William Faulkner and William Spratling, *Sherwood Anderson and Other Famous Creoles* (New Orleans, 1926; Austin: U of Texas P, 1966); Joseph Blotner, *Faulkner: A Biography,* vol. 1 (New York: Random, 1974); Carvel Collins, ed., *Helen: A Courtship and Mississippi Poems* (Tulane U and Yoknapatawpha P, 1981); Carvel Collins, ed., The *Creole Sketches of William Faulkner*; Works Progress Administration, *New Orleans City Guide*; and Violet Harrington Bryan, "The Image of New Orleans in the Fiction of George Washington Cable and William Faulkner: A Study of Place in Fiction."

16.   Editorial, "The Ephemeral Sex," *The Double Dealer* 1 (Mar. 1921): 85.

17.   Editorial, "Burning Question," *The Double Dealer* 1 (May 1921): 173.

18.   Editorial, "The Dominant Petticoat," *The Double Dealer* 1 (June 1921): 218.

19.   See Susan Gilbert and Sandra Gubar, *No Man's Land,* vol. 1 (New Haven: Yale UP, 1988), and Anne Goodwyn Jones, "Gone with the Wind and Others: Popular Fiction, 1920–1950," *The History of Southern Literature,* eds. Louis D. Rubin et al. (Baton Rouge: Louisiana State UP, 1985), 363–74.

20.   Sherwood Anderson, "New Orleans, *The Double Dealer* and the Modern Movement in America" 126.

21.   William Faulkner, *New Orleans Sketches,* ed. Carvel Collins (New York: Random, 1958).

22.   See John N. Duvall, "Faulkner's Critics and Women: The Voice of the Community," in *Faulkner and Women,* ed. Doreen Fowler and Ann J. Abadie (Oxford: UP of Mississippi): 41–57. Duvall argues that many of Faulkner's critics have not been attentive to the author's ideological use of language; he

refers to the Bakhtin/Volosinov definition of language as the fundamental object in the study of ideologies (*Marxism and the Philosophy of Language,* 1929, by V. N. Volosinov, with collaboration by M. M. Bakhtin).

23. In his image of New Orleans as courtesan, Faulkner projects the etymological associations of the word as a woman attached to the court (from the Italian *cortegiano, cortegiana*). In the *Oxford English Dictionary,* 1989, the quotations included reflect the complexity of the term, which refers both to the strumpet, or woman of pleasure, and the woman of sophistication and tradition: cf. J. H. Blunt, 1868: "The ambitious courtesan who now ruled the King"; Ebsworth, 1880: "We might have shown the Courtezanship, not only of Stuart times, but also during the reign of the Virgin Queen."

24. David Weimer, *The City as Metaphor* (New York: Random, 1966), 1–14.

25. For informed descriptions of the New Orleans scene during the birth of jazz, see Louis Armstrong, *Satchmo: My Life in New Orleans*; Frederick Turner, *Remembering Song: Encounters with the New Orleans Jazz Tradition* (New York: Viking, 1982); Allan Lomax, *Jelly Roll.* Ted Gioia, *The Imperfect Art: Reflections on Jazz and Modern Culture* (New York: Oxford UP, 1987), points out correspondences between jazz form and production and the form and production of modern literature and art.

26. See Herbert Asbury, *The French Quarter* (New York: Alfred A. Knopf, 1936), 264–95; Lyle Saxon, *Fabulous New Orleans.*

27. Collins, introd., *New Orleans Sketches* xxvi.

28. Frederick L. Gwynn, "Faulkner's Prufrock—And Other Observations," *Journal of English and Germanic Philosophy* 52 (1953): 60–70.

29. Blotner 29.

30. Wisdom Collection, No. 198, Special Collections, Howard-Tilton Library, Tulane University.

31. See Cleanth Brooks, *William Faulkner: Toward Yoknapatawpha and Beyond* (New Haven: Yale UP, 1978); Carvel Collins, introd., *Helen: A Courtship*; Bryan, "The Image of New Orleans in the Works of George Washington Cable and William Faulkner."

32. William Faulkner, *Mosquitoes* (1927; New York: Washington Square P, 1985), 14. All quotations from Mosq*uitoes* will be from this edition, hereafter cited parenthetically in the text.

33. Brooks, *William Faulkner: Toward Yoknapatawpha and Beyond* 120–21.

34. William Faulkner, *Absalom, Absalom!* (1936; New York: Vintage, 1986): 123, 134. All quotations from the novel will be from this edition; hereafter page notations will be cited parenthetically in the text.

35. The contrast between Charles Bon and Clytie is symbolized by the change that Clytie makes immediately in Charles Valery St. Étienne's clothes on bringing the young boy back to Sutpen's Hundred from New Orleans. She covered his Fauntleroy suit, "the delicate garments of his pagehood," with the "harsh and shapeless denim cut to an iron pattern and sold by the millions— that burlesque uniform and regalia of the tragic burlesque of the sons of Ham" (246). See Elizabeth S. Muhlenfeld, "Shadows with Substance and Ghosts

Exhumed: The Women in Absalom, Absalom!" Mississippi Quarterly 25 (Summer 1972): 289–304.

36.   See Monroe K. Spears, *Dionysus and the City: Modernism in Twentieth-Century Poetry* (New York: Oxford UP, 1970), 93–104, and Malcolm Bradbury, "The Cities of Modernism," in *Modernism, 1890–1930,* ed. Malcolm Bradbury and James McFarlane (New Jersey: Humanities P, 1978), 96–104.

37.   Compare with Walker Percy's version of the creation myth in Love in the Ruins, which is discussed in chap. 5. See also Gary Harrington, *Faulkner's Fables of Creativity: The Yoknapatawpha Novels* (Athens: U of Georgia P, 1990).

38.   Joseph Blotner, *Faulkner: A Biography* (New York: Random, 1974), vol. 1: 93–94; Osbert Burdett, *The Beardsley Period: An Essay in Perspective* (London: Bodley, 1925).

39.   Brooks, *William Faulkner: Toward Yoknapatawpha and Beyond* 317.

40.   See Nancy Blake, "Creation and Procreation: The Voice and the Name, or Biblical Intertextuality in *Absalom, Absalom!*" in *Intertextuality in Faulkner,* ed. Michael Gresset and Noel Polk (Jackson: UP of Mississippi, 1985): 128–42.

5. Shaping Patterns of Myth and Folklore: The Federal Writers' Projects

1.   Lyle Saxon's other books include four romantic histories, *Father Mississippi* (1927), *Old Louisiana* (1928), *Fabulous New Orleans* (1929), and *Lafitte the Pirate* (1930), and the novel *Children of Strangers* (1937).

2.   Marcus Christian was acknowledged in the preface of *Gumbo Ya-Ya* (1945) for his contributions, though not listed as an editor: "Marcus B. Christian, who was Supervisor of the all-Negro Writers' Project, also contributed to the book, as did Edmund Burke." Other African Americans were mentioned: Joseph Louis Gilmore (valet of Lyle Saxon), Charles Barthelemy Rousseve, author of *The Negro in Louisiana* (New Orleans: Xavier UP, 1937), Albert W. Dent, president of Dillard University, and Sister Anastasia of the Convent of the Holy Family—ironically listed in that order (vii). Editors of *Gumbo Ya-Ya,* listed on the title page, were Lyle Saxon, Edward Dreyer, and Robert Tallant. Christian published *I Am New Orleans,* a long poem, separately, in 1968 and 1976.

3.   Lyle Saxon, *The Friends of Joe Gilmore* (New York: Hastings House, 1948), 134.

4.   Cathy Chance Harvey, "Lyle Saxon: A Portrait in Letters, 1917–1945," diss., Tulane U, 1980: 67–76.

5.   Faulkner and Spratling, *Sherwood Anderson and Other Famous Creoles* (New Orleans, 1926).

6. James W. Thomas, "Lyle Saxon's Struggle with *Children of Strangers,*" *Southern Studies 16 (Spring 1990)*: 27–40.

7. See François Mignon, *Plantation Memo: Plantation Life in Louisiana 1750–1970,* ed. Ora Garland Williams (Baton Rouge: Claitor's, 1972); Oliver Ford III, "Ada Jack Carver: A Critical Biography," diss., U of Connecticut, 1975; and the Marcus Christian Collection, the Archives and Manuscript Department of the Earl K. Long Library, University of New Orleans.

8. Donald M. Lawson, "Caroline Dormon: A Renaissance Spirit of Twentieth-Century Louisiana," *Louisiana History* 24 (Spring 1983): 121–39.

9. Ford, "Ada Jack Carver" x. Cammie Henry kept over a hundred large scrapbooks of Louisiana writers and artists who participated in the Melrose coterie until her death in 1948; the material is now housed at Northwestern University, Natchitoches, Louisiana.

10. Quoted in Cathy Chance Harvey, "Dear Lyle/Sherwood Anderson," *Southern Studies* 18 (Fall 1979): 336.

11. Harvey, "Dear Lyle/Sherwood Anderson" 336–37.

12. Donald M. Lawson, "Caroline Dormon: A Renaissance Spirit of Twentieth-Century Louisiana," *Louisiana History* 24 (Spring 1983): 123.

13. Lyle Saxon, *Children of Strangers* (New Orleans: Robert Crager, 1937), 231. All subsequent references will be to this edition; page numbers noted parenthetically in text.

14. Saxon, *Children of Strangers* 272.

15. Robert Tallant, "My Fabulous Friend—Lyle Saxon," *Times-Picayune,* Magazine Section, Nov. 21, 1948.

16. Harvey 354.

17. Marcus B. Christian Collection, the Archives and Manuscripts Department of the Earl K. Long Library of the University of New Orleans. All unpublished manuscripts, source material, correspondence, and poetry of Marcus Christian will be found in the UNO Archives, hereafter cited as "MCC."

18. MCC.

19. MCC.

20. Biographical data from MCC.

21. There are 1,175 poems in the MCC; see also Joseph Logsdon, "Marcus Bruce Christian," *A Dictionary of Louisiana Biography,* ed. Glenn R. Conrad, (New Orleans: Louisiana Historical Association, 1988), vol. 1: 1778–79.

22. Arna Bontemps, "Why I Returned Home," in *Black Voices: An Anthology of Afro-American Literature,* ed. Abraham Chapman (New York: New American Library, 1968), 321–31.

23. James B. LaFourche, "Lyle Saxon Passes," *Louisiana Weekly,* Apr. 20, 1946; Logsdon 1778–79.

24. Robert Tallant, *Voodoo in New Orleans* (1946; Gretna, LA: Pelican, 1974), and *The Voodoo Queen: A Novel* (1956; Gretna, LA: 1983.

25. John W. Blassingame acknowledges Marcus Christian as an important resource in writing his *Black New Orleans 1860–1880* (Chicago: U of Chicago P), 1973. See his preface.

26.   MCC. Christian's determination to reconstruct the histories by adding the contributions of blacks presages the current thinking behind the work of Henry Louis Gates and others to reform the canon of American literature.

27.   Armand Lanusse, Les Cenelles, (1845); Robert Tallant, *The Romantic New Orleanians* (New York: Dutton, 1950), 289.

28.   MCC.

29.   MCC; also *Phylon* 7.3 (1946).

30.   Tallant, *Voodoo in New Orleans* 4.

31.   MCC.

32.   MCC.

33.   Tallant, *Voodoo in New Orleans* 17.

34.   Tallant, *Voodoo in New Orleans* 28–29.

35.   Lafcadio Hearn, "The Last of the Voudous," *Harper's Weekly,* Nov. 7, 1885; C. D. Warner, *Studies in the South and West*; Tallant, *Voodoo in New Orleans* 32; Ishmael Reed, *The Last Days of Louisiana Red* (New York: Random, 1974).

36.   Helene d'Aquin, *Souvenirs d'Amerique et de France Par Une Creole* (Paris: Perisse Frères, 1882).

37.   Henry C. Castellanos, *New Orleans As It Was: Episodes of Louisiana Life* (1895; 2d ed. New Orleans: L. Graham, 1905); William G. Nott, "Marie Leveau, Long High Priestess of Voodooism in New Orleans," *Times-Picayune,* Nov. 19, 1922; Lyle Saxon, *Fabulous New Orleans* (New York: Century, 1929); MCC.

38.   Zora Neale Hurston, *Mules and Men,* foreword by Arnold Rampersad (New York: Harper and Row, 1935), xviii, 183.

39.   MCC.

40.   MCC.

41.   MCC.

42.   Hurston, *Mules and Men* 193.

43.   MCC.

44.   George Washington Cable, "Creole Slave Songs," *Century Magazine* 31 (Apr. 1886): 807–28.

45.   MCC, n.d.

46.   "Lagniappe," *Times-Picayune,* Mar. 20, 1956; MCC.

47.   Roark Bradford, *Ol' Man Adam an' His Chillun: Being the Tales They Tell about the Time When the Lord Walked the Earth Like a Natural Man* (New York: Harper & Brothers, 1928); Roark Bradford, *John Henry* (New York: Harper & Brothers, 1931).

48.   MCC; James Cloyd Bowman, *John Henry: The Rambling Black Ulysses* (Chicago: Albert Whitman and Co., 1942).

49.   MCC.

50.   MCC.

51.   MCC.

52.   MCC.

53.   The word *zigaboo* was resurrected in Spike Lee's movie *School Daze* (1988).

54.   Langston Hughes, "The Negro Artist and the Racial Mountain," in *Black*

Expression, ed. Addison Gayle, Jr. (New York: Weybright and Talley, 1969), 263.

55. Margaret Walker, *For My People* (1940); rpt. *This Is My Century: New and Collected Poems* (Athens: U of Georgia P, 1989). Walker was born in New Orleans and spends a good deal of time in the city. She was also involved with the New Orleans Negro Writers' Project. In New Orleans at the beginning of her career, she met Langston Hughes, who encouraged her to continue her writing.

56. Tom Dent considers Christian to have been one of his mentors; as the son of Dillard University's president, Albert W. Dent, he found himself regularly in the university's library studying and talking with Christian. Brenda Marie Osbey also knew Christian personally and was influenced and encouraged by him as a poet; personal interviews with the author.

6. Abstractions of Time and Place: Williams and Percy

1. Tennessee Williams, *Memoirs* (Doubleday, 1975): 1–4; W. Kenneth Holditch, "The Last Frontier of Bohemia: Tennessee Williams in New Orleans, 1938–1983," *Mississippi Quarterly* 23 (2): 1–37.

2. Tennessee Williams, *27 Wagons Full of Cotton and Other One-Act Plays* (Norfolk, Conn.: New Directions, 1945); *One Arm and Other Stories* (Norfolk, Conn.: New Directions, 1948).

3. Williams, "The Lady of Larkspur Lotion," *27 Wagons* 69.

4. See Thomas J. Richardson, "The City of Day and the City of Night: New Orleans and the Exotic Unreality of Tennessee Williams," *Tennessee Williams: A Tribute,* ed. Jac Tharpe (Jackson: UP of Mississippi, 1977), 634.

5. Richardson 635.

6. Williams, "One Arm" in *Collected Stories,* ed. Gore Vidal (New York: New Directions, 1985), 175.

7. "One Arm" 188.

8. Williams, "The Angel in the Alcove," *Collected Stories* 121.

9. *Collected Stories* 123.

10. Richardson 633.

11. The apartment was the residence of Dick Orme. Williams, *Memoirs* 109–11.

12. Williams, *A Streetcar Named Desire* (New York: New American Library, 1947), 13. All future references will be to this edition of the play; page notations will be noted parenthetically in the text. The set directions read: "You can almost feel the warm breath of the brown river beyond the river warehouses with their faint redolences of bananas and coffee. A corresponding air is evoked by the music of Negro entertainers at a barroom around the corner. In this part of New Orleans you are practically always just around the corner ... from a tinny piano being played with the infatuated fluency of brown fingers. This 'Blue Piano' expresses the spirit of the life which goes on here."

13.   Robert Tallant, *Mrs. Candy and Saturday Night* (Garden City, NY: Doubleday, 1947), 84–85.

14.   John M. Roderick, "From 'Tarantula Arms' to 'Della Robbia Blue': The Tennessee Williams Tragicomic Transit Authority," in T*ennessee Williams's* A Streetcar Named Desire: *Modern Critical Interpretations,* ed. Harold Bloom (New York: Chelsea House, 1988), 99.

15.   Milly S. Barranger, "New Orleans as Theatrical Image in Plays by Tennessee Williams," *Southern Quarterly* 23.2 (1985): 40.

16.   See Gilbert Debusscher, 'Minting Their Separate Wills': Tennessee Williams and Hart Crane," in *Tennessee Williams: Modern Critical Views* (New York: Chelsea House, 1987), ed. Bloom, 115.

17.   Williams, *Suddenly, Last Summer* in *The Theatre of Tennessee Williams* (New York: New Directions, 1971), vol. 3: 396. All future references to this play will be made to this edition; parenthetical page numbers will be given in the text. *Suddenly, Last Summer* and *Something Unspoken* were presented together under the title *Garden District* in New York on Jan. 7, 1958.

18.   See Donald Spoto, *The Kindness of Strangers: The Life of Tennessee Williams* (Boston: Little, Brown, 1985), 123, 219–24.

19.   Williams, "Desire and the Black Masseur," in *Collected Stories* 211.

20.   See Camille Paglia. *Sexual Personae: Art and Decadence from Nefertiti to Emily Dickinson* (New Haven: Yale UP, 1990), 53, 263, 434–35. Paglia describes the killing of Sebastian as in the tradition of homoerotic martyr, the eating of his flesh a kind of ritual *sparagmos,* and the archaic incest of mother-cults which appear also in Poe and James.

21.   Michael Kobre, "The Consolations of Fiction: Walker Percy's Dialogic Art." *New Orleans Review* 16 (Winter 1989): 52.

22.   Walker Percy, *The Moviegoer* (New York: Farrar, Straus, 1961), 6. All subsequent references to *The Moviegoer* will be from this edition; page numbers will be noted parenthetically in the text.

23.   Michael Swindle, "At Court with Walker Percy," *New Orleans* 23.4 (Jan. 1989): 41.

24.   See Morton Inger, *Politics and Reality in an American City: The New Orleans School Crisis of 1960* (New York: Center for Urban Education, 1968).

25.   Robert Coles, *Walker Percy: An American Search* (Boston: Little, Brown, 1978): x–xvii. In *Children of Crisis I: A Study of Courage and Fear* (Boston: Little, Brown, 1967), Coles described his work with black children in New Orleans as they desegregated the public schools in 1960.

26.   Coles, *Walker Percy* xi–xii.

27.   Walker Percy, "The Man on the Train," *Message in the Bottle* (New York: Farrar, Straus, 1954), 83.

28.   Walker Percy, "From Facts to Fiction," *Washington Post Book Week* (Dec. 25, 1966): 5, 9; rpt. *The Writer* (Oct. 1967): 27.

29.   "From Facts to Fiction" 27.

30.   Walker Percy, "New Orleans, Mon Amour," *Harper's* 237 (Sept. 1968): 88.

31.   The Boston Club is described in the WPA's *New Orleans City Guide* 287–88:

"824 Canal St., reputedly the second oldest club in the United States, was founded in 1841 by a group of mercantile and professional men for the purpose of enjoying more privacy in playing Boston, a card game much in favor at that time. . . . Old Negro servants, in the employ of the club for many years, administer to the needs of the members. . . . Women are entertained at a dance on New Year's Eve. On Mardi Gras day the club is host to the Queen of Carnival. It is here, while the socially elite view the scene from a balcony constructed across the facade of the club, that Rex toasts his queen with a goblet of champagne. A buffet supper is usually served after the evening parade of Comus." See references to such elitist white male business and social clubs in Kate Chopin's "In and Out of Old Natchitoches" and *The Awakening.* The Boston Club remains much the same to this day.

32. Rex is considered King of Carnival. The Krewe of Rex began in 1872 with the visit of the Russian Duke Alexis Romanoff Alexandrovitch, and the royal anthem of Rex, "If Ever I Cease to Love," was chosen because it was a favorite of Duke Alexis. The King is chosen secretly each year from its membership of prominent businessmen. Rex chose the motto "Pro Bono Publico," and has maintained a slight liaison with the mayor's office and the Chamber of Commerce, while the older organizations were completely private, closed affairs. See *The City Guide* 182–84.

33. See Sandra M. Gilbert and Susan Gubar, *No Man's Land* (New Haven: Yale UP, 1988), vol. 1: 12–32, for a discussion of modernist male writers' treatment of "the woman problem," which, they write, "must have seemed like part of the shredding fabric of patriarchal authority" (22). "The liberated Miss Nancy Ellicott of T. S. Eliot's 'Cousin Nancy' (1917), who not only 'smoked / And danced all the modern dances' but also seemed to attempt to destroy the earth itself, 'Strode across the hills and *broke* them'" (31). Gilbert and Gubar note that "such a no man's land of mad women and unmanned or maddened women" appears repeatedly in the works of D. H. Lawrence, T. S. Eliot, and their contemporaries, among them William Faulkner and Ernest Hemingway.

34. Max Webb, "Binx Bolling's New Orleans: Moviegoing, Southern Writing, and Father Abraham," *The Art of Walker Percy,* ed. Panthea Reid Broughton (Baton Rouge: Louisiana State UP, 1979): 20.

35. Walker Percy, "The Diagnostic Novel: On the Uses of Modern Fiction," *Harper's* 272 (June 1986): 39–45.

36. Walker Percy, "Notes for a Novel about the End of the World," *The Message in the Bottle* 101. *Love in the Ruins: The Adventures of a Bad Catholic at a Time Near the End of the World* (New York: Farrar, Straus, 1971). All references to *Love in the Ruins* will be from this edition; page references will be noted parenthetically in the text.

37. John Edward Hardy, *The Fiction of Walker Percy* (Urbana: U of Illinois P, 1987), 106.

38. Hardy 110.

39. Michael Pearson, "The Double Bondage of Racism in Walker Percy's Fiction," *Mississippi Quarterly* 41 (Fall 1988): 481.

40. Walker Percy, "Notes for a Novel about the End of the World" 117.

41. See next chapter for a discussion of Reed's representation of New Orleans in his novels.

42. Webb 18.

43. See James W. Tuttleton, "The Physician-Writer and the Cure of the Soul," *New Orleans Review* 16 (Winter 1989): 33; Cleanth Brooks, "Walker Percy and Modern Gnosticism," *Southern Review* 13 (1977): 677–87.

44. Martin Luschei, *The Sovereign Wayfarer: Walker Percy's Diagnosis of the Malaise* (Baton Rouge: Louisiana State UP, 1972).

45. Joseph Dewey, *In a Dark Time: The Apocalyptic Temper in the American Novel of the Nuclear Age* (West Lafayette, Ind.: Purdue UP, 1990). Dewey discusses Percy's portrayal of the apocalyptic temper of the contemporary period in *Love in the Ruins* and *The Thanatos Syndrome.*

7. African-American Dialogues and Revisionist Strategies: Dent, Reed, Kein, and Osbey

1. Thomas C. Dent, Richard Schechner, and Gilbert Moses, eds., *The Free Southern Theater by the Free Southern Theater* (Indianapolis, Ind.: Bobbs-Merrill, 1969).

2. John O'Neal, "Motion in the Ocean," *Tulane Drama Review* 12 (Summer 1968): 77.

3. O'Neal 71. See also Genevieve Fabre, "The Free Southern Theatre, 1963–1979," *Black American Literature Forum* 17.2 (Summer 1983): 55–59.

4. Much of my information about the civil rights movement in New Orleans is the result of personal interviews with Tom Dent, author of the forthcoming *Southern Journey: An Oral History of the Civil Rights Movement and the Contemporary South,* to be published by Harcourt, Brace, Jovanovich, and Dr. Henry Mitchell, optometrist, and co-founder of the Consumer's League in New Orleans.

5. See Henry C. Lacey, *To Raise, Destroy, and Create: The Poetry, Drama, and Fiction of Imamu Amiri Baraka (LeRoi Jones)* (Troy, NY: Whitston, 1981), 50–52, for a discussion of the Um*bra* poets.

6. Tom Dent, "Ten Years After Umbra," *Magnolia Street* (1976, 1987), 22–23.

7. Tom Dent, personal interview, 1989. Tom discussed sitting in the old Dillard Library, where Christian was a librarian, and discussing Black New Orleans authors and their works, as well as folklore and history. Christian also always had a printing press in his office or home, so that he could get his works printed. He believed that self-printing was often the only way that a black writer could get anything out.

8. Jerry W. Ward, Jr. "Tom Dent Talking: New Orleans as a Resource of Genius," 3.

9. Thomas C. Dent, editorial, *Echoes from the Gumbo,* Dec. 1968: 3. Also see Ward, "Tom Dent Talking."

10. Ward, "Tom Dent Talking" 8.

11. Maulana Ron Karenga, "Meats and Sea-Foods," *Echoes from the Gumbo* (Dec. 1968): 6.

12. Val Ferdinand (Kalamu ya Salaam), "Food for Thought," *Echoes from the Gumbo* (Dec. 1968): 4.

13. Tom Dent, "A Message for Langston," *Nkombo* 2.4 (Dec. 1969): 33.

14. Octave Lilly published the book of poetry *Cathedral in the Ghetto* in 1972; Richard Haley, poet and civil rights activist, whom James Baldwin discussed meeting at the Florida Agricultural and Mechanical University (FAMU) during the hectic early days of the civil rights movement in his essay "They Can't Turn Back," continued to write poetry until his death in 1989.

15. *Nkombo* (Apr. 1974): 64. See Houston Baker, *Blues, Ideology, and Afro-American Literature: A Vernacular Theory* (Chicago: U of Chicago P, 1984), for a discussion of how the blues matrix informs structures and themes of much of African American literature.

16. LeRoi Jones, "Black Dada Nihilismus," *The Dead Lecturer* (New York: Grove P, 1964).

17. Congo Square Writers' Workshop, *Bamboula* (1976). See also Ward, "Tom Dent Talking." Dent said the Congo Square Writers' Workshop "was a descendent of the writing workshop I had with the Free Southern Theater, which was a descendent of the Umbra workshop. But it was more than a writing workshop, obviously. It was a fellowship of people who had the same artistic yearnings, if not artistic production. It was a fellowship of friends. More importantly, I look upon it as a fellowship of broader cultural and artistic consciousness and interrelationships than is ordinarily possible in a place like New Orleans" (2).

18. Dent, preface, *Magnolia Street* (1976).

19. Michael Pearson, "The Double Bondage of Racism in Walker Percy's Fiction," Mississippi Quarterly 41 (Fall 1988): 479–96.

20. See William Ivy Hair, *Carnival of Fury: Robert Charles and the New Orleans Race Riot of 1900* (Baton Rouge: Louisiana State UP, 1976), a biography of the black laborer who shot twenty-seven whites (seven policemen) in several encounters with New Orleans police in July 1900.

21. Jerry W. Ward, Jr., introd., *Blue Lights and River Songs* by Tom Dent (Detroit: Lotus P, 1982).

22. Dent, "So You Leave the Project to Look for Work," *Blue Lights and River Songs* (Detroit: Lotus P, 1982).

23. Dent, "Ritual Murder," *Callaloo* (Feb. 1978): 67–81. *Ritual Murder* was first performed at the Ethiopian Theatre in the summer of 1976 and was directed by Chakula Cha Jua. All future references to the play will be from this edition; page notations will be given parenthetically in the text.

24. John Kennedy Toole, *A Confederacy of Dunces* (New York: Grove P, 1980).

25. John M. Roderick, "From 'Tarantula Arms' to 'Della Robbia Blue,'" 99.

26. Ishmael Reed, *Shrovetide in Old New Orleans* (1978; New York: Atheneum, 1989), 26.

27. Reed, *Shrovetide.*

28. Reed, *Shrovetide* 252–54.

29.   Henry Louis Gates, Jr., *The Signifying Monkey: A Theory of African-American Literary Criticism* (New York: Oxford UP, 1988), 51. Gates bases his theory of "the signifying monkey" on Ishmael Reed's "formal revision and critique of the Afro-American literary tradition ... especially as Reed manifested his critique in his third novel, *Mumbo-Jumbo*" (ix). See pp. 50–54 for a definition of signifying as double-voicedness and pp. 217–38 for his discussion of *Mumbo Jumbo*.

30.   Reginald Martin, *Ishmael Reed and the New Black Aesthetic Critics* (London: MacMillan, 1988), 74–75.

31.   Reed, *Shrovetide* 9.

32.   Ishmael Reed, *The Last Days of Louisiana Red* (New York: Random House, 1974).

33.   Reed, *Shrovetide* 31.

34.   Reed, *The Last Days of Louisiana Red,* epigraph: "Gumbo à la Creole."

35.   Mark Shadle, "A Bird's Eye View: Ishmael Reed's Unsettling of the Score by Munching and Mooching on the Mumbo Jumbo Work of History," *North Dakota Quarterly* 54 (Winter 1986): 21.

36.   Ishmael Reed, "Neo-Hoo-Doo Manifesto," *New and Collected Poems* (New York: Atheneum, 1988): 21.

37.   Theodore O. Mason, Jr., "Performance, History, and Myth: The Problem of Ishmael Reed's *Mumbo-Jumbo,*" *Modern Fiction Studies* 34 (Spring 1988): 98.

38.   Mason 100.

39.   See Larry McCaffery, *The Metafictional Muse: The Works of Robert Coover, Donald Barthelme, and William H. Gass* (Pittsburgh: U of Pittsburgh P, 1982) for a discussion of the stylistic devices used by writers of the period 1965–75, their increased audience self-consciousness, "experimentalism in the direction of reflexive, nonreferential works" that fall into a group of writers that he calls "metafictional."

40.   Joe Weixlmann, "Culture Clash, Survival, and Transformation: A Study of Some Innovative Afro-American Novels of Detection," *Mississippi Quarterly* (Winter 1984): 21–31.

41.   Sybil Kein, *Gombo People: Poesie Creole de la Nouvelle Orleans,* Leo J. Hall, Grosserand Superior Printers, 1981.

42.   Sybil Kein, "Comme Ye Dit: The Use of the Creole Language in 19th and 20th Century Literature," presented at the Modern Language Association Convention, Dec. 1988, New Orleans, Louisiana.

43.   Violet Harrington Bryan, "Evocations of Place and Culture in the Works of Four Contemporary Black Louisiana Writers: Brenda Marie Osbey, Sybil Kein, Elizabeth Brown-Guillory, and Pinkie Gordon Lane," *Louisiana Literature* 4 (Fall 1987): 53–55.

44.   Sybil Kein, *Delta Dancer* (Detroit: Lotus, 1984).

45.   Kein, "Fragments from the Diary of Amelie Patine . . . ," *Delta Dancer* 20–21.

46.   Sybil Kein, personal interview, July 30, 1986.

47. Alice Dunbar-Nelson, "The Stones of the Village," *The Works of Alice Dunbar-Nelson,* ed. Gloria T. Hull, vol. 3. See chap. 3 for a discussion of this work.

48. Kein, "Toucoutou," *Delta Dancer* 19.

49. Kein, "Letter to Madame Linde from Justine, Her Creole Servant," *Delta Dancer* 34–35.

50. The Cajuns are descendants of the Acadian exiles who arrived in Louisiana in the second half of the eighteenth century from Nova Scotia in search of their religious freedom. See Naomi Griffiths, *The Acadians: Creation of a People* (New York, 1969) for a discussion of their history. Also see Glenn R. Conrad, ed. *The Cajuns: Essays on Their History and Culture* (Lafayette, LA: Center for Louisiana Studies, U of Southwestern Louisiana, 1983). In reference to the poems "Cofaire" and "La Chaudriere Pele La Gregue . . . ," it is important to know that the Creoles are Creoles of color, or African-American.

51. Kein, "Cofaire," *Delta Dancer* 61–62.

52. Brenda Marie Osbey, *Ceremony for Minneconjoux,* Callaloo Poetry Series (Lexington: UP of Kentucky, 1983); *In These Houses* (Middletown, Conn.: Wesleyan UP, 1988); *Desperate Circumstance, Dangerous Woman: A Narrative Poem* (Brownsville, OR: Story Line P, 1991). For an informative study of the history of the Faubourg Tremé, see the six-part series: Brenda Marie Osbey, "Faubourg Tremé: Community in Transition," New Orleans Tribune, 6.12 (Dec. 1990), 7.1 (Jan. 1991), 7.8 (Aug. 1991), and forthcoming.

53. Violet Harrington Bryan, "An Interview with Brenda Marie Osbey," The Mississippi Quarterly 40 (Winter 1986–87): 33–45.

54. Bryan, "Interview with Osbey" 38.

55. Bryan, "Evocations of Place and Culture" 50–52.

56. Osbey. Telephone interview, Dec. 26, 1988.

57. Brenda Marie Osbey, personal interview, Aug. 11, 1991.

58. See Violet Harrington Bryan, "Narratives of Community: The Poetry of Brenda Marie Osbey," a paper presented at the Modern Language Association Convention, Dec. 28, 1988, New Orleans.

59. Paul Ricoeur, Time *and Narrative* (Chicago: U of Chicago P, 1954), 28.

60. Kein, *Sérénade Creole,* Master Tracks Audio Productions.

61. Calvin C. Hernton, "The Tradition." *Parnassus* (Spring 1985): 518–50.

Conclusion

1. Roland Barthes, "Myth Today," *Mythologies,* trans. Annette Lavers (New York: Hill and Wang, 1972), 112.

2. Brenda Marie Osbey, "Writing the Words, *Ceremony for Minneconjoux* 80–82.

3. For a discussion of the poetry of Tom Dent, see chap. 7. See also Robert O. Stephens, "Cable's Bras Coupé and Merimée's *Tamango*: The Case of the Missing Arm," *Mississippi Quarterly* 35 (Fall 1982): 387–405.

4.   Anselm Strauss, *Images of the American City* (New Brunswick, NJ: Transaction, 1976); Yi-Fu Tuan, To*pophilia* (Englewood Cliffs, NJ: Prentice-Hall, 1974), Sp*ace and Place* (Minneapolis: U of Minnesota P, 1977), "Attitudes Towards the Environment: Themes and Approaches," in D. Lowenthal, *Environmental Perception and Behavior* (Chicago: U of Chicago P, 1967); D. C. D. Pocock, *Humanistic Geography and Literature* (Croom Helm, London, 1981); Leonard Lutwack, *The Role of Place in Literature* (Syracuse: Syracuse UP, 1984); Shortridge, "The Concept of the Place-Defining Novel in American Popular Culture," *Professional Geographer* 43.3 (1991): 280–91.

5.   Clifford Geertz, *The Interpretation of Cultures* (New York: Basic Books, 1973), 5.

6.   Brenda Marie Osbey, "Faubourg Tremé: Community In Transition, Part I: Early History," New Orleans Trib*une,* 6.12 (Dec. 1990): 15.

7.   Osbey, "Faubourg Tremé: Community in Transition, Part III: The Beginning of the End," New Orleans Trib*une,* 7.1 (Jan. 1991): 16.

8.   See *State v. Treadaway,* 126 La. 300, 52 So. 500 (1910). Also see *Sunseri v. Cassagne,* La. 195, 196 So. 7 (1940), and *Messina v. Ciaccio,* La. App. 290 So. 2d 339 (1974). The cases were pointed out to me by Robert E. Harrington on August 14, 1991.

9.   W. E. B. DuBois, *The Souls of Black Folk* (1903; New York: Dodd, Mead, 1961), 3.

10.   See William Ivy Hair, *Carnival of Fury: Robert Charles and the New Orleans Race Riot of 1900* (Baton Rouge: Louisiana State UP, 1976).

11.   Anne Goodwyn Jones, *Tomorrow Is Another Day* 356.

12.   Faulkner, *Absalom, Absalom!* 110.

13.   Elizabeth S. Muhlenfeld, "Shadows with Substance and Ghosts Exhumed: The Women in *Absalom, Absalom!*" *Mississippi Quarterly* 25 (Summer 1972): 238. Also see Thadious Davis, Faulkner's *"Negro": Art and the Southern Context* (Baton Rouge: Louisiana State UP, 1983), 180–83.

14.   Williams, *A Streetcar Named Desire* 117.

15.   Walker Percy, "New Orleans, Mon Amour," *Harper's Magazine* 237 (Sept. 1, 1968): 81.

16.   Grace King, "The Balcony," *Balcony Stories* (1892; Ridgewood, NJ: Gregg, 1968), 2.

Bibliography

Ш

Primary Sources

Adams, Edward Clarkson. *Nigger to Nigger*. New York: Scribners, 1928.

Anderson, Sherwood. *Dark Laughter*. New York: Boni and Liveright, 1925.

———. "A Meeting South." *The Dial* (Spring 1925). Rpt. in *Sherwood Anderson: Short Stories*. Ed. Maxwell Geismar. New York: Hill and Wang, 1962. 170–80.

Armstrong, Louis. *Satchmo: My Life in New Orleans*. 1954. New York: DaCapo, 1986.

Basso, Etolia S., ed. *The World from Jackson Square*. New Orleans: Tulane UP, 1968.

Bontemps, Arna. "Why I Returned Home." *Black Voices: An Anthology of Afro-American Literature*. Ed. Abraham Chapman. New York: New American Library, 1968. 321–31.

Boucicault, Dion. *The Octoroon, or Life in Louisiana. Plays by Dion Boucicault*. Ed. Peter Thomson. Cambridge: Cambridge UP, 1984.

Bradford, Roark. *Ol' Man Adam an' His Chillun*. New York: Harper, 1928.

———. *John Henry*. New York: Harper, 1931.

Cable, George W. *Creoles and Cajuns, Stories of Old Louisiana*. Ed. Arlin Turner. Garden City, NJ: Doubleday, 1959.

———. The *Creoles of Louisiana*. New York: Scribners, 1884.

———. *Dr. Sevier*. New York: Osgood, 1884.

———. *The Grandissimes*. 1880. Rev. ed. New York: Scribner's, 1907.

———. *Madame Delphine*. New York: Scribner's, 1881.

———. "The Negro Question in the United States." *Contemporary Review* (Mar. 1888); rpt. in *The Negro Question*. Ed. Arlin Turner. Garden City, NY: Doubleday, 1958.

———. *Old Creole Days*. New York: Scribners, 1879.

———. "A Southern White Man." New Orleans *Bulletin* Sept. 26, 1875.

———. *The Strange True Stories of Louisiana*. New York: Scribner's, 1889.

Chesnutt, Charles. *Conjure Woman*. 1899. Ann Arbor: U of Michigan P, 1969.

———. "The Future American." *Boston Transcript* Aug. 18, Aug. 25, Sept. 1, 1900. Charles Chesnutt Collection, Special Collections Dept., Fisk University Library.

———. *The House Behind the Cedars*. 1900. Ridgewood, NJ: Gregg P, 1968.

————. "An Inside View of the Negro Question." Incomplete typescript, n.d. Charles Chesnutt Collection. Special Collections Dept., Fisk University Library.

————. "Paul Marchand, F.M.C." Unpublished manuscript. Charles Chestnutt Collection, Special Collections Dept., Fisk University Library.

————. "Post Bellum, Pre-Harlem," *The Crisis* 40 (June 1931): 193–94.

————. *The Short Fiction of Charles Chesnutt.* Ed. Sylvia Lyons Render. Washington, DC: Howard UP, 1974.

————. "What Is a White Man?" The *Independent* 30 (May 1889).

Chesnutt, Helen. *Charles Waddell Chesnutt.* Chapel Hill: U of North Carolina P, 1952.

Chopin, Kate. *The Complete Works.* Ed. Per Seyersted. Baton Rouge: Louisiana State UP, 1969.

————. *A Kate Chopin Miscellany.* Ed. Per Seyersted. Natchitoches, LA: Northwestern State UP, 1979.

Christian, Marcus. *I Am New Orleans.* 1968, 1976.

————. *Negro Ironworkers of Louisiana*, 1718–1900. Gretna, LA: Pelican, 1972.

————. Unpublished manuscripts, correspondence, poetry. Marcus Christian Collection. Archives and Manuscripts Dept., Earl K. Long Library, University of New Orleans.

Clemens, Samuel [Mark Twain]. *Life on the Mississippi.* 1883. New York: Harper and Row, 1968.

Congo Square Writers' Workshop. *Bamboula.* New Orleans, 1976.

Crane, Hart. *White Buildings: Poems.* New York: Boni and Liveright, 1926.

Dent, Tom. *Blue Lights and River Songs.* Detroit: Lotus P, 1982.

————. *Magnolia Street.* 1976, 1987.

————. "Ritual Murder." *Callaloo*, Feb. 1978: 67–81.

DuBois, W. E. B. *The Souls of Black Folk.* 1903. New York: Dodd, Mead, 1961.

Dunbar, Paul Laurence. *Clorindy, or the Origin of the Cakewalk.* Music by Will Cook. New York: Witmark, 1898.

Dunbar-Nelson, Alice. "April Is On the Way." *Ebony and Topaz.* 1927. Rpt. in *The Works of Alice Dunbar-Nelson.* Ed. Gloria T. Hull. Vol. 2. Schomburg Library of Nineteenth-Century Black Women Writers. New York: Oxford UP, 1988. 89–91.

————. *Give Us Each Day: The Diary of Alice Dunbar-Nelson.* Ed. Gloria T. Hull. New York: W. W. Norton, 1984.

————. *The Goodness of St. Rocque and Other Stories.* New York: Dodd, Mead, 1899.

————. "The Pearl in the Oyster." *The Southern Workman.* 1900. Rpt. in *The Works of Alice Dunbar-Nelson.* Ed. Gloria T. Hull. Vol. 3. Schomburg Library of Nineteenth-Century Black Women Writers. New York: Oxford UP, 1988. 51–64.

————. "People of Color in Louisiana, Part I, II." *Journal of Negro History,* Jan. 1917. Rpt. in *An Alice Dunbar-Nelson Reader.* Ed. R. Ora Williams, Washington, DC: UP of America, 1976.

———. *Violets and Other Tales.* Boston: Monthly Review P, 1895.

———. *The Works of Alice Dunbar-Nelson.* Ed. Gloria T. Hull. 3 vols. Schomburg Library of Nineteenth-Century Black Women Writers. New York: Oxford UP, 1988.

Echoes from the Gumbo. BLKARTSOUTH (New Orleans). Dec. 1968.

Evans, Augusta Jane. Macaria. 1863. New York: Dillingham, 1887.

Faulkner, William. *Absalom, Absalom!* 1936. *Absalom, Absalom! The Corrected Text.* New York: Vintage, 1986.

———. "Carcassonne." *Collected Stories.* New York: Random, 1934.

———. *Helen: A Courtship and Mississippi Poems.* Ed. Carvel Collins. New Orleans: Tulane U and Yoknapatawpha P, 1981.

———. *Mosquitoes.* 1927. New York: Washington Square P, 1985.

———. *New Orleans Sketches.* Ed. Carvel Collins. New York: Random, 1958.

———. *Pylon.* 1935. New York: Vintage, 1987.

Faulkner, William, and William Spratling. *Sherwood Anderson and Other Famous Creoles.* 1927. Austin: U of Texas P, 1966.

Federal Writers' Project of the Works Progress Administration. *New Orleans City Guide.* Boston: Houghton Mifflin, 1938.

Fuller, Sara S., ed. Th*e Paul L. Dunbar Papers.* Ohio Historical Society, Columbus. Microfilm ed., 1972.

Grue, Lee Meitzen. *French Quarter Poems.* New Orleans: Long Measure P, 1979.

Guillaume, Alfred J., Jr. "Joanni Questi, *Monsieur Paul.*" *Louisiana Literature* 1–3 (Spring 1984): 22–37.

Hearn, Lafcadio. *An American Miscellany.* Ed. Albert Mordell. 2 vols. New York: Dodd, Mead, 1924.

———. *Fantastics and Other Fancies.* Ed. Charles Woodward Hutson. Boston: Houghton Mifflin, 1914.

———. "The Last of the Voudous." *Harper's Weekly* Nov. 7, 1885.

Hurston, Zora Neale. *Mules and Men.* 1935. New York: Harper and Row, 1990.

Kane, Harnett. *Queen New Orleans: City by the River.* New York: W. Morrow, 1949.

Kein, Sybil. "An American South." Manuscript.

———. *Delta Dancer.* Detroit: Lotus, 1984.

———. *Gombo People: Poesie Creole de la Nouvelle Orleans.* Leo J. Hall, 1981.

———. *Sérénade Creole.* Master Tracks Audio Productions. 1986.

King, Grace. *Balcony Stories.* 1892. Ridgewood, NJ: Gregg P, 1968.

———. "Bonne Maman." *Harper's New Monthly Magazine* July 1886. Rpt. in Grace King, *Tales of a Time and Place.* New York: Macmillan, 1892.

———. "The Little Convent Girl." *Century* 46, n.s. 24 (May–Oct. 1893): 547–51. Rpt. in *Balcony Stories.* 1892.

———. "Monsieur Motte," *New Princeton Review,* Apr. 1886. *Monsieur Motte.* New York, 1888.

———. *Memories of a Southern Woman of Letters.* New York: Macmillan, 1932.

———. *New Orleans: The Place and the People.* New York: Macmillan, 1895.

Lanusse, Armand, ed. *Les Cenelles*. 1845. Trans., ed. Regine Latortue and Gleason
　　R. W. Adams. Boston: G. K. Hall, 1979.
Lilly, Octave. *Cathedral in the Ghetto*. New York: Vantage, 1970.
Lomax, Allan. *Mister Jelly Roll: The Fortunes of Jelly Roll Morton, Creole and
　　Inventor of Jazz*. New York: Grosset and Dunlap, 1950.
Nkombo. BLKARTSOUTH (of Free Southern Theater). New Orleans. 1968–74.
Osbey, Brenda Marie. *Ceremony for Minneconjoux*. Lexington: UP of Kentucky,
　　Callaloo Poetry Series, 1983.
―――. *Desperate Circumstance, Dangerous Woman*. Brownsville, Oreg.: Story
　　Line P, 1991.
―――. *In These Houses*. Middletown, Conn.: Wesleyan UP, 1988.
Percy, Walker. *Love in the Ruins: The Adventures of a Bad Catholic at a Time Near
　　the End of the World*. New York: Farrar, 1971.
―――. *Message in the Bottle*. New York: Farrar, 1954.
―――. *The Moviegoer*. New York: Farrar, 1961.
―――. "New Orleans, Mon Amour." *Harper's Magazine* Sept. 1, 1968: 80–82, 86,
　　88, 90.
―――. *The Thanatos Syndrome*. New York: Ballantine Books, 1987.
Reed, Ishmael. *The Last Days of Louisiana Red*. New York: Random, 1974.
―――. *Mumbo Jumbo*. New York: Atheneum, 1972.
―――. *New and Collected Poems*. New York: Atheneum, 1988.
―――. *Shrovetide in Old New Orleans*. New York: Atheneum, 1989.
―――. *Yellow Back Radio Broke-Down*. New York: Atheneum, 1988.
Rice, Anne. *The Feast of All Saints*. New York: Ballantine, 1979.
Saxon, Lyle. *Children of Strangers*. New Orleans: Robert Crager, 1937.
―――. *Fabulous New Orleans*. New York: Appleton-Century, 1928.
―――. *The Friends of Joe Gilmore*. New York: Hastings House, 1948.
Saxon, Lyle, Edward Dreyer, and Robert Tallant. *Gumbo Ya-Ya*. New York:
　　Bonanza Books, 1945.
Shaik, Fatima. *The Mayor of New Orleans: Just Talking Jazz*. Berkeley: Creative
　　Arts Book Co., 1989.
Spencer, Herbert. *The Study of Sociology*. New York: Appleton, 1882.
Tallant, Robert. *Mrs. Candy and Saturday Night*. Garden City, New York:
　　Doubleday, 1947.
―――. *The Romantic New Orleanians*. New York: Dutton, 1950.
―――. *Voodoo in New Orleans*. 1946. Gretna, LA: Pelican, 1974.
―――. *The Voodoo Queen: A Novel*. 1956. Gretna, LA: Pelican, 1983.
Tinker, Edward Larocque. *Toucoutou*. New York: Dodd, Mead, 1928.
Toole, John Kennedy. *A Confederacy of Dunces*. Foreword by Walker Percy. New
　　York: Grove, 1980.
Tourgée, Albion. *Bricks Without Straw*. New York: Fords, Howard and Hulbert,
　　1886.
―――. *A Fool's Errand*. New York: Fords, Howard and Hulbert, 1879.
Walker, Margaret. *For My People*. 1940. Rpt. in her *This Is My Century: New and
　　Collected Poems*. Athens: U of Georgia P, 1989.

Williams, Tennessee. *Collected Stories*. Ed. Gore Vidal. New York: New Directions, 1985.

―――. *Garden District* ("Suddenly, Last Summer" and "Something Unspoken"). Presented Jan. 7, 1958, New York.

―――. *One Arm and Other Stories*. Norfolk, Conn.: New Directions, 1948.

―――. *A Streetcar Named Desire*. New York: New American Library, 1947.

―――. *Memoirs*. New York: Doubleday, 1975.

―――. *Suddenly, Last Summer. The Theatre of Tennessee Williams*. Vol. 3. New York: New Directions, 1971.

―――. *27 Wagons Full of Cotton and Other One-Act Plays*. Norfolk, Conn.: New Directions, 1945.

Secondary Sources

Aaron, Daniel. *The Unwritten War*. Madison: U of Wisconsin P, 1987.

Alexander, Alland, Jr. *Human Nature: Darwin's View*. New York: Columbia UP, 1985.

Alexander, Richard D. *Darwinism and Human Affairs*. Seattle: U of Washington P, 1979.

Allain, Helene d'Aquin. *Souvenirs d'Amerique et de France, par un creole*. Paris, 1883.

Alland, Alexander, Jr. *Human Nature: Darwin's View*. New York: Columbia UP, 1985.

Anderson, Sherwood. "New Orleans, *The Double Dealer*, and the Modern Movement in America." *The Double Dealer* 3 (Mar. 1922): 119–26.

Appiah, Anthony. "The Uncompleted Argument: DuBois and the Illusion of Race." *Critical Inquiry* 12 (Autumn 1985): 21–36. Rpt. in *"Race," Writing, and Difference*. Ed. Henry Louis Gates, Jr. Chicago: U of Chicago P, 1986.

Aptheker, Bettina. *Woman's Legacy: Essays on Race, Sex, and Class in American History*. Amherst: U of Massachusetts P, 1982.

Asbury, Herbert. *French Quarter*. New York: Knopf, 1936.

Baker, Houston A. *Blues, Ideology, and Afro-American Literature: A Vernacular Theory*. Chicago: U of Chicago P, 1984.

Bakhtin, M. M. "Discourse and the Novel." *The Dialogic Imagination*. Trans. Caryl Emerson and Michael Holquist. Austin: U of Texas P, 1981.

Bannister, Robert C. *Social Darwinism: Science and Myth in Anglo-American Social Thought*. Philadelphia: Temple UP, 1979.

Barranger, Milly S. "New Orleans as Theatrical Image in Plays by Tennessee Williams." *Southern Quarterly* 23.2 (Winter 1985): 38–54.

Barthes, Roland. "Myth Today." *Mythologies*. Trans. Annette Lavers. New York: Hill and Wang, 1979.

Bassett, John Earl. "Faulkner's *Mosquitoes*: Toward a Self-Image of the Artist." *The Southern Literary Journal* 12 (Spring 1980): 49–64.

Basso, Etolia S., ed. *The World from Jackson Square*. New Orleans: Tulane UP, 1968.

Bauer, Dale M. *Feminist Dialogics: A Theory of Failed Community.* Albany: State U of New York P, 1988.

Bell, Caryn Ann. "Critics of the Color Line: George W. Cable and Charles W. Chesnutt." M.A. thesis. U of New Orleans, 1979.

Berkove, Lawrence I. "The Free Man of Color in *The Grandissimes* and Works by Harris and Twain." *Southern Quarterly* 18.4 (1980): 60–73.

Berthoff, Warner. *The Ferment of Realism: American Literature 1884–1919.* New York: Free P, 1965.

––––––. *Hart Crane: A Re-Introduction.* Minneapolis: U of Minnesota P, 1989.

Berzon, Judith. *Neither White Nor Black: The Mulatto Character in American Fiction.* New York: New York UP, 1978.

Blair, Karen J. *Clubwoman as Feminist: True Womanhood Redefined, 1864–1914.* New York: Holmes and Meier, 1980.

Blake, Nancy. "Creation and Procreation: The Voice and the Name, or Biblical Intertextuality in *Absalom, Absalom!*" *Intertextuality in Faulkner.* Eds. Michel Gresset and Noel Polk. Jackson: UP of Mississippi, 1985.

Blassingame, John. *Black New Orleans: 1860–1880.* Chicago: U of Chicago P, 1973.

Bloom, Harold, ed. *Tennessee Williams: Modern Critical Views.* New York: Chelsea House, 1987.

––––––. *Tennessee Williams's* A Streetcar Named Desire: *Modern Critical Interpretations.* New York: Chelsea House, 1988.

Blotner, Joseph. *Faulkner: A Biography.* 2 vols. New York: Random, 1974.

Bonner, Thomas, Jr. "Christianity and Catholicism in the Fiction of Kate Chopin." *Southern Quarterly* 20.2 (Winter 1982): 118–25.

Bontemps, Arna, ed. *American Negro Poetry.* New York: Farrar, Straus and Giroux, 1963.

Bradbury, Malcolm. "The Cities of Modernism." *Modernism, 1890–1930.* Ed. Malcolm Bradbury and James McFarlane. New Jersey: Humanities P, 1978. 96–104.

Brawley, Benjamin. The *Negro in Literature and Art in the U.S.* New York: Duffield, 1930.

Bremer, Sydney. "Chicago's Lost Sisters." *Women Writers and the City.* Ed. Susan Squier. Knoxville: U of Tennessee P, 1986.

Brooks, Cleanth. "Walker Percy and Modern Gnosticism." *Southern Review* 13 (1977): 677–87.

––––––. *William Faulkner: Toward Yoknapatawpha and Beyond.* New Haven: Yale UP, 1978.

Broughton, Panthea Reid. *The Art of Walker Percy, Stratagems for Being.* Baton Rouge: Louisiana State UP, 1979.

Brown, Dorothy H., and Barbara C. Ewell. "Prologue." *New Orleans Review,* 15 (Spring 1988): 5–6.

Brown, Sterling A. "Folk Life of the Negro." *Black Expression: Essays by and about Black Americans in the Creative Arts.* Ed. Addison Gayle. New York: Weybright and Talley, 1970.

————. *The Negro in American Fiction and Negro Poetry and Drama.* 1937. Rpt. as *Negro Poetry and Drama and the Negro in American Fiction.* New York: Atheneum, 1978.

————, Arthur P. Davis, and Ulysses Lee, eds. *The Negro Caravan: Writings by American Negroes.* 1941. New York: Arno P and New York Times, 1969.

Brownell, Blaine A., and David R. Goldfield, eds. *History: The Growth of Urban Civilization in the South.* Port Washington, NY: National University Publications, 1977.

Bryan, Violet Harrington. "Creating and Re-creating the Myth of New Orleans: Grace King and Alice Dunbar-Nelson." PO*MPA* (1987): 185–96.

————. "Evocations of Place and Culture in the Works of Four Contemporary Black Louisiana Writers: Brenda Osbey, Sybil Kein, Elizabeth Brown-Guillory, and Pinkie Gordon Lane." *Louisiana Literature* 4 (Fall 1987): 49–65.

————. "Frances Joseph-Gaudet. Black Philanthropist." *Sage: A Scholarly Journal on Black Women* 3.1 (Spring 1987): 46–49.

————. "i touch memory with the tips of my fingers." Review of *Desperate Circumstance, Dangerous Woman: A Narrative Poem. The New Orleans Tribune* 7.10 (Oct. 1991): 16.

————. "The Image of New Orleans in the Fiction of George Washington Cable and William Faulkner: A Study of Place in Fiction." Diss. Harvard U, 1981.

————. "An Interview with Brenda Marie Osbey." *Mississippi Quarterly* 40.1 (Winter 86–87): 33–45.

————. "Land of Dreams: Image and Reality in New Orleans." *Urban Resources* 1 (Spring 1984): 29–35.

————. "Narratives of Community: The Poetry of Brenda Marie Osbey." Paper Presented at Modern Language Association Convention. Dec. 28, 1988, New Orleans.

————. "Narratives of Community: Review of Brenda Marie Osbey's *In These Houses.*" *New Laurel Review* 16 (1988): 124–28.

————. "New Orleans Black Ethnicity: A Historical Perspective." *The State of Black New Orleans* (1986): 81–102.

————. "Promoting Black New Orleans Culture." *The State of Black New Orleans* (1986): 61–73.

Buerkle, Jack, and Danny Barker. *Bourbon Street Black: The New Orleans Jazzmen.* New York: Oxford UP, 1973.

Burdett, Osbert. *The Beardsley Period: An Essay in Perspective.* London: Bodley, 1925.

"Burning Question." *The Double Dealer* 1 (May 1921): 173.

Bush, Robert, ed. *Grace King of New Orleans.* Baton Rouge: Louisiana State UP, 1973.

————. *Grace King: A Southern Destiny. Baton Rouge: Louisiana State UP, 1983.*

Campbell, Michael. "The Negro in Cable's *The Grandissimes.*" *Mississippi Quarterly* 27.2 (1974): 165–78.

Carnegie, Andrew. "The Gospel of Wealth." *North American Review* 148 (June

1889) and 149 (Dec. 1889). Rpt. in *The Gospel of Wealth and Other Timely Essays.* Cambridge, Mass: Harvard UP, 1965.

Carter, Hodding, ed. *The Past as Prelude: New Orleans 1718–1968.* New Orleans: Tulane UP, 1968.

Castellanos, Henry C. *New Orleans As It Was: Episodes of Louisiana Life.* 1895. 2d ed. New Orleans: L. Graham, 1905.

Castille, Philip, ed. *Southern Literature in Transition: Heritage and Promise.* Memphis: Memphis State UP, 1983.

Christian, Barbara. *Black Women Novelists: The Development of a Tradition.* Westport, Conn.: Greenwood, 1980.

Cixous, Hélène. "The Laugh of the Medusa." Trans. Keith Cohen and Paula Cohen. *Signs: Journal of Women in Culture and Society* 1.4 (1976): 875–93.

Clarke, John Henrik. *American Negro Short Stories.* New York: Hill and Wang, 1966.

Clark, William Bedford. "Cable and the Theme of Miscegenation in *Old Creole Days* and *The Grandissimes.*" *Mississippi Quarterly* 30 (1977): 597–609.

Clayton, Ronnie W. "A History of the Federal Writers' Project in Louisiana." Diss. Louisiana University and Agricultural and Mechanical College, 1974.

Cleman, John. "The Art of Color in George W. Cable's *The Grandissimes.*" *American Literature* 47 (Spring 1975): 396–410.

Cohn, David. Review of *Darkwater* by W. E. B. DuBois. *The Double Dealer* 1 (June 1921): 254.

Coles, Robert. *Walker Percy: An American Search.* Boston: Little, Brown, 1978.

Collins, Carvel, ed. *Helen: A Courtship and Mississippi Poems, by William Faulkner.* New Orleans: Tulane U and Yoknapatawpha P, 1981.

———, ed. *The New Orleans Sketches of William Faulkner.* New York: Random, 1958.

Conrad, Glenn R., ed. *The Cajuns: Essays on Their History and Culture.* Lafayette, LA: Center for Louisiana Studies, U of Southwestern Louisiana, 1983.

Conway, Jill. "Women Reformers and American Culture, 1870–1930." *Journal of Social History* 5 (Winter 1971–72): 164–77.

Craig, Evelyn Anita. *Black Drama of the Federal Theatre Era.* Amherst: U of Massachusetts P, 1980.

Crane, Hart. "Black Tambourine." *The Double Dealer* 1 (June 1921): 232.

Cunningham, Virginia. *Paul Lawrence Dunbar and His Song.* New York: Biblo and Tanner, 1947.

"Darwinism in Literature." *Galaxy* 15 (1873): 695.

Davis, Angela Y. *Women, Race and Class.* New York: Vintage-Random, 1983.

Davis, Rebecca Harding. "Here and There in the South." *Harper's New Monthly Magazine,* Sept. 1887: 593–605.

Day, Douglas. "Borges, Faulkner, and *The Wild Palms.*" *Virginia Quarterly Review* 56 (Winter 1980): 109–18.

Debusscher, Gilbert. "Minting Their Separate Wills: Tennessee Williams and Hart Crane." *Tennessee Williams: Modern Critical Views,* ed. Bloom. 113–30.

Dent, Thomas C., Richard Schechner, and Gilbert Moses, eds. *The Free Southern*

Theater by the Free Southern Theater. Indianapolis, Ind.: Bobbs-Merrill, 1969.

Dent, Thomas C. "Black Theater in the South: Report and Reflections." *The Theater of Black Americans.* Ed. Errol Hill. New York: Applause Theater Book Publishers, 1987.

————. Personal interview with the author. Oct. 1988.

Desdunes, Rodolphe Lucien. *Nos Hommes et Notre Histoire.* Montreal, 1911. Published as *Our People and Our History.* Trans. Sister Dorothea McCants. Baton Rouge: Louisiana State UP, 1973.

Desmond, John F. "Disjunctions of Time: Myth and History in *The Thanatos Syndrome.*" *New Orleans Review* 16.4 (Winter, 1989): 61–71.

Detiege, Sister Audrey Marie. *Henriette Delille, Free Woman of Color: Foundress of the Sisters of the Holy Family.* New Orleans: Sisters of the Holy Family, 1976.

Dewey, Joseph. *In A Dark Time: The Apocalyptic Temper in the American Novel of the Nuclear Age.* West Lafayette, Ind.: Purdue UP, 1990.

Dill, Bonnie Thornton. "The Dialectics of Black Womanhood." *Signs* 4.3 (Spring 1979): 543–55.

Donovan, Josephine. *Feminist and Literary Criticism: Exploration in Theory.* Lexington: UP of Kentucky, 1975.

Dreyfus, Hubert L., and Paul Rakinowski. *Michel Foucault: Beyond Structuralism and Hermeneutics.* Chicago: U of Chicago P, 1982.

DuBois, Ellen Carrol, et al. *Feminist Scholarship: Kindling in the Groves of Academe.* Urbana: U of Illinois P, 1985.

DuBois, W. E. B. *The Souls of Black Folk.* 1903. New York: Dodd, Mead, 1963.

Duvall, John N. "Faulkner's Critics and Women: The Voice of the Community." *Faulkner and Women.* Eds. Doreen Fowler and Ann J. Abadie. Jackson: UP of Mississippi, 1986. 41–47.

Dyer, Joyce C. "Gouvernail, Kate Chopin's Sensitive Bachelor." *Kate Chopin.* Ed. Harold Bloom. New York: Chelsea House, 1987. 61–70.

————. "Techniques of Distancing in the Fiction of Kate Chopin." *Southern Studies* 24 (Spring 1985): 69–81.

Egan, Joseph. "Lions Rampant: Agricola Fusilier and Bras-Coupé as Antithetical Doubles in *The Grandissimes.*" *Southern Quarterly* 18.4 (1980): 74–80.

Elfenbein, Anna Shannon. "Kate Chopin's *The Awakening*: An Assault Upon American Racial and Sexual Mythology." *Southern Studies* 26.3 (Fall, Winter 1987): 304–12.

————. *Women on the Color Line: Evolving Stereotypes and the Writings of George Washington Cable, Grace King, Kate Chopin.* Charlottesville: UP of Virginia, 1989.

Ellman, Mary. *Thinking About Women.* New York: Harcourt, 1968.

"Ephemeral Sex." Editorial. *The Double Dealer* 1 (Mar. 1921): 85.

Evans, Augusta Jane. *Macaria.* 1863. New York: Dillingham, 1887. Excerpt rpt. in "Married Belles: What A Woman Says." New Orleans *Tribune,* Mar. 29, 1865.

Evans, Sally Kittredge. "Free Persons of Color." *The Creole Faubourgs.* Vol. 4 of *New Orleans Architecture,* ed. Roulhac Toledano, Sally Kittredge Evans, and Mary Louise Christovich. Gretna, LA: Pelican, 1974. 25–36.

Evans, Sara. P*ersonal Politics: The Roots of Women's Liberation in the Civil Rights Movement and the New Left.* New York: Knopf, 1979.

Evans, William W. "Naming Day in Old New Orleans: Charactonyms and Colloquialisms in George Washington Cable's *The Grandissimes* and *Old Creole Days.*" *Names: Journal of the American Name Society* 30.3 (1982): 183–91.

Everett, Donald. "Free Persons of Color in New Orleans, 1803–1865." Diss. Tulane U, 1952.

Ewell, Barbara. *Kate Chopin.* New York: Ungar, 1985.

Fabre, Genevieve. "The Free Southern Theatre, 1963–1979." *Black American Literature Forum* 17.2 (Summer 1983): 55–59.

Fanger, Donald. *Dostoevsky and Romantic Realism.* Chicago: U of Chicago P, 1965.

Feibleman, James K. "Literary New Orleans Between World Wars." *The Southern Review* 1 NS (July 1965): 702.

Ferdinand, Val [Kalamu ya Salaam]. "Food for Thought." *Echoes from the Gumbo.* Dec. 1968: 4.

Ferguson, Sally Ann H. "Chestnutt's 'The Conjurer's Revenge': The Economics of Direct Confrontation." *Obsidian* 7 (Summer–Winter 1981): 37–42.

Fiehrer, Thomas Marc. "The African Presence in Colonial Louisiana: An Essay on the Continuity of Caribbean Culture." *Louisiana's Black Heritage.* Ed. Robert R. MacDonald, John R. Kemp, and Edward F. Haas. New Orleans: Louisiana State Museum, 1979. 3–31.

Fluck, Winfried. "Tentative Transgressions: Kate Chopin's Fiction as a Mode of Symbolic Action." *Studies in American Fiction.*

Foner, Laura. "The Free People of Color in Louisiana and St. Domingue: A Comparative Portrait of Two Three-Caste Slave Societies." *Journal of Social History* 3 (1970): 406–30.

Ford, Oliver III. "Ada Jack Carver: A Critical Biography." Diss. U of Connecticut, 1975.

Franklin, John Hope. *From Slavery to Freedom: A History of the Negro in America.* 3d. ed. New York: Random, 1967.

Frisby, James R., Jr. "New Orleans Writers and the Negro: George Washington Cable, Grace King, Ruth McEnery Stuart, Kate Chopin, and Lafcadio Hearn, 1870–1900." Diss. Emory University, 1972.

Furman, Nelly. "The Study of Women and Language: Comment on Vol. 3, No. 3." *Signs* 4 (Fall 1978).

Gates, Henry Louis, Jr. *The Signifying Monkey: A Theory of African-American Literary Criticism.* New York: Oxford UP, 1988.

Gaudet, Marcia. "Kate Chopin and the Lore of Cane River's Creoles of Color." *Xavier Review.*

Gayle, Addison, *The Black Aesthetic.* New York: Doubleday, 1971.

Geertz, Clifford. "Ideology as a Cultural System." *The Interpretation of Cultures.* New York: Basic Books, 1973.

Giddings, Paula. *When and Where I Enter: The Impact of Black Women on Race and Sex in America.* Toronto: Bantam, 1984.

Gilbert, Sandra. "The Second Coming of Aphrodite." *Kate Chopin.* Ed. Harold Bloom. New York: Chelsea House, 1987. 89–114.

Gilbert, Sandra, and Susan Gubar. *The Mad Woman in the Attic: The Women Writer and the Nineteenth-Century Literary Image.* New Haven: Yale UP, 1979.

———. *No Man's Land.* 2 vols. *New Haven: Yale UP, 1988.*

Gioia, Ted. *The Imperfect Art: Reflections on Jazz and Modern Culture.* New York: Oxford UP, 1987.

Griffiths, Naomi. *The Acadians: Creation of a People.* New York, 1969.

Gwin, Minrose C. *Black and White Women of the Old South: The Peculiar Sisterhood in American Literature.* Knoxville: U of Tennessee P, 1985.

Gwynn, Frederick L. "Faulkner's Prufrock and Other Observations." *Journal of English and Germanic Philosophy* 52 (1953): 60–70.

Hackenberry, Charles. "Meaning and Models: The Uses of Characterization in Chesnutt's *The Marrow of Tradition* and *Mandy Oxendine.*" *American Literary Realism* 17 (Autumn 1984): 193–202.

Hair, William Ivy. *Carnival of Fury: Robert Charles and the New Orleans Race Riot of 1900.* Baton Rouge: Louisiana State UP, 1976.

Harrington, Gary. *Faulkner's Fables of Creativity: The Yoknapatawpha Novels.* Athens: U of Georgia P, 1990.

Harvey, Cathy Chance. "Dear Lyle/Sherwood Anderson." *Southern Studies* 18 (Fall 1979): 320–38."

———. Lyle Saxon: A Portrait in Letters, 1917–1945." Diss. Tulane University, 1980.

Hearn, Lafcadio. "The Last of the Voudoos." *Harper's Weekly* Nov. 7, 1885. Rpt. in *An American Miscellany* 2, ed. Albert Mordell. New York: Dodd, Mead, 1924.

Henderson, Stephen. *Understanding the New Black Poetry, Black Speech, and Black Music as Poetic References.* New York: Morrow, 1973.

"Herbert Spencer in America." *Century* 24 (Sept. 1882): 789.

Hernton, Calvin. "The Tradition." *Parnassus* (Spring 1985): 518–50.

Hobson, Linda Whitney. *Understanding Walker Percy.* Columbia: U of South Carolina P, 1988.

Hofstadter, Richard. *Social Darwinism in American Thought.* Rev. ed. Boston: Beacon, 1955.

Hogue, Lawrence Hogue. *Discourse and the Other: The Production of the Afro-American Text.* Durham, N.C.: Duke UP, 1986.

Holditch, W. Kenneth. "The Last Frontier of Bohemia: Tennessee Williams in New Orleans, 1938–1983." *Southern Quarterly* 23.2 (Winter 1985): 1–37.

———. "The Singing Heart: A Study of the Life and Work of Pearl Rivers." *Southern Quarterly* 20 (Winter 1982): 87–117.

———. "Lust and Languor in the Big Easy: The Literary Mystique of New Orleans." *New Orleans Ethnic Cultures.* Ed. John Cooke. New Orleans: Committee on Ethnicity in New Orleans, 1978.

Holly, Allie Miller. "Alice Ruth Moore Dunbar-Nelson: The Individual." Presentation at the Delta Sigma Theta Regional Conference New Orleans, Jan. 1968.

Hughes, Langston. "The Negro Artist and the Racial Mountain." *Black Expression: Essays by and about Black Americans in the Creative Arts.* Ed. Addison Gayle. New York: Weybright and Talley, 1970.

Hull, Gloria T. "Afro-American Women Poets: A Bio-Critical Survey." *Shakespeare's Sisters: Feminist Essays on Women Poets.* Ed. Sandra M. Gilbert and Susan Gubar. Bloomington: Indiana UP, 1979. 174+.

———. *Color, Sex and Poetry: Three Women Writers of the Harlem Renaissance.* Bloomington: Indiana UP, 1987.

———, ed. *Give Us Each Day: The Diary of Alice Dunbar-Nelson.* New York: Norton, 1984.

———. "Shaping Contradictions: Alice Dunbar-Nelson and the Black Creole Experience." *New Orleans Review* 5 (Spring 1988): 34–37.

———, ed. The Works of Alice Dunbar-Nelson. 3 vols. Schomburg Black Women Writers Series. New York: Oxford UP, 1988.

Inger, Morton. *Politics and Reality in an American City: The New Orleans School Crisis of 1960.* New York: Center for Urban Education, 1968.

Jackson, Joy J. *New Orleans in the Gilded Age: Politics and Urban Progress 1880–1896.* Baton Rouge: Louisiana State UP, 1969.

Johnson, Karen Ramsay. "Gender, Sexuality, and the Artist in Faulkner's Novels." *American Literature* 61.1 (Mar. 1989): 1–15.

Jones, Anne Goodwyn. "*Gone With the Wind* and Others: Popular Fiction, 1920–1950." *The History of Southern Literature.* Eds. Louis D. Rubin, Jr., et al. Baton Rouge: Louisiana State UP, 1985. 363–74.

———. *Tomorrow Is Another Day: The Woman Writer in the South, 1859–1936.* Baton Rouge: Louisiana State UP, 1981.

Jones, LeRoi. "The Myth of a 'Negro Literature.'" *Black Expressions; Essays by and about Black Americans in the Creative Arts.* Ed. Addison Gayle, Jr. New York: Weybright and Talley, 1970.

Jones, Suzanne W. "*Absalom, Absalom!* and the Custom of Storytelling: A Reflection of Southern Social and Literary History." *Southern Studies* 24.1 (Spring 1985): 82–112.

———. "Place, Perception and Identity in *The Awakening.*" *Southern Quarterly* 25 (Winter 1987): 108–19.

———. "Two Settings: The Islands and the City." *Approaches to Teaching Chopin's "The Awakening."* Ed. Jerry Koloski. New York: Modern Language Association, 1988.

Juncker, Clara. "The Mother's Balcony: Grace King's Discourse of Femininity." *New Orleans Review* 15 (Spring 1988): 39–46.

Kane, Harnett. *Queen New Orleans: City by the River.* New York: W. Morrow, 1949.

Karenga, Maulana Ron. "Meats and Sea-Foods." *Echoes from the Gumbo,* Dec. 1968: 4.

Kein, Sybil. "Comme Ye Dit: The Use of the Creole Language in 19th and 20th

Century Literature." Paper presented at the Modern Language Association
    Convention, New Orleans, LA, Dec. 1988.
———. Personal interview with the author. July 30, 1986.
Kobre, Michael. "The Consolations of Fiction: Walker Percy's Dialogic Art." *New
    Orleans Review* 16.4 (Winter 1989): 45–52.
Lacey, Henry C. *To Raise, Destroy, and Create: The Poetry, Drama, and Fiction of
    Imamu Amiri Baraka (LeRoi Jones).* Troy, NY: Whitston, 1981.
Latortue, Regine, and R. W. Gleason., eds. and trans. *Les Cenelles: A Collection of
    Poems by Creole Writers of the Early Nineteenth Century.* Boston: Hall,
    1979.
Lattin, Patricia Hopkins. "Childbirth and Motherhood in *The Awakening* and in
    'Athénaise.'" *Approaches to Teaching Chopin's "The Awakening."* Ed.
    Bernard Kolowski. New York: Modern Language Association, 1988. 40–46.
———. "Kate Chopin's Repeating Characters." *Mississippi Quarterly* (Winter
    1979): 19–37.
Lawson, Donald M. "Caroline Dormon: A Renaissance Spirit of Twentieth-Century
    Louisiana." *Louisiana History* 24 (Spring 1983): 121–39.
Lentricchia, Frank, and Thomas McLaughlin, eds. *Critical Terms for Literary Study.*
    Chicago: U of Chicago P, 1990.
Lerner, Gerda, ed. *Black Women in White America: A Documentary History.* New
    York: Random, 1972.
———. "Early Community Work of Black Club Women." *Journal of Negro
    History* 59 (Apr. 1974): 158–67.
Lewis, A. Lawson, "Tom More and Sigmund Freud." *New Orleans Review* 16.4
    (Winter 1989): 27–31.
Lewis, Peirce F. *New Orleans: The Making of an Urban Landscape.* Cambridge,
    MA: Ballinger, 1976.
Lind, Ilse Dusoir. "The Design and Meaning of Absalom, Absalom!" *William
    Faulkner: Three Decades of Criticism.* Ed. Frederick J. Hoffman and Olga
    Vickery. East Lansing: Michigan State UP, 1960.
Loggins, Vernon. *The Negro Author: His Development in America to 1900.* Port
    Washington, NY: Kennikat P, 1964.
Logsdon, Joseph. "Marcus Bruce Christian." A *Dictionary of Louisiana Biography*
    1. Ed. Glenn R. Conrad. Louisiana Historical Association, 1988.
Luschei, Martin. *The Sovereign Wayfarer: Walker Percy's Diagnosis of the Malaise.*
    Baton Rouge: Louisiana State UP, 1972.
Lutwack, Leonard. *The Role of Place in Literature.* Syracuse: Syracuse UP, 1984.
McCaffrey, Larry. *The Metafictional Muse: The Works of Robert Coover, Donald
    Barthelme, and William H. Gass.* Pittsburgh: U of Pittsburgh P, 1982.
McClure, John. Review of *Cane* by Jean Toomer. *The Double Dealer* 6 (Jan. 1924):
    26–27.
McDowell, Deborah. Introd. to Pass*ing* and *Quicksand,* by Nella Larsen. New
    Brunswick, NJ: Rutgers UP, 1987.
McHaney, Thomas L. "Faulkner and Modernism: Why Does It Matter?" *New*

Directions in Faulkner Studies. Ed. Doreen Fowler and Ann J. Abadie. Jackson: UP of Mississippi, 1984.

Martin, Reginald. *Ishmael Reed and the New Black Aesthetic Critics*. London: MacMillan. 1988.

Martinez, Maurice M. "Black Indians: Their Heritage Is Rooted in Mardi Gras." *The National Leader* 24 (Mar. 1983): 18–20.

Mason, Theodore O. "Performance, History, and Myth: The Problem of Ishmael Reed's *Mumbo-Jumbo*." *Modern Fiction Studies* 34 (Spring 1988): 97–109.

Matheus, John. "Tiyette: A Play in One Act." *Plays and Pageants from the Life of the Negro*. Ed. Willis Richardson. Washington, DC: Associated Publishers, 1930.

May, John R. "Local Color in Kate Chopin's *The Awakening*." *Southern Review* 6.4 (Fall 1970): 1031–40.

Meese, Elizabeth. *Crossing the Double-Cross: The Practice of Feminist Criticism*. Chapel Hill: U of North Carolina P, 1986.

Mencken, H. L. "The Sahara of the Bozart." *Prejudices: Second Series,* 1917. Rpt. in *Prejudices: A Selection*. Ed. James Farrell. New York: Vintage, 1958. 70–79.

Merrill, Susan, ed. W*omen Writers and the City: Essays in Feminist Literary Criticism*. Knoxville: U of Tennessee P, 1984.

Mignon, François. *Plantation Memo: Plantation Life in Louisiana 1750–1970*. Ed. Ora Garland Williams. Baton Rouge: Claitor's, 1972.

Miller, Jordan Y., ed. *Twentieth-Century Interpretations of "A Streetcar Named Desire."* Englewood Cliffs, NJ: Prentice-Hall, 1971.

Mills, Gary B. Th*e Forgotten People: Cane River's Creoles of Color*. Baton Rouge: Louisiana State UP, 1977.

Muhlenfeld, Elisabeth S. "Shadows with Substance and Ghosts Exhumed: The Women in *Absalom, Absalom!*" *Mississippi Quarterly* 25 (Summer 1972): 289–304.

Neal, Larry. "The Black Arts Movement." *The Black Aesthetic*. Ed. Addison Gayle. New York: Doubleday, 1971. 257–74.

Nigro, August J. *The Diagonal Line: Separation and Reparation in American Literature*. Selinsgrove, Pa.: Susquehanna UP, 1984.

Olsen, Otto H., ed. *The Thin Disguise: Plessy v. Ferguson*. New York: Humanities P, 1967.

Olsen, Tillie. *Silences*. New York: Delacorte, 1978.

O'Neal, John. "Motion in the Ocean." *Tulane Drama Review* 12 (Summer 1968).

Osbey, Brenda Marie. "Faubourg Tremé: Community in Transition." *New Orleans Tribune*. Part 1, 6.12 (Dec. 1990): 14–16; Part 2, "Solidifying the Community" 7.1 (Jan. 1991): 12–14; Part 3, "The Beginning of the End" 7.8 (Aug. 1991): 14–16; Part 4, "The Fall of Tremé" 7.9 (Sept. 1991): 14–15; Part 5, "A New Era" 7.11 (Nov. 1991): 20–21; Part 6, "The Making of a Ghetto" 7.12 (Dec. 1991): 20–21.

———. Personal interview with the author. Aug. 11, 1991.

———. Telephone interview with the author. Dec. 26, 1988.

Paglia, Camille. *Sexual Personae: Art and Decadence from Nefertiti to Emily Dickinson.* New Haven: Yale UP, 1990.

Parrington, Vernon Louis. Main Currents in American Thought: *An Interpretation of American Literature from the Beginning to 1920.* New York: Harcourt, Brace, 1930.

Pattee, Fred Lewis. *A History of American Literature Since 1870.* New York: Century, 1915.

Pearson, Michael. "The Double Bondage of Racism in Walker Percy's Fiction." *Mississippi Quarterly* 41.4 (Fall 1988): 479–96.

Percy, Walker. "The Diagnostic Novel: On the Uses of Modern Fiction." *Harper's* 272 (June 1986): 39–45.

———. "From Facts to Fiction." *Washington Post Book Week,* Dec. 25, 1966. Rpt. in *The Writer,* Oct. 1967: 27–28.

———. "The Man on the Train." *The Message in the Bottle.* New York: Farrar, Straus, and Giroux, 1954. 83–100.

———. "New Orleans, Mon Amour." *Harper's* 237 (Sept. 1968): 80–82, 86, 88, 90.

———. "Notes for a Novel about the End of the World." *The Message in the Bottle.* New York: Farrar, Straus and Giroux, 1954. 101–18.

———. "Symbol, Consciousness, and Intersubjectivity." *The Message in the Bottle.* New York: Farrar, Straus and Giroux, 1954. 265–76.

Petro, Peter. *Modern Satire: Four Studies.* New York: Mouton Publishers, 1982.

Petry, Alice Hall. "A Fable of Love and Death: The Artistry of Cable's 'Jean-ah Poquelin.'" *The Southern Literary Quarterly* 15 (Spring 1983): 87–99.

———. *A Genius in His Way: The Art of Cable's "Old Creole Days."* Rutherford: Fairleigh Dickinson UP, 1988.

Pocock, D. C. D. *Humanistic Geography and Literature.* London: Croom Helm, 1981.

Pryse, Marjorie, and Hortense J. Spillers. *Conjuring: Black Women, Fiction and Literary Tradition.* Bloomington: Indiana UP, 1985.

Reddick, Laurence D. "The Negro in the New Orleans Press, 1850–1860: A Study in Attitudes and Propaganda." Diss. U of Chicago, 1941.

Reinecke, "The National and Cultural Groups of New Orleans, 1718–1918." *New Orleans Ethnic Cultures.* Ed. John Cooke. New Orleans: Committee on Ethnicity in New Orleans, 1978. 6–25.

Render, Sylvia Lyons. *Charles W. Chesnutt.* Boston: Twayne-Hall, 1980.

Reuss, Carol. "Dear Dorothy Dix." *New Orleans Review* 15 (Spring 1988): 77–83.

Richardson, Thomas. "The City of Day and the City of Night: New Orleans and the Exotic Unreality of Tennessee Williams." *Tennessee Williams: A Tribute.* Ed. Jac Tharpe. Jackson: UP of Mississippi, 1977: 631–42.

———, ed. *'The Grandissimes': Centennial Essays.* Jackson: UP of Mississippi, 1981.

———. "Local Color in Louisiana." *The History of Southern Literature.* Ed. Louis D. Rubin, Jr. Baton Rouge: Louisiana State UP, 1985. 199–208.

Ricoeur, Paul. *Time and Narrative.* Chicago: U of Chicago P, 1954.

Ringe, Donald. "The Double Center: Character and Meaning in Cable's Early
    Novels." *Studies in the Novel* 5 (1973): 52–62.
———. "Narrative Voice in Cable's *The Grandissimes.*" *Southern Quarterly* 18
    (1980): 13–22.
Roderick, John M. "From 'Tarantula Arms' to 'Della Robbia Blue': The Tennessee
    Williams Tragicomic Transit Authority." *Tennessee Williams's* A Streecar
    Named Desire: *Modern Critical Interpretations,* ed. Bloom. 93–101.
Ross, Stephen M. "Oratory and the Dialogical in *Absalom, Absalom! Intertextuality
    in Faulkner.* Ed. Michel Gresset and Noel Polk. Jackson: UP of Mississippi,
    1985. 74–81.
Rouquette, Adrien Emmanuel. *Critical Dialogue Between Aboo and Caboo in a
    New Orleans Book or A Grandissime Ascension.* New Orleans: Great
    Publishing House of Sam Slick Allspice, 1880.
Roussève, Charles Barthelemy. *The Negro in Louisiana: Aspects of His History and
    His Literature.* New Orleans: Xavier UP, 1937.
Rubin, Louis D., Jr. *George Washington Cable: The Life and Times of a Southern
    Heretic.* New York: Pegasus Western, 1969.
———, et al., eds. *The History of Southern Literature.* Baton Rouge: Louisiana
    State UP, 1985.
Said, Edward W. *The Work, The Text and The Critic.* Cambridge: Harvard UP,
    1983.
St. Julien, Aline. *Colored Creole: Color Conflict and Confusion in New Orleans.*
    New Orleans: Ahidiana-Habari, 1977.
Schwartz, Lawrence H. *Creating Faulkner's Reputation: The Politics of Modern
    Literary Criticism.* Knoxville: U of Tennessee P, 1988.
Searight, Sarah, *New Orleans.* New York: Stein and Day, 1973.
Seyersted, Per, ed. *The Complete Works of Kate Chopin.* 2 vols. Baton Rouge:
    Louisiana State UP, 1969.
———. *Kate Chopin: A Critical Biography.* Baton Rouge: Louisiana State UP,
    1969.
Seyersted, Per, and and Emily Toth, eds. *A Kate Chopin Miscellany.* Natchitoches,
    LA: Northwestern State UP, 1979.
Shadle, Mark. "A Bird's Eye View: Ishmael Reed's Unsettling of the Score by
    Munching and Mooching on the Mumbo Jumbo Work of History." *North
    Dakota Quarterly* 54 (Winter 1986): 21.
Shannon, Anna Williams. "Women in the Color Line: Subversion of Female
    Steretypes in the Fiction of Cable, King, and Chopin." Diss. U of Nebraska,
    1979.
Shortridge, James. "The Concept of the Place-Defining Novel in American Popular
    Culture." *Professional Geographer* 43.3 (1991): 280–91.
Showalter, Elaine. *A Literature of Their Own.* Princeton: Princeton UP, 1977.
———, ed. *The New Feminist Criticism: Essays on Women, Literature, and Theory.*
    New York: Pantheon, 1985.
Skaggs, Peggy. "Three Tragic Figures in Kate Chopin's *The Awakening.*" *Louisiana
    Studies* 13 (Winter 1974): 345–64.

Smith, Barbara. "Toward a Black Feminist Criticism." *But Some of Us Are Brave*.
    Ed. Gloria T. Hull et al. Old Westbury, NY: Feminist P, 1982.
Smith, Lillian. *Killers of the Dream*. 1961. Rev. ed. New York: Norton, 1971.
Smith, Michael P. *Spirit World: Pattern in the Expressive Folk Culture of Afro-
    America*. New Orleans: New Orleans Urban Folklife Society, 1984.
Smith-Rosenberg, Carroll. "The Female World of Love and Ritual Relations
    between Women in Nineteenth-Century America." *Signs* 1.1 (Autumn 1975):
    1–29.
Smyth, Joseph Hilton. Review of The Weary Blues by Langston Hughes. *The
    Double Dealer* 8 (May 1926): 358.
Spencer, Herbert. *The Study of Sociology*. New York: Appleton, 1882.
Spears, Monroe K. *Dionysus and the City: Modernism in Twentieth-Century Poetry*.
    New York: Oxford UP, 1970.
Spoto, Donald. *The Kindness of Strangers: The Life of Tennessee Williams*. Boston:
    Little, Brown, 1985.
Squier, Susan Merrill. *Women Writers and the City*. Knoxville: U of Tennessee P,
    1984.
Stein, Allen F. *After the Vows Were Spoken: Marriage in American Literary
    Realism*. Columbus: Ohio State UP, 1984.
Stephens, Robert O. "Cable and Turgenev: Learning How to Write a Modern
    Novel." *Studies in the Novel* 15.3 (Fall 1983): 237–48.
————. "Cable's Bras Coupé and Merimée's "Tamango: The Case of the Missing
    Arm." *Mississippi Quarterly* 35.4 (Fall 1982): 387–405.
Sterkx, H. E. *The Free Negro in Ante-Bellum Louisiana*. Rutherford, NJ: Fairleigh
    Dickinson UP, 1972.
Strauss, Anselm. *Images of the American City*. New Brunswick, NJ: Transaction,
    1976.
Summer, William Graham. *Social Darwinism: Selected Essays*. Englewood Cliffs,
    NJ: Prentice Hall, 1963.
Swindle, Michael. "At Court with Walker Percy." *New Orleans* 23.4 (Jan. 1989):
    38–42, 76–77.
Tallant, Robert. Gumbo Ya-Ya: A Collection of Louisiana Folk *Tales*. New York:
    Bonanza Books, 1945.
————. "My Fabulous Friend—Lyle Saxon." New Orleans *Times-Picayune
    Magazine*. Nov. 21, 1948. 8–9.
————. *The Romantic New Orleanians*. New York: Dutton, 1950.
————. *Voodoo in New Orleans*. 1946. Gretna, LA: Pelican, 1974.
Taylor, Helen. "The Case of Grace King." *Southern Review* 18 (Fall 1982):
    685–702.
————. *Gender, Race, and Region in the Writings of Grace King, Ruth McEnery
    Stuart, and Kate Chopin*. Baton Rouge: Louisiana State UP, 1989.
Thomas, James W. "Lyle Saxon's Struggle with Children of Strangers." *Southern
    Studies* 16 (Spring 1990): 27–40.
Tinker, Edward Larocque. "Cable and the Creoles." *American Literature* 5
    (1933–34): 311–26.

————. *Toucoutou.* New York: Dodd, Mead and Co., 1928.

Tocqueville, Alexis de. *Democracy in America.* ed. Phillips Bradley, 2 vols. New York: Random, 1945.

Toth, Emily. *Kate Chopin.* New York: William Morrow, 1990.

————. "Kate Chopin's New Orleans Years." *New Orleans Review* 15 (Spring 1988): 53–60.

Touchstone, Blake. "Voodoo in New Orleans." *Louisiana History* 13 (Fall 1972): 371–86.

Tregle, Joseph G., Jr. "Early New Orleans Society: A Reappraisal." *Journal of Southern History* 18 (1952): 32–33.

Tuan, Yi-Fu. "Attitudes towards the Environment: Themes and Approaches." *Environmental Perception and Behavior.* Chicago: U of Chicago P, 1967.

————. *Space and Place.* Minneapolis: U of Minnesota P, 1977.

————. *Topophilia.* Englewood Cliffs, NJ: Prentice-Hall, 1974.

Turner, Arlin, ed. C*reoles and Cajuns: Stories of Old Louisiana.* Garden City, NY: Doubleday, 1959.

————. *George W. Cable.* Baton Rouge: Louisiana State UP, 1966.

————. "George W. Cable's Beginnings as a Reformer." *Journal of Southern History* 17 (May 1951): 136–61.

————. "A Novelist Discovers a Novelist: The Correspondence of H. H. Boyesen and George W. Cable." *Western Humanities Review* 5 (Autumn 1951): 346.

Turner, Frederick. *Remembering Song: Encounters with the New Orleans Jazz Tradition.* New York: Viking, 1982.

Tuttleton, James W. "The Physician, Writer and the Cure of the Soul." *New Orleans Review* 16.4 (Winter 1989): 17–21.

Wagner, Jean. *Black Poets of the United States.* Urbana: U of Illinois P, 1973.

Walker, Nancy. "Feminist or Naturalist: The Social Context of Kate Chopin's *The Awakening.*" *Southern Quarterly* 17.2 (1979): 95–103.

Wall, Cheryl A., ed. *Changing Our Own Words: Essays on Criticism, Theory, and Writing by Black Women.* New Brunswick, NJ: Rutgers UP, 1989.

Ward, Jerry W., Jr. Introduction. Bl*ue Lights and River Songs.* By Tom Dent. Detroit: Lotus P, 1982.

————. "Tom Dent Talking: New Orleans as a Resource of Genius." *Xavier Review* 6.1 (1986): 1–11.

Waring, George E. "George W. Cable," Century *Magazine* 23 (Feb. 1882): 603.

Warner, Charles Dudley. "New Orleans." *Harper's New Monthly Magazine* 74 (Dec. 1886): 186–206.

Washington, Mary Helen. *Invented Lives.* New York: Anchor, 1987.

Watson, James G. "Faulkner in Fiction." *Southern Quarterly* 20 (Fall 1981): 46–63.

————. "New Orleans, *The Double Dealer* and 'New Orleans.'" *American Literature* 56 (May 1984). 214–26.

Webb, Bernice Larson. "Cable's Handling of the Mutilated Black Prince in *The Grandissimes.*" *Revue de Louisiane* 11.2 (Winter 1982): 101–6.

Webb, Max. "Binx Bolling's New Orleans: Moviegoing, Southern Writing, and

Father Abraham." *The Art of Walker Percy*. Ed. Panthea Reid Broughton. Baton Rouge: Louisiana State UP, 1979.

Weimer, David. *The City as Metaphor*. New York: Random, 1966.

Weixlmann, Joe. "Culture Clash, Survival, and Transformation: A Study of Some Innovative Afro-American Novels of Detection." *Mississippi Quarterly* (Winter 1984): 21–31.

Whiting, Eleanor. "Woman's Work and Wages." *Lippincott's Magazine* (May 1898): 670–77.

Whitlow, Roger. "Alice Dunbar-Nelson: New Orleans Writer." *Regionalism and the Female Imagination*. Ed. Emily Toth. New York: Human Sciences P, 1985. 186–206.

———. "The Ordeal of George W. Cable." *The New Yorker* 33 (Nov. 9, 1957).

Wideman, John Edgas. "Charles Chesnutt and the WPA Narrative: The Oral and Literate Roots of Afro-American Literature." *The Slave's Narrative*. Ed. Charles T. Davis and Henry Louis Gates, Jr. New York: Oxford UP, 1985. 59–78.

Wilson, Edmund. *Patriotic Gore: Studies in the Literature of the American Civil War*. New York: Oxford UP, 1966.

Woodward, C. Vann. *The Burden of Southern History*. New York: New American Library, 1969.

———. *Origins of the New South: 1877–1913*. Baton Rouge: Louisiana State UP, 1951. 159–63.

———. *The Strange Career of Jim Crow*. 1955. New York: Oxford UP, 1964.

Woolf, Cynthia Griffin. "Thanatos and Eros: Chopin's *The Awakening*." *American Quarterly* 25 (Oct. 1973): 449–71.

Wright, Richard. "The Literature of the Negro in the U.S." *Black Expression; Essays by and about Black Americans in the Creative Arts*. Ed. Addison Gayle. New York: Weybright and Talley, 1970.

Young, James O. *Black Writers of the Thirties*. Baton Rouge: Louisiana State UP, 1973.

Young, Thomas Daniel. "The Fugitives: Ransom, Davidson, Tate." *History of Southern Literature*. Ed. Louis D. Rubin, Jr. Baton Rouge: Louisiana State UP, 1985. 319–32.

Ziff, Larzer. *The American 1890's: Life and Times of a Lost Generation*. New York: Viking, 1966.

Index